THE PATH of the
BAAL SHEM TOV

THE PATH of the
BAAL SHEM TOV

EARLY CHASIDIC
TEACHINGS AND CUSTOMS

DAVID SEARS

A JASON ARONSON BOOK

ROWMAN & LITTLEFIELD PUBLISHERS, INC.
Lanham • Boulder • New York • Toronto • Oxford

A JASON ARONSON BOOK

ROWMAN & LITTLEFIELD PUBLISHERS, INC.

Published in the United States of America
by Rowman & Littlefield Publishers, Inc.
A wholly owned subsidiary of The Rowman & Littlefield Publishing Group, Inc.
4501 Forbes Boulevard, Suite 200, Lanham, Maryland 20706
www.rowmanlittlefield.com

PO Box 317
Oxford
OX2 9RU, UK

Copyright © 1997 by David Sears
First Rowman & Littlefield edition 2004

British Library Cataloguing in Publication Information Available

Library of Congress Cataloging-in-Publication Data

Sears, David.
    The path of the Baal Shem Tov : early Chasidic teachings and customs / David
Sears.
        p.   cm.
    Includes bibliographical references and index.
    ISBN 1-56821-972-5 (paperback)
    1. Ba'al Shem Tov, ca. 1700–1760—quotations.   2. Hasidism.   3. Parables,
Hasidic.   4. Judaism—Hasidic rite—liturgy.   I. Title.
BM755.I8S33   1997
296.8'332—dc20   96-9445

Printed in the United States of America

Dedicated
to the memory of

Miriam (Bas Yonah HaLevi) Hayum
(26 Elul 5755–1995)

Wise with simple faith,
joyous even in the midst of adversity,
and kind without desiring anything in return,
she was, in many ways, the kind of person
the Baal Shem Tov wanted us all to be

Contents

Part II Customs of the Baal Shem Tov

Part III Letters of the Baal Shem Tov

Preface

Chasidim often call their approach to Divine service the *derech haBaal Shem Tov*—"the path of the Baal Shem Tov." Perhaps there is a *limud*, an instructive concept, contained in this choice of words. Judaism is often presented as a belief system or a body of laws and rituals to be observed by a certain group of people. It is true that the rabbis go to great lengths to clarify these beliefs and practices. But such a description still misses the point. Judaism is dynamic, not static. It is not so much a dogma as a path that leads to the supreme purpose: knowledge of God.

One of the symptoms of our exile is that this perception of Judaism as a path often has been forgotten. Thus, the condition of exile is compared to sleep. When one sleeps, not only is one's consciousness diminished, but it is impossible to move or progress. The *ge'ulah* (Messianic Redemption) is compared to an awakening from sleep, from spiritual unconsciousness and inertia.[1]

As history entered its last phase before the *ge'ulah*, the greatest Jewish mystic since the Ari *z"l* appeared in Eastern Europe. His task was to awaken the Jewish people from their fitful slumber and inspire them to stretch out their limbs and move, spiritually. The Baal Shem Tov came to pave a path (or at least to clear away the debris that obscured the old one) by which everyone could realize life's ultimate goal.

It is difficult to adequately portray the Baal Shem Tov's path in an anthology such as this. Spontaneous and inspired revelations of the soul, these teachings resist the formalism of the written word. If the Baal Shem Tov did compose written works, aside from a handful of letters, none of them has survived. (According to one tradition, all his manuscripts were lost during his attempted voyage to the Holy Land.) In any case, the full import of what the Baal Shem Tov wished to communicate could only be grasped in the master's presence.[2] Nevertheless, disciples such as Rabbi Yaakov Yosef of Polonoye and Rabbi Moshe Chaim Ephraim of Sudylkov did preserve many of the Baal Shem Tov's teachings. Thus, although we no longer can hear from the Master's lips *d'varim k'gachalei eish*—"words like coals of fire"—it is still possible to reconstruct the channels through which he imparted his lofty perceptions.

---

1. *Tehillim* 126.
2. Note *Likkutei Moharan* I, 19:1.

Naturally, teachings recorded by different disciples vary in both style and content. Some are clear; others, cryptic. Where necessary, a word or two of clarification has been added in brackets, but these remarks should not be taken as definitive. Although the material has been arranged thematically, within each category it follows no special order. Therefore, the reader should feel free to put aside whatever seems difficult until a later time.

This book also has a few inconsistencies that should be mentioned. My original intent was to collect a sampling of the Baal Shem Tov's teachings, customs, and spiritual practices, not tales or legends about him. But sometimes a good story proved to be irresistible. The notes, too, are a bit idiosyncratic. In a popular work such as this, source references are usually limited to the texts cited by the author. However, in some cases additional sources (especially from the works of the Baal Shem Tov's great-grandson, Rabbi Nachman of Breslev, and later Chasidic leaders) have been included for those who wish to explore further. These exceptions to the rule merely reflect my personal interests; hopefully they will prove useful to others, as well.

Rabbinic interpretation (d'rush) heavily relies upon wordplays, which also figure prominently in Chasidic thought. These should not be viewed as mere literary sleights of hand; invariably, they reflect the deeper implications of the Torah. Thus, on the verse: "Is not My word like fire, declares God, and like a hammer that shatters the rock?" our Sages commented: "[The Torah] separates into many sparks."[3] Wordplays are hard to translate, and I have probably not always succeeded in rendering them effectively. But if the reader will consider them patiently, the effort will not go unrewarded.

The word mysticism means different things to different people; therefore, a clarification of terms may be in order. The Random House Dictionary of the English Language defines mysticism as "the doctrine of an immediate spiritual intuition of truths believed to transcend ordinary understanding, or of a direct, intimate union of the soul with God through contemplation and love." It is in this sense that the word is used in this book.

Last of all, it is important to note that a number of teachings attributed to the Baal Shem Tov are also attributed to Rabbi Dov Ber, the Maggid of Mezeritch, or other disciples. Therefore, this work has been subtitled, "Early Chasidic Teachings and Customs," to imply more than one author. However, everything included here is imbued with the spirit of the Chasidic movement's founder.

---

3. *Sanhedrin* 34a, citing *Yirmiyahu* 23:29.

Acknowledgments

Many teachers and friends helped in one way or another during the course of this project. Rabbi Chaim Avraham Horowitz, the Bostoner Rebbe of New York, *shlita*, first encouraged me to try my hand at the craft of translation and commissioned my first efforts. I would also like to thank Rabbi Pinchos Dovid Horowitz, *sh'lita*, Bostoner Rebbe of Flatbush and *rosh yeshiva* of Darchei Noam, for showing me and countless other *talmidim* the *ne'imus haTorah* in true Chasidic spirit. Their mother, Rebbetzin Leah Fradel Horowitz, a direct descendant of the Ziditchov dynasty, also shared some of her vast knowledge of Chasidic history with me. The Mashgiach Ruchani of Yeshivas Darchei Noam, Rabbi Shlomo Eisenblatt, *sh'lita*, was kind enough to review an early draft of the book. Rabbi Shmuel Teich, the P'shemishler Rebbe, *sh'lita*, looked over the entire work and offered many helpful suggestions. Rabbi Avraham Yehoshua Bick, the Medzhibuzher Rav, *sh'lita*, pointed out several problem issues which I hope were satisfactorily resolved. Rabbi Ben Zion Strasser, the Nitra Dayan, *sh'lita*, reviewed the manuscript during the last few weeks before Pesach—no small favor from an active *posek*. Rabbi Shlomo Aharon Gottleib, a gifted teacher of *Likkutei Moharan*, introduced me to many concepts of the Baal Shem Tov, which ultimately led me to undertake this project. Rabbi Zvi Davis provided his scholarly acumen, as well as the use of his computer to perhaps his most technophobic friend—I don't know how I could have finished this book without him. Rabbi Rachmiel Steinberg, Shmuel Greenbaum, Yaacov Sternbach and Avraham Klapper also were extremely helpful in the computer-related aspects of the project. Rabbi Yonah Horowitz and my long-standing *chavrusa*, David Zeitlin, spent a number of hours poring over the translation (although responsibility for any errors remains with me). Rabbi Yisrael Moskowitz, Rabbi Eliezer Shore, Rabbi Shmuel Heitler, Leibel Estrin, Fischel Bresler and Andy Statman also read through various drafts of the manuscript and helped in many ways. After living in the urban *sh'tetl* of Borough Park for many years, I must thank my mother, Mrs. Grace Sears, for ensuring that I can still speak English (more or less)—and Jack Pulaski for teaching me how to write it. Chava Shulman, Mrs. Tzirel Newman, and Mrs. Malka Davis typed in numerous additions and corrections to the final draft. The encouragement of Arthur Kurzweil, Vice-President of Jason Aronson Inc., and the efforts of his staff enabled me to finish this project at last. To all of the above—and, not least of all, to my supportive and forbearing wife, Shira Sara—I am grateful.

Rabbi Pinchas of Koretz often used to thank God that he had been born after the *Zohar* had been revealed to the world. Although I have hardly scratched their surface, I feel the same way about the teachings of the Baal Shem Tov and his disciples. There is no way that I can adequately thank God for leading me to the light of Chasidus and for mercifully enabling me to complete this book.

May the Torah always remain with our children and grandchildren—*ad bias Goel Tzedek*, amen.

Introduction

It is hard for us to imagine what Jewish life was like before the Baal Shem Tov. Chasidim and non-Chasidim may still differ on many issues: their approach to prayer and Torah study, the mysteries of Kabbalah and the plight of the masses, the role of the *tzaddik* (righteous man), etc. However, most of today's so-called Misnagdim (opponents of Chasidism) not only respect the founder of the Chasidic movement but have been influenced by his teachings.

This was not always the case. While England's colonists in America were fomenting a political revolution, the Jewish world of Eastern Europe was already in the throes of a spiritual revolution: the Chasidic movement. In the wake of the havoc wreaked by the false Messiah, Shabbsai Tzvi, and the Chmielnitzki pogroms of the late 1600s, the Jewish people were left shattered in body and soul. The level of Torah education was abysmal, and even among Torah scholars the bitterness of *galus* (exile) was deeply felt. In the midst of this darkness, a ray of light appeared. People began to speak of a *Baal Shem*—a master of Divine mysteries—named Rabbi Yisrael Ben Eliezer, who lived in the Carpathian foothills in the village of Ilust. At first simple folk began to visit him; then Torah scholars came, as well.

The Baal Shem Tov's spiritual magnetism reached far and wide. His disciples made further disciples, and his path in Divine service spread like wildfire throughout the sleepy Jewish hamlets of Eastern Europe. To this day, one can sense an almost palpable charisma in the Baal Shem Tov's teachings, in the tales he told, as well as those told about him—even his name evokes a sense of awe. During the first few generations of the Chasidic movement, hundreds of thousands of Jews became Chasidim, often in spite of fierce opposition. At the time of the Holocaust, approximately half of Europe's Orthodox Jewish population was Chasidic. What precious commodity did so many individuals spanning the entire spectrum of the Jewish people gain from the Baal Shem Tov and his disciples?

Perhaps the answer is: life. There is an amazing, not to say incredible, legend that the Baal Shem Tov's *tzitzis* (strings ritually tied to a four-cornered garment) possessed a life of their own and could move at will.[1]

---

1. *Divrei Shalom, Ki Savo.*

In all of Jewish history, this legend is probably without precedent. What special connection exists between the *mitzvah* (commandment) of *tzitzis* and the Baal Shem Tov?

The Torah states that one should gaze upon the *tzitzis* and remember all of God's commandments. Concerning this, our Sages taught that the *mitzvah* of *tzitzis* symbolically includes all the rest.[2] With this in mind, the legend about the Baal Shem Tov's *tzitzis* becomes particularly meaningful—for the main point of the Baal Shem Tov's teachings was to bring the *mitzvos* to life, to pick up the fallen spirit of the Jewish people, and to show everyone how to come closer to God.

THE BIRTH OF CHASIDISM

Orphaned at an early age, the Baal Shem Tov never forgot his father's last instructions: "Yisrael, do not fear anyone or anything in this world but the Creator. And love every Jew with all your heart and soul, regardless of who or what he is."

Even during his youth, Yisrael turned to God, spending much time in the fields and forests praying, reciting psalms, and talking to the Creator in his own language. Like many other Jewish mystics from the Patriarchs to the Ari *z"l*, he chose to forsake the company of his peers, seeking to refine himself in solitude.[3] Although the local community provided for his education up to the age of *bar mitzvah*, Yisrael disguised his piety and continued to study Torah at night or where others could not observe him.

After his marriage to the sister of the prominent scholar Rabbi Avraham Gershon Kitover, he withdrew from the world altogether, sustaining himself as a clay-digger in the Carpathian mountains. There he fasted, studied, meditated, prayed. His wife, Chana, was devoted to him in every way, sharing privation and hardship without complaint. This prolonged retreat lasted for ten years, during which an angelic mentor, Achiyah HaShiloni,[4] initiated Yisrael into the mysteries of Torah.[5]

---

2. Rashi on *Bamidbar* 15:39, citing *Midrash Tanchuma*.

3. *Shivchei Baal Shem Tov* 4,5; *Likkutei Dibburim* 1, 5B:26–30.

4. According to tradition, Achiyah HaShiloni was among those who left Egypt with Moshe Rabbeinu. He was a prophet in the period of David HaMelech and Shlomo HaMelech and also taught the prophetic mysteries to Eliyahu HaNavi. See *I Melachim* 11:29, 14:2; *Bava Basra* 121b; *Yerushalmi Eiruvin* 5:1, 22b; *Zohar* I:4b, III:309a; *Zohar Chadash* 19a.

5. *Kesser Shem Tov* 143; *Toldos Yaakov Yosef, Balak*; *Zohar Chai, Bereishis*.

According to Chasidic tradition, they began with the first words of *Bereishis* (Genesis), and when they reached the Torah's final words, *l'eiynei kol Yisrael*—"before the eyes of all Israel"—Rabbi Yisrael Baal Shem Tov was told that the time had come for him to return to the world. Like Moshe Rabbeinu at the Burning Bush, he now understood that the ultimate purpose of his retreat had been for a greater revelation, which would lift up the crushed spirits of the Jewish people and open the gates of holiness for them all.

In 1734, at the age of thirty-six, the Baal Shem Tov began to teach publicly, to heal the sick in body and soul, and to attract his first disciples. Some sought him out for remedies; others turned to him for *kameyos* (Kabbalistic amulets); and people from all walks of life solicited his advice and blessings. But perhaps the most widely needed succor the Baal Shem Tov had to offer was his unique path of meditation and Divine service (the nature of which is portrayed by the contents of this book).

There is no single element in the doctrine of Chasidism which does not have a precedent in Torah. Earlier Kabbalists had expressed most of the key ideas employed by the Baal Shem Tov. However, the *gefihl*, the essential spirit of the Baal Shem Tov's approach, springs from life itself. The immediacy, directness, and profound humanity of his teachings, animated by the pervasive awareness of the Divine Presence as an experiential reality, is totally new.

Despite its mysticism, the Kabbalah can be a highly technical field of study. Here, too, the Baal Shem Tov was not content with mere intellectual proficiency. A narrative included in the early Chasidic anthology *Kesser Shem Tov* highlights this point. It describes the first meeting between the Baal Shem Tov and Rabbi Dov Ber, the Maggid of Mezeritch, who was destined to become the most influential Chasidic master of the next generation. Disappointed by their initial encounter, the Maggid returned to the local inn and told his coachman that he would like to leave later that night, as soon as the moon appeared.

At midnight, while Rabbi Dov Ber was preparing himself for the journey, the Baal Shem Tov sent his attendant to summon him. When he came to the Baal Shem Tov, the master asked, "Do you know how to study Torah?"

The Maggid said, "Yes."

Then the Baal Shem Tov continued, "I have indeed heard that you know how to study Torah. Do you also possess knowledge of Kabbalah?"

Again, the Maggid said, "Yes."

The Baal Shem Tov instructed his attendant to bring him a copy of *Eitz Chayim* [one of the most profound Kabbalistic works of the Ari *z"l*], and proceeded to show the Maggid a certain section of that text. Rabbi Dov Ber studied it and then explained its meaning to the Baal Shem Tov. But the Baal Shem Tov replied, "You do not know anything at all!"

He studied it a second time and then told the Baal Shem Tov, "The explanation I gave is correct. If you know a better one, tell it to me, and we will see who possesses the truth."

Thereupon the Baal Shem Tov said, "Stand on your feet!" and the Maggid arose.

The passage under discussion mentions the names of various angels. As soon as the Baal Shem Tov read it aloud, the room became filled with light, fire began to flash all around them, and they actually perceived the angels mentioned.

Afterwards, the master commented to Rabbi Dov Ber, "The meaning of the text was as you had stated. However, there was no soul in your learning."[6]

The Baal Shem Tov was not satisfied with conceptual knowledge alone, and the fact that within two generations some of the greatest Torah scholars in Europe had joined the Chasidic movement demonstrated that they were looking for something deeper, too.

THE BAAL SHEM TOV'S DOCTRINE

One of the most central themes in the Baal Shem Tov's teachings is *deveykus* (cleaving to God). It is discussed in virtually every context, from one's most mundane activities to Kabbalistic practices intended only for exceptional *tzaddikim*. However, the vehicle for *deveykus* that is most relevant to the widest spectrum of the Jewish people is the daily prayer service itself.

Again, the idea that prayer can provide a vehicle for mystical experience is not new. The Ari *z"l* taught that each section of the morning prayer service corresponds in ascending order to one of the four "worlds" or levels of reality discussed in the Kabbalah. And in the *Tur*, the early codifier, Rabbi Yaakov ben Asher, states:

It is taught that when one prays, he must focus his attention ... This means that he must be aware of the words he utters and bear in mind that the

---

6. *Kesser Shem Tov* 424.

Shechinah is before him, as it is written, "I have placed God before me at all times."[7] One must concentrate and remove all distracting thoughts, so that his consciousness and intention remain pure during prayer ... This was the practice of the pious and the diligent: they would meditate and concentrate in their prayers until they divested themselves of physicality, and the spirit of higher perception would overcome them until they nearly reached the level of prophecy.[8]

Not only did the Baal Shem Tov feel that such practices are still relevant, but he encouraged even the average person to engage in them. Although we are far from the level of those to whom the above passage refers, our spiritual potential may be greater than we suspect:

Deveykus ... is the key that opens all locks. And this [advice]—to attach yourself to the words of prayer and Torah—applies to everyone. For every Jew, even the most common Jew, can come to experience the loftiest deveykus.[9]

With his various Torah discourses, practical instructions, words of encouragement, and personal testimonies, the Baal Shem Tov attempted to enable every Jew, according to his degree of holiness and purity, to reach the greatest heights. Reading the Baal Shem Tov's letter to Rabbi Gershon Kitover,[10] one recalls the words of Moshe Rabbeinu, "Would that all of God's people were prophets, that God would put His spirit upon them!"[11]

The Baal Shem Tov beheld Godliness in a blade of grass and intuited the Divine will in the smallest coincidence. His approach emphasizes God's immanence. Because God imbues everything with life, it is possible to apprehend the fundamental unity of all creation through every object and event. However, God is neither limited by creation nor coextensive with it. His Essence remains shrouded in mystery, beyond mortal conception. As our Sages taught, "God is the place of the world, but the world is not His place."[12] God transcends all worlds, physical and

---

7. *Tehillim* 16:8.

8. *Tur, Orach Chaim* 98.

9. Letter of R. Yosef Yitzchak of Lubavitch, cited in *Kesser Shem Tov, Hosafos, Noach*, 10.

10. This letter, included in the present anthology, states that Moshiach will come when the Baal Shem Tov's teachings have become widely disseminated, and the entire Jewish people can experience ascents of the soul and perform mystical unifications.

11. *Bamidbar* 11:29.

12. *Bereishis Rabba* 68:10.

spiritual. The only way we can relate to this aspect of Divinity is through simple *emunah* (faith)—and at the level of action, through fulfilling God's will. In order to "connect" to God's transcendence, one must transcend the limits of the human mind.[13]

The question is, how can mortal man know the Divine will? Without an act of revelation, this knowledge would be impossible. The revelation to the patriarchs, matriarchs, and prophets was a direct communication from God; the revelation to the entire Jewish people (and, through them, to the rest of the world) is through the Torah. Because the Torah expresses God's will and wisdom, it combines both the possibility and impossibility of knowledge. The Torah's depths can be explored forever, yet the root of knowledge always remains beyond us. Thus, the Baal Shem Tov taught:

> "God's Torah is perfect (*temimah*); it restores the soul" (*Tehillim* 19:8). God's Torah is perfect, for no one in the world has touched it yet. This is because "it restores the soul" of the person who continually approaches it with fresh enthusiasm. When one studies God's Torah with simplicity (*temimus*), as if he had never done so before, then it restores the soul.[14]

Notwithstanding his directives to apprehend Godliness in every nuance of the here and now, the Baal Shem Tov never downplays the primacy of Torah study and the performance of *mitzvos*. On the contrary, he recognizes them as the vehicle for our most perfect relationship to God—they are the marital bond between God and the Jewish people. Therefore, according to the Baal Shem Tov, the spiritual task of each and every Jew is to study Torah and perform the *mitzvos* with love and fear of God. For this reason, it became customary among many Chasidim to precede any holy undertaking with the Kabbalistic formula, *L'sheim yichud Kud'sha B'rich Hu u'Shechintei b'dichilu u'richimu.* . . . ("For the sake of the unification of the Holy One, blessed be He, and the Divine Presence, in love and in awe, the One who is hidden and concealed—in the name of all Israel.")[15]

The Torah makes it possible for Godliness to be grasped through the very limitations of intellect; the fulfillment of the Torah's command-

---

13. *Mishneh Torah, Hilchos Yesodei HaTorah*, Chapter 7; *Likkutei Moharan* I:24; *Sefer HaTanya*, Chapter 18.

14. *Vay'chal Moshe, Tehillim* 19.

15. See R. Elimelech of Lizhensk, *Tzetel Kattan* 4; *Noam Elimelech, Devarim*. Also note the ruling of R. Chaim of Chernowitz, printed in some editions of his *Sha'arei Tefillah*, which refutes the Nodah B'Yehudah's critique of this practice.

ments makes it possible for Godliness to be expressed through the very limitations of action. However, this can only take place when one approaches the Torah with *emunah* (faith). The verse states, "All Your *mitzvos* are *emunah*."[16] In other words, the transcendental quality of *emunah* is the root of Divine service.

The Baal Shem Tov's emphasis on *deveykus* even while engaged in Torah study contained an implicit critique of the attitude that prevailed in the Torah centers of that time. The *mitzvah* to study Torah *lishmah* (for its own sake) generally had been understood to mean that one should exert himself to correctly grasp the material at hand in order to perform the Divine will, rather than for ulterior motives such as prestige or winning arguments.[17] This issue was much debated during the nineteenth century, notably in *Nefesh HaChaim* by Rabbi Chaim of Volozhin, founder of the modern Lithuanian *yeshiva* system, and in *Yesod HaAvodah* by Rabbi Avraham of Slonim, a prominent Chasidic leader who lived in Lithuania, the stronghold of the Misnagdim.

The Baal Shem Tov and his followers pointed out that the common approach to learning, even with ulterior motives held in check, remains earthbound, ensnared in a mentality of *nitzatchon*—the winning of an intellectual battle. *B'chol d'rachecha da'eyhu*—"Know Him in all your ways"[18]—also means in the midst of intellectual exertion. At the very least, the Baal Shem Tov wanted one to pause from time to time in order to meditate upon God.[19] However, he also urged his disciples to cleave to God through the Torah itself:

> The proper *kavanah* (intention) for Torah study is to attach oneself in holiness and purity to the letters of thought and speech. That is, one should bind his *nefesh*, *ruach*, *neshamah*, *chayah* and *yechidah* (the five levels of the soul) to the holiness of "the candle of *mitzvos* and the light of Torah,"[20] the letters which enlighten and shine and impart true and eternal Godly

---

16. *Tehillim* 119:86.

17. Interestingly, R. Nachman of Breslev seems to define the study of Torah "*lishmah*" in this sense, while denouncing those who separate intellectual achievement from right action (*Likkutei Moharan* I:31); elsewhere, he states that the purpose of Torah study should be for the sake of "*yishuv ha'olam*": in order to make the world a civilized place (ibid., II:78). However, like the Baal Shem Tov, R. Nachman taught that one should approach his studies calmly and with patience, not trying to understand everything perfectly or all at once (*Sichos HaRan* 76).

18. *Mishlei* 3:6.

19. See *Likkutei Amarim of R. Menachem Mendel of Vitebsk*, 51.

20. *Mishlei* 6:23.

life. When one finally merits to understand and attaches himself to the holy letters, he will be able to perceive through the medium of the letters themselves—even to know future events. Thus, it is written that [the words of Torah] "enlighten the eyes."[21] For they enlighten the eyes of those who cleave to them in holiness and purity like the lights of the Urim and Tumim [on the breastplate of the Kohen Gadol].[22]

Yet this was never an all-or-nothing imperative. In practice, both Chasidim and Misnagdim fully appreciated that most of us will only rarely taste the sublime experience of *deveykus* during the rigorous intellectual process of Torah study. The fact that the Chasidim nevertheless preserved such an ideal, despite its loftiness, reflected a difference in educational approach. Torah study must be clearly addressed as an intrinsically spiritual task, or it may easily degenerate into an exercise in cleverness.

Similarly, there are other forms of Divine service mentioned in the Baal Shem Tov's teachings that are beyond the reach of the ordinary person. The ascent from one supernal realm to another is something most of us are not likely to experience often, no matter how diligently we concentrate on the words of prayer. Another such issue is the elevation of unholy or extraneous thoughts to their source in the world of the *sefiros*. Since "nothing exists but Him,"[23] one must transform "darkness to light," to use the *Zohar*'s phrase. It is possible to relate to God even where He is hidden; ultimately, everything is workable. The question is: Who can linger in these spiritual danger zones and emerge unscathed? In the view of most later Chasidic leaders, only a person with a "pure body," i.e., one who has overcome all physical desires, can accomplish this feat. For the rest of us, the only way to deal with unholy thoughts is with simple faith and detachment. As Rabbi Shneur Zalman of Liadi wrote, "One who wrestles with a filthy opponent is bound to become soiled."[24]

Instead of struggling with negativity, one should pursue the positive; rather than confronting evil directly, one should simply do good.[25] There is a humorous story that puts the matter in Chasidic perspective.

---

21. *Tehillim* 19:8–9.

22. *Sod Yachin U'Boaz*, Chapter 2.

23. *Devarim* 4:35.

24. *Sefer HaTanya*, Chapter 28; also see *Likkutei Moharan* I, 5:4; I:64; I:72; II:51; *Likkutei Halachos, Hilchos Tefillin* 6:32–37.

25. *Chayei Moharan* 447.

Early every morning, while everyone was asleep, the holy Rabbi Meir of Premishlan would arise, put a towel and a change of clothing in a sack, and leave his village in order to immerse in a nearby mountain spring. Once, two thieves, still awake from the last night's misadventures, saw the *tzaddik* as he left the main road and began to climb up the craggy mountainside. Of course, they immediately assumed that he was carrying a bag of gold and silver coins, which he was about to hide in a secret place.

Unobserved by Reb Meir, they began to follow him. But while the *tzaddik* danced up the boulders and hopped across the crevices, the thieves huffed and puffed and struggled to keep up, until at last they lost their footing and came tumbling to the ground. Encountering the hapless pair on his way home, Reb Meir helped them back to the village to nurse their aching bones.

"How could it be that an old man like you can climb such a precipice like a mountain goat, while my comrade and I can't go halfway without falling on our heads?" asked one of the thieves.

"When one is bound Above," the *tzaddik* replied, "he will not fall below."

That is all well and good if a person is a *tzaddik*, you may say. But the converse of Reb Meir's statement is also true: if you are bound below—if you are already sunken in evil passions and confusions— you cannot rise Above. Without some fundamental connection to the sphere of holiness, all the positivity in the world ultimately won't enable you to withstand the power of your lower nature. According to the Baal Shem Tov and his followers, the solution for most of us is by attachment to the *tzaddikim*.

THE ROLE OF THE CHASIDIC REBBE

There is a famous Chasidic adage attributed to Rabbi Shlomo of Karlin. It is written, "*V'tzaddik b'emunaso yichyeh*"—"And the *tzaddik* lives by his faith."[26] The word *yichyeh* (lives) may also be read *y'chayeh* (gives life). In other words, the *tzaddik* can elevate and transform those on a lower level if they have faith in his ability to do so. This principle became

---

26. *Chavakuk* 2:4.

the basic dynamic of both the spiritual path and the social system which the Baal Shem Tov and his disciples developed.[27]

The focal point in Chasidic life is the *tzaddik*. He is the ferryman who can enable one to traverse the turbulent waters of this world, the *ish haElokim*, the Godly man, who, like Moshe Rabbeinu, is uniquely empowered to bring man closer to God, and God closer to man. As such, his territory is not only the world of *nigleh*—worldly matters and the dimension of Torah that deals with them. The Chasidic *rebbe* also must be a master of *nistar*—the inner world and the inner dimension of Torah. One could argue that the Baal Shem Tov's model of Jewish leadership hearkens back to an ancient prototype: although he has exchanged his sackcloth for satin brocade, the Chasidic *rebbe* wears the mantle of the prophets.[28] (In this connection, it is interesting to note that the Baal Shem Tov's personal mentor, Achiyah HaShiloni, was not only a prophet, but a teacher of prophets.)

In truth, the Chasidic concept of the *tzaddik* is firmly rooted in traditional Judaism. The Talmud and Midrashim are replete with tales of *tzaddikim* and their miraculous powers, self-sacrifice and love for the Jewish people. Rather, it is the *tzaddik*'s role as a communal leader that is distinctive.

The *Zohar* describes Shabbos as the central point of the week, since the other six days receive their blessings from its holiness.[29] It also compares the *tzaddik* to Shabbos, since both are set apart from the mundane and both reflect the ultimate goal of creation.[30] The Baal Shem Tov united these two concepts when he made the *tzaddik*—and his Shabbos *tisch*—the center of Chasidic life.[31]

First and foremost, the *tzaddik* exemplifies what every Jew should strive to be.[32] He has labored and persevered until, having overcome all worldly desires, his only desire is for God.[33] Therefore, his thought, speech, and action have become a vehicle for the Divine will and wisdom. The *tzaddik* is a living *Sefer* Torah. Thus, our Sages taught: "Those who stand up for a Torah scroll but not for a Torah sage are fools."[34]

---

27. Also note *Likkutei Moharan* I, 13:2; ibid., 62:7; *Sichos HaRan* 63.

28. *Likkutei Moharan* II, 8:8.

29. *Zohar* II, *Yisro*, 88a.

30. *Zohar* III, *Naso*, 144b.

31. *Degel Machaneh Ephraim*, *Tzav*.

32. *Niddah* 30b.

33. *Zohar* I:4a; *Likkutei Moharan* I:8; I:52; ibid., II:7; *Sichos HaRan* 136; *Shivchey HaRan* 23; *Avodas Yisrael*, *T'rumah*, 31b; *Sefer HaTanya* I:10.

34. *Makkos* 22b.

In his role as a spiritual guide, the *tzaddik* stands in the world of *tikkun* (perfection) and reaches out to those still struggling to overcome their inner darkness. His enlightenment does not remove him from the human dilemma; in fact, the *tzaddik* may feel the pain of others more than they do themselves.[35] Bound to the Source of life, he works unceasingly to perfect all of creation. Even mundane matters are within his sphere of concern—for everything must fulfill its spiritual destiny. The *tzaddik* has purged every trace of evil from his heart; therefore, his perspective is unclouded by any trace of ego or desire. His intervention in the affairs of others is an act of love.[36]

Thus, to borrow a Kabbalistic paradigm, the *tzaddik* represents the goal in the midst of the process, the central point of holiness in the midst of the profane.[37]

THE INNER ESSENCE

In a larger sense, it is this revelation of the central and innermost point that is the unique contribution of Chasidism. *P'nimius HaTorah*—the mystical dimension—is the root and inclusive principle of the entire Torah. The *tzaddik*, too, is the root and inclusive principle of all Jewish souls.[38] The *Midrash Tanchuma* states that the Torah refers to Moshe by the name "Yisrael" because he represented the entire Jewish people.[39] Since the *tzaddik* embodies this collective innermost point, he can relate to the innermost point of each and every Jew. In Kabbalistic literature (and especially in the writings of the Chabad school of Chasidism), this is called *yechida*—"oneness"—the point where we are all the same,

---

35. *Sichos HaRan* 188.

36. *Avodas Yisrael, Likkutim, Ta'anis; Divrei Emes, Noach,* 13b; *Chayei Moharan* 471.

37. *Sichos HaRan* 72, citing *Mishlei* 19:21.

38. *Sha'ar HaPesukim* 2:3, citing *Bamidbar* 11:21.

39. Rashi on *Bamidbar* 21:21, citing *Midrash Tanchuma.* Also note *Berachos* 58a: "R. Chanina recited the blessing to be said upon seeing 600,000 Jews when he beheld his mentors, R. Papa and R. Huna, son of R. Yehoshua." Ramban (*Milchamos,* ad loc.) explains that there are great sages who comprehend all the viewpoints of the entire Jewish people. Their prototype is Yehoshua Bin Nun, whom the Torah describes as "the man who has *ruach* (spirit) within him," because he knew how to relate to the spirit of each and every individual (*Bamidbar* 27:18; Rashi, ad loc.). For a discussion of this concept in Chasidic thought, see *Degel Machaneh Ephraim, Mas'ei; Likkutei Moharan* I, 34:4.

without distinctions.[40] Therefore, he can express true *ahavas Yisrael* (love of the Jewish people).

Once, when my own teacher, Rabbi Elazar Mordechai Kenig, of Tzefat, Israel, was visiting New York, the name of a certain rabbi was mentioned in conversation. "You can see that he must be very great in *p'nimius haTorah*," Rabbi Kenig said, "because he can reach so many different types of Jews."

The Gemara teaches that just as we put on *tefillin*, so does the Creator, so to speak, put on *tefillin*:

> Rabbi Nachman Bar Yitzchak asked Rabbi Chiya bar Avin, "What is written in the *tefillin* of the Master of the Universe?" And he replied, "Who is like Your people, Israel, one nation on the earth?"[41] . . . The Holy One, blessed be He, said to Israel, "You have made me One in the world, and I will make you one in the world."[42]

The corollary of God's Oneness is the oneness of the Jewish people.[43] The *tzaddikim*, too, are compared to the *tefillin* because they alone can truly grasp the secret of this oneness. Thus, it is no accident that Chasidic doctrine specifically stresses the realization of God's Oneness within all of creation, *p'nimius haTorah*, *tzaddik*, and *ahavas Yisrael*. They are really facets of the same fundamental truth.[44]

"The Torah, the Jewish people and the Holy One, blessed be He, are all one."[45] This unity is a *metzius*—a fact. But how may it be realized in the heart of every person? According to the Baal Shem Tov, the key is love. Thus, he proclaimed: "I have come to this earth to introduce a new way of serving God that is really very old. There are three things for which a person must strive: love of God, love of his fellow Jew, and love of Torah. And there is no need for self-mortification."[46] It is love which binds together that which is separate and brings about a revelation of a higher and essential unity. This sort of simple but profound truth char-

---

40. *Zohar* I:81a; ibid., 206a; *Eitz Chaim, Sha'ar* 42; ibid., 6:5, 40:10, 49:12, 45:1; R. Shneur Zalman of Liadi, *Likkutei Torah, Balak*, 70a; R. Dov Ber of Lubavitch, *Imrei Binah, Sha'ar Krias Shema*, Chapter 8.

41. *Divrei HaYomim* 27:21.

42. *Berachos* 6a.

43. *Degel Machaneh Ephraim, Va'eschanan*, 198b.

44. See *Likkutei Moharan* II:67.

45. Based on *Zohar* III, 73a.

46. *Butzina D'Nehora*, cited in *Sefer Baal Shem Tov, Mishpatim*, 17.

acterizes the Baal Shem Tov's mysticism and his approach as a teacher of the Jewish people.

The compiler of the *Sefer Baal Shem Tov* points out that *HaRav Yisrael Ben Eliezer* bears the same *gematria* (numerical value) as the verse, "Hear, O Israel, the Lord, our God, the Lord is One."[47] In the merit of the holy Baal Shem Tov and those who follow in his ways, may God have mercy on the "one nation on earth" and redeem us physically and spiritually from our long and bitter exile. "On that day, God will be One and His Name will be One,"[48] speedily, in our days, *amen*.

47. *Devarim* 6:4; see *Sefer Baal Shem Tov, Va'eschanan,* note 14.
48. *Zechariah* 14:9.

I

Teachings of the Baal Shem Tov

Ahavas Yisrael

Ahavas Yisrael (love of the Jewish people) is the first gate which leads to the courtyard of the Creator (*Likkutei Dibburim* II, p. 412).

The Baal Shem Tov once reproached an itinerant preacher who had delivered a fiery sermon to a group of simple villagers. "How can you speak evil of the Jewish people?" he cried. "All day long a Jew trudges through the marketplace until dusk, when he becomes anxious and says, 'It's getting late for *minchah* (the afternoon prayer).' So he runs off somewhere to pray and doesn't even know what he is saying—but nevertheless, the very angels tremble at his words" (*Shiv'chei Baal Shem Tov* 128).

The Maggid [of Mezeritch] taught: The Baal Shem Tov often used to say that love of the Jewish people is the same thing as love of God. The verse states, "You are children unto the Lord, your God."[1] When one loves the father, one loves the children (*HaYom Yom*, p. 81).

"Israel in whom I will praise Myself . . . " (*Yeshayahu* 49:3). God cannot be praised—for who can comprehend His Essence? Therefore, God brought the Jewish people into existence in order to praise Himself. Just as a father praises himself because of his children, so does the Holy One, Blessed be He, praise Himself because of Israel (*Kisvei Kodesh*, cited in *Sefer Baal Shem Tov, Ki Savo* 4).

"You shall love your neighbor as yourself," (*Vayikra* 19:18), is a reflection of the *mitzvah*, "You shall love the Lord, your God."[2] When one loves another Jew, he loves the Holy One, blessed be He. For [the soul of] a Jew is a "portion of God Above,"[3] and when one loves a fellow

---

1. *Devarim* 14:1.
2. *Devarim* 6:5.
3. *Shefa Tal* 1a.

3

Jew, he loves his innermost essence. Thus, he loves the Holy One, blessed be He, as well (*HaYom Yom* 78).

"[God told Avraham:] Look to the heavens and count the stars . . . Thus shall be your offspring" (*Bereishis* 15:15). The Baal Shem Tov explained: The stars appear very small, but in heaven they are really very large. The same is true of the Jewish people. In this world, they appear very small. But in the Supernal World, they are really very great (Rabbi Tzvi Hirsch of Ziditchov, *Beis Yisrael, Lech Lecha* 36, cited in *Sefer Baal Shem Tov, Lech Lecha* 27).

The Baal Shem Tov taught: The Holy One, blessed be He, sends a soul to the world to live seventy or eighty years, just to do another Jew a favor, materially in general or spiritually in particular (*Likkutei Dibburim* III, p. 1126, cited in *Kesser Shem Tov, Hosafos*, 130).

The Baal Shem Tov said that a heartfelt chapter of *Tehillim*, the effort expended in doing another Jew a favor, whether material or spiritual, and love of one's fellow Jew are keys which can unlock the gates to the Heavenly Palaces of mercy, healing, salvation and livelihood (*Sefer HaSichos* 5700, p. 73, cited in *Kesser Shem Tov, Hosafos*, 127).

The Baal Shem Tov taught: God loves every Jew as if he were an only child, born to his parents in their old age—and even more (*Likkutei Sichos* III, p. 982).

The Baal Shem Tov once said: "When a Jew sighs in compassion for the grief of another Jew, this breaks through even the most impenetrable barriers of those who denounce us Above. And when a Jew enthusiastically shares in another Jew's rejoicing and blesses him, God receives

it like the prayer of Rabbi Yishmael Kohen Gadol in the Holy of Holies"
(*Sefer HaSichos* 5703).

The Baal Shem Tov once told his disciple, the Rav of Kolomaye (father of the *tzaddik*, Rabbi Nachman of Kolomaye): "I love the Jew whom you might consider to be the lowest of the low more than you love your only son" (*Leket Imrei P'ninim* 208b).

The entire Jewish people are one. [This collectivity] has a physical aspect (*chomer*) and spiritual aspect (*tzurah*). And just as the body needs the soul, so does the soul need the body. Therefore, [one who is in the category of *tzurah*] should not separate himself from [those who are in the category of *chomer*]; rather, he should bind himself to them and watch over them with a compassionate eye in order to return them to the ways of virtue (*Toldos Yaakov Yosef, Kedoshim*).

"'For you shall be [like] a desirable land,' says the Lord of Hosts" (*Malachi* 3:12). Just as the greatest wise men cannot fathom all the treasures of nature with which God has endowed the earth—for everything comes from the earth—similarly, no one can apprehend all the treasures the Jewish people contain; for they are God's "desirable land."

The Baal Shem Tov concluded: "I would like to enable the Jewish people to yield the kind of produce which God's 'desirable land' can surely give" (*HaYom Yom*, p. 54, cited in *Kesser Shem Tov, Hosafos* 44).

Among the teachings [Rabbi Shneur Zalman of Liadi] brought back from his first visit to [the Maggid of] Mezeritch were two different interpretations of the verse "Remember, O God, what has become of us; look and behold our disgrace" (*Eichah* 5:1). The Baal Shem Tov, whose soul rests in the Garden of Eden, delivered these two different interpretations of the same verse on two separate occasions, albeit with the same preface. He began by discussing the sanctity of the physical birth of all

Jews, whether male or female, without distinction. The Baal Shem Tov spoke at length, lucidly describing God's holy love for the Jewish people—not only their souls but their bodies, as well. God loves every Jew equally, from the greatest Torah scholar to the humblest commoner. His love is no greater for the foremost Torah scholar than for the common man, nor any less for the Jewish commoner than for the greatest Torah scholar. The Baal Shem Tov went on to explain how this Divine love is for the essence of all Jews and Judaism. "Torah scholar" and "commoner" are merely two terms for one who knows and one who does not know. These terms only apply to one's manifest abilities. However, regarding the essence of all Jews and Judaism, everything is the same.

All Jews have their source in the Divine name of forty-five letters—*Mah* [which bears the numerical value of forty-five]. [This Divine name is] of the World of *Atzilus* (Emanation), as the discourse, "*Pasach Eliyahu . . .*" states, "The Divine name *Mah* is the path of *Atzilus*."[4] Bringing strong proofs from the laws of family purity, circumcision, and the injunction to save endangered lives, the Baal Shem Tov explained that all Jews are equally loved by God.

After giving this preface, the Baal Shem Tov once observed a large group of accomplished Torah scholars who were intensely involved in scholarly debate and in presenting their *chiddushim* (original Torah interpretations). He saw that everyone was only preoccupied with himself, well pleased with his own accomplishments. To that assembly, the Baal Shem Tov said: "'Remember, O God, what (*mah*) has become of us . . .' Remember, O God, what has become of the *Mah* [i.e., the essential simplicity and oneness] of our souls. 'Look and behold our disgrace.' Look and make us witness our own disgraceful state."

On another occasion, [the Baal Shem Tov visited] a small town inhabited by unlettered simple folk, who, due to their love for their fellow Jews, performed the *mitzvah* of redeeming captives with *mesiras nefesh* (self-sacrifice). The Baal Shem Tov told his disciples, "'Remember, O God, what (*mah*) has become of us . . .' Remember, O God, what has come about because of the *Mah* of their souls. 'Look and behold our disgrace (*cherpah*).' Look at how they risk their lives [*mecharef* means both risk and disgrace[5]] out of love for the Jewish people!" (*Sefer HaMa'amarim: Yiddish*, p. 212).

---

4. *Tikkunei Zohar, Hakdamah* II; *Likkutei Moharan* II:82.
5. See Radak, *Sefer HaSherashim, cheref*; Radak and Rashi on *Shoftim* 5:18; Radak on II *Shmuel* 23:9.

"Until Avraham the world existed in darkness." (*Bereishis Rabba*—Vilna edition 2:3). The *tzaddikim* of that period did not teach their contemporaries the paths of God, nor did they beseech mercy for their sakes. "When Avraham came, [the light] began to shine."[6] He began to teach his generation the paths of Divine service and to demonstrate *mesiras nefesh* (self-sacrifice) in awakening God's mercy on behalf of his fellowmen. He even prayed and sought mercy for the wicked and the sinful: the people of Sodom and Amorah.

Nevertheless, in the days of Avraham the masses (including Yishmael) were called "a nation comparable to a donkey."[7] But regarding the descendants of Yisrael, the masses are called *am ha'aretz* ("people of the earth")—that is, a nation comparable to the earth.

Everyone treads upon the earth. [However, despite its lowliness,] the earth has been graced by God with the power of growth, so that it yields produce and thereby sustains all living creatures; within it may be found treasures of gold and silver and all things the world holds dear. Similarly, [the *Midrash* says] of the Jewish people, "'Your cheek (*reikaseich*) is like a split pomegranate . . .'[8] Even your empty ones (*reikaseich*) are as full of *mitzvos* as a pomegranate [is full of seeds]."[9] How much more are those who uphold the *mitzvos* whole-heartedly and with simple faith—the *am ha'aretz*—a people comparable to the earth. This is what [the Torah means when] it states, "For you shall be [like] a desirable land . . ."[10] (*Sefer HaZichronos* I, p. 342, cited in *Kesser Shem Tov, Hosafos*, 98).

Our master, the Baal Shem Tov, once said: The Jewish people are the *tefillin* of the Master of the Universe. The Gemara states, "What is written in the *tefillin* of the Master of the Universe? 'And who is like

6. *Shemos Rabba* 15:26.
7. *Vayikra Rabba* 20:2.
8. *Shir HaShirim* 4:3.
9. *Shir HaShirim Rabba*, ad loc.
10. *Malachi* 3:12.

unto Your people, Yisrael, one nation in the world.'"[11] For the Jewish
people draw forth God's Oneness into the world.

Tefillin contain two basic components: those of the head and those
of the hand [which are worn opposite the heart]. The Jewish people,
who are God's *tefillin*, also include *tefillin* of the head—thinkers and
Torah scholars—and *tefillin* of the hand—simple Jews who [neverthe-
less] possess fine character traits.

The blessing recited upon affixing the *tefillin* states, "Who has sanctified us with His *mitzvos* and commanded us . . ." God made us, the
Jewish people, holy with His *mitzvos*. This blessing is recited over both
the *tefillin* of the hand and those of the head; then they both must be
affixed.[12] But first one must put on the *tefillin* of the hand, and then the
tefillin of the head.

In the *tefillin* [of the Master of the Universe], those of the hand
comprise the Divine service of the common folk, and those of the head
comprise the Divine service of Torah scholars. [However,] the act [which
corresponds to] putting on these *tefillin* is the acceptance of the Kingdom of Heaven by ordinary Jews. This is even higher than the Divine
service of those gifted with the knowledge and apprehension of Torah.
(*Sefer HaSichos* 5700, p. 133, cited in *Kesser Shem Tov, Hosafos* 70).

I heard from my grandfather (the Baal Shem Tov): When the Holy
One, blessed be He, created His world, it was unable to endure. Everything would have reverted to nothingness had He not created the Children of Israel. [When He did so,] the world was able to endure.[13]

The name Yisrael alludes to this. The letter *reish* corresponds to
the *sefirah* of *chochmah* (wisdom).[14] The letter *lamed* corresponds to the
sefirah of *binah* (understanding).[15] And the letter *alef* corresponds to the

---

11. *Berachos* 6a.
12. See Part Two of this volume, "Customs of the Baal Shem Tov," for variant
traditions concerning this blessing.
13. See *Likkutei Moharan* 1:52.
14. *Reish* can also mean "beginning." In the Kabbalistic description of creation,
this is related to the *sefirah* of *chochmah* (wisdom), as implied by *Tehillim* 111:10, "The
beginning is wisdom . . ."
15. *Lamed* is related to *limud*, "instruction," which suggests *binah*, the next *sefirah*
in the process of creation.

sefirah of *daas* (knowledge).[16] [Together, these three *sephiros* express the Divine Intellect which animates the universe.] The remaining two letters, *yud* and *shin*, spell the word *yesh* (somethingness). The world was created *yesh m'ayin* (something from nothing). These two letters allude to the "somethingness" which enables the world to endure—the Jewish people. The name Yisrael thus indicates that they preserve all of creation, for without them, everything would revert to its original state of nothingness. The "somethingness" of the Jewish people sustains the "somethingness" of the rest of creation. However, this is true when a Jew possesses only enough "somethingness" to fulfill his role in sustaining the universe. If he has more, none of the above applies.

This was the gist of my grandfather's awesome words. There is nothing else to say, for "all words are spent,"[17] due to the depth of the perception and the inability of those who wish to grasp it. According to my limited understanding, the entire Torah is contained in this teaching (*Degel Machaneh Ephraim, Va'eschanan*).

[R. Pinchos of Koretz] told R. Mendel of Brod that the Baal Shem Tov taught his disciples: One must always strive to perfect the world. But one who does so may be compared to a broom which is used to sweep out a courtyard and becomes soiled in the process. Although he may help to purify the world, some of its evil may cling to him. Still, one must descend to *Gehenna*, if necessary, for the sake of the Jewish people. This is alluded to by the Gemara's concept of "transgressing for the sake of God."[18] One might have thought that by acting for the sake of God, he would not have to descend to *Gehenna*. However, the Baal Shem Tov revealed that this is not so. Even though a broom is used to clean the house, it becomes dirty, and must be thoroughly washed until it becomes clean again. Similarly, a person may have done much to perfect the world, but he should not become proud—for who knows what may cleave to him? (*Imrei Pinchos, Darchei Avodas Hashem* 29).

---

16. *Alef* is related to knowledge, as in Job 33:33, "And I shall cause you to know (*va'aleph'cha*) wisdom." *Daas* is the third *sefirah* in the process of creation.

17. *Koheles* 1:8.

18. *Horayos* 10b; *Nazir* 23b.

Beginning Anew

"You are Him, the Lord, our God . . ." (*Siddur, "Ein K'Elokeinu"*). When a person thinks that he is close to God and uses the term "You," he is really far from God. [Thus, it is followed] by the term "Him," which implies concealment. But when one thinks that he is far from God and uses the term "Him," he is really very close. [Thus, it is followed] by "the Lord, our God" (*Kesser Shem Tov* 29).

"Those who were lost in Ashur will come, as well as those who were exiled in the land of Mitzrayim . . ." (*Yeshayahu* 27:13). I heard this teaching in the name of the venerable and saintly man of God, our master, Rabbi Yisrael Baal Shem Tov of Medzhibuzh: When a person thinks that he is blameless in the eyes of Heaven, perfect in all his ways and lacking nothing in his Divine service, he is utterly lost and will never get back on his feet again, may the Merciful One spare us. To be sure, he has not even begun to serve God and has no idea of the truth; he will perish without wisdom and live in falsehood all his days.

Not so the *tzaddik*. He knows the truth and recognizes the loftiness of the Creator. The more he accomplishes and the greater the level he attains, the more he recognizes God's loftiness. He sees that his Divine service has always been deficient; for [no one] is greater than Moshe Rabbeinu, who before his death declared, "You have just begun to show Your servant Your greatness . . ."[1] [Moshe Rabbeinu] felt that all of his Divine service hitherto had been merely a beginning; he considered himself to be in exile before Him, God forbid, as if he had not yet attained the level of a *tzaddik*.

Concerning this, the verse states, "Those who were lost in Ashur will come . . ." That is, those who were in the land of Ashur, who felt content (*me'ushurim*) with all their deeds, are lost. However, those who took themselves to be in the land of Mitzrayim—[this word also may be read as] *meitzar yam*, "the straits of the sea"—and had not yet attained a high spiritual level are described as exiled, not lost. [Because they feel

---

1. *Devarim* 4:23.

far from God, they are always beginning to serve him anew.][2] (*Ahavas Dodim, Shir HaShirim*).

"Do not cast us away when we are old . . ." (*Tehillim* 71:9). Sometimes a person feels inspired to undertake a certain holy task, either in Torah study or prayer. But this enthusiasm does not remain with him. It soon falls away, and, instead, the *mitzvah* he wanted to perform suddenly seems old to him, like a familiar routine. Concerning this, the verse states, "Do not cast us away" from our enthusiasm, for then "we are old," and [our Divine service] seems like a familiar routine. Rather, may it always be new (*Sifsei Tzaddikim, Pekudei*).

"And you shall appoint for yourselves cities; Cities of Refuge they shall be for you . . ." (*Bamidbar* 35:11). The Baal Shem Tov taught: The three Cities of Refuge allude to thought, speech, and action. One must flee [to them] from the Avenger—the evil angel who wants to deter him from serving the Creator. [Therefore,] one must fortify himself with holy thoughts, holy words, and good deeds. Even if they are not so luminous and pure, they are better than nothing, for [by virtue of them] one nevertheless performs his Master's will (*Kedushas Levi, Likkutim* 109b).

---

2. See R. Elimelech of Lizhensk, *Likkutei Shoshanah* 98a.

Bris Milah

[Our Sages taught:] When David HaMelech entered the bath-house and saw himself standing naked, he cried, "Woe unto me, that I stand naked of *mitzvos*!" Then he reminded himself of the mark of circumcision upon his flesh and his mind became calm. Upon leaving, he recited a song of praise to God: "To the choirmaster, on the eight-stringed harp (*sh'minis*), a psalm of David . . . "[1] This alludes to the *mitzvah* of circumcision, which is performed on the eighth day (*sh'minis*) (*Menachos* 43b).

One might wonder why David HaMelech did not remind himself of his *peyos* and beard, which also are *mitzvos*. I heard an explanation of this in the name of Rabbi Yisrael Baal Shem Tov: When [the Gemara says that] David HaMelech entered the bath-house, it did not refer to a physical bath-house. Rather, he entered into contemplation in order to examine himself and cleanse himself of transgression; as the verse states, "When God will have washed away the filth of the daughters of Tzion . . ."[2] And he saw himself standing naked, without any *mitzvos*— for he felt that he did not possess a single *mitzvah* free from selfish motives. Even his *peyos* and beard seemed to possess a trace of unholy motivation; for his *peyos* and beard were very beautiful, and because of them he looked handsome to others. Then David HaMelech reminded himself of the mark of circumcision in his flesh. When his father had circumcised him on the eighth day, he had lacked sufficient knowledge to conceive of unholy thoughts. Also, as he grew up, the mark of circumcision remained hidden from others. Therefore, this *mitzvah* was pure (*Rav Yaivi, Tehillim* 12).

---

1. *Tehillim* 12:1.
2. *Yeshayahu* 4:4.

Charity

"As for me, in righteousness (*tzedek*) I will behold Your face ..." (*Tehillim* 17:15). I heard in the name of the Baal Shem Tov that when one gives a coin to a poor person, he performs a unification [of the Divine Name YHVH]. The coin represents the letter *yud* [which is a small point]. The five fingers of the giver allude to the letter *hey* [which is equivalent to the number five]. His extended arm is comparable to the letter *vav*. And the receiver's five fingers correspond to the last letter *hey*. In this way, one draws forth Divine mercy [which is represented by the Divine Name YHVH] (*Mevaser Tzedek, R'ei*).

"Just as (*mah*) He is merciful and gracious, so you should be merciful and gracious" (*Shabbos* 133b). The word *rachum* (merciful) contains the same letters as the word *chomer* (physicality). How could the Holy One, blessed be He, bestow His mercy upon something gross and physical—and how could He be perceived by even the most refined level of physical thought? Only if God constricts Himself in order to relate to the physical world can He bestow His mercy upon us. And what causes this constriction? An act of mercy on the part of man. Then the Holy One, blessed be He, puts on His garment and constricts Himself, so to speak, and shows us mercy. Thus [the statement of our Sages may be rendered,] "For what reason (*mah*) is He merciful and gracious? Because you are merciful and gracious"[1] (*Tzava'as HaRivash* 112).

Once the Baal Shem Tov took his son, Rabbi Tzvi [who was still a young boy], along with him to visit the local rabbi. The lad looked about and saw many silver vessels there. On their way home, the Baal Shem Tov said to his son, "Surely, you are envious because your father doesn't own any silver vessels."

"Yes," his son replied.

---

1. See *Sichos HaRan* 89.

He then said, "If your father had money for silver vessels, it would be better spent to provide for the poor, and anything left could be given to charity" (*Shiv'chei Baal Shem Tov* 122).

I heard from [Rabbi Gedaliah of Linitz] that the Baal Shem Tov never kept money overnight. When he returned from his travels, he would pay his debts and contribute the rest of his money to charity the very same day (*Shiv'chei Baal Shem Tov* 123).

"And when you spread forth your hands, I will hide My eyes from you; also, when you pray at length, I will not listen, for your hands are full of blood" (*Yeshayahu* 1:15).

The Baal Shem Tov explained: The main forms of Divine service are the service of the mind and the service of the heart; that is, Torah study and prayer. By exerting oneself in these two forms of Divine service, one's character traits and one's conduct in worldly matters will automatically be what they should be.

Nevertheless, one's hands can still be "full of blood." One may give to the poor with a generous hand but not feel the other person's plight. This is bloodshed. Thus, the verse states, "And when you spread forth your hands," when you extend your hands to another and generously give charity, which is a service of the heart, nevertheless, "I will hide My eyes from you." I will not pay attention to this, for it is not a true form of Divine service. True Divine service entails feeling another person's plight. "Also, when you pray at length . . ." which [in comparison to charity] is a service of the mind—this is not true Divine service, because one does not really feel compassion for the other person. "Your hands are full of blood." That is, your character traits—even the good character traits—are full of blood (Rabbi Yosef Yitzchak of Lubavitch, *Sefer HaMa'amarim: Yiddish*, p. 216).

The Baal Shem Tov used to give more than one-fifth of his income to charity. He was once asked, "Does the Torah not state that one should not distribute (*y'vazbeiz*) more than a fifth?"[2]

---

2. *Kesubos* 50a.

He replied, "The word *y'vazbeiz* is related to the word *bizah* [plunder, as in wartime]. If one does not really wish to give, but must wage war with himself in order to plunder and rend the money from his own possession—in that case, the Torah states, 'Do not distribute (*y'vazbeiz*) more than a fifth.' But if one gives with joy and delight, how is charity unlike any other pleasure or necessity on which one spends money?"[3] (*Orach L'Chaim, Terumah* and *V'Tzivah HaKohen,* Chapter 15, cited in *Likkutei Sichos* I, p. 170).

"He gave charity to the destitute . . ." (*Tehillim* 112:9). The Baal Shem Tov said: God gave the trait of being charitable to the destitute (*Ner Yisrael* I, *Tehillim,* p. 207).

I heard it said in the name of our master, the holy Rabbi Yisrael Baal Shem Tov: [Most of] the *mitzvos* a person performs with improper motives would be better left undone—with the exception of giving charity. Even if this *mitzvah* is not performed in the most perfect manner, one still performs a *mitzvah,* since a poor person will benefit from it[4] (*Turei Zahav, R'ei*).

---

3. Also see *Sefer HaTanya, Iggeres HaTeshuvah* 93a; *Iggeres HaKodesh* 115b.

4. See Rashi on *Vayikra* 5:17; *Sifra* on *Vayikra* 12:12. Another version of this teaching mentions three things that are praiseworthy, even with improper motives: charity (for the reason stated above); immersion in the *mikveh,* which, regardless of a person's intent, effects *taharah* (ritual purification); and teaching Torah, which enables the student to become knowledgeable. See *Imrei Pinchos,* 1098.

Children

Rabbi Rephael of Bershad taught: A man whose son had gone astray once came to the Baal Shem Tov. "Love him even more," the Baal Shem Tov advised, "and this will help him to return to God" (*Midrash Pinchas* 38b).

During his years of concealment, the Baal Shem Tov [used to escort children back and forth from *cheder*]. Sometimes he would rest his holy hand on the heart of a child and say, "May you be a warm-hearted Jew" (*Likkutei Dibburim* III, p. 1054).

The Maggid of Mezeritch once remarked, "If only I could kiss the *Sefer* Torah with the same love that the Baal Shem Tov used to show a little child who had started reciting his *alef-beis*!" (*Sippurei Chasidim, Shir HaShirim*).

"And Yitzchak loved Esav because that which he trapped was in his mouth" (*Bereishis* 25:28). Rashi explains homiletically that this verse refers to the mouth of Esav, for he trapped [Yitzchak, his father,] and deceived him with his words. Rabbi Michel of Zlotchov heard from his master, the holy Baal Shem Tov: From the day that Esav deceived Yitzchak, even *tzaddikim* cannot see evil in their own children (*Zohar Chai, Vayeishev,* 346a).

Criticism

One could not see a deficiency in someone else if he did not bear a trace of it within himself[1] (*Kesser Shem Tov* 116).

For oneself, one must always maintain a critical eye; for others, never (*Sippurei Tzaddikim* 24, 1).

When one speaks with others, he should not look to see whether or not their thoughts constantly cleave to the Creator—for the very act of looking damages the soul. However, regarding people who are what they should be, whose thoughts do constantly cleave to the Creator, one should gaze at them. This will enable one's soul to acquire an additional measure of holiness (*Tzava'as HaRivash* 50).

The saintly man of God, Rabbi Yisrael Baal Shem Tov, once encountered one of the outstanding *tzaddikim* of the generation who used to rebuke the masses [during his sermons]. "How can you give reproof?" the Baal Shem Tov asked. "All of your days you have never known what it is to sin, nor do you associate with your fellow creatures enough to understand their transgressions" (*Amtachas Binyamin, Koheles*; cited in *Sefer Baal Shem Tov, Kedoshim* 16).

I heard from my master (the Baal Shem Tov) a simple adage that encompasses everything: If you wish to belittle any creature, belittle yourself. And if you wish to praise anyone, praise God all the more (*Toldos Yaakov Yosef, Vayeishev*).

---

1. Also see R. Shmuel of Slonim, *Divrei Shmuel, Bechukosai*.

Dancing

[Rabbi Shneur Zalman of Liadi] said that the following was the first teaching about Simchas Torah which the Baal Shem Tov related to his disciples:

Jews are usually sleepy on Simchas Torah. In general, Shabbos and Yom Tov are times when people pray later than on weekdays. And on Simchas Torah in particular, one sleeps a bit more because of the *hakafos* (dancing with the Torah scrolls) and the festive meal. However, angels do not have such forms of Divine service; so, naturally, on Simchas Torah they get up as early as usual. They want to sing God's praises, but, lacking human souls, they are unable to do so. [Our Sages taught that the Ministering Angels do not begin to sing praises in Heaven until the Jewish people have sung on earth below.] Thus, the verse states, "When the morning stars [i.e., the Jewish people] sang together . . ." and then concludes ". . . all the sons of God [i.e., the angels] shouted for joy."[1] So there they are, awake, roaming about the Garden of Eden—and sometimes they come across things they do not recognize: shoe-soles, sandals. [The angels] are utterly bewildered: they are used to finding *tzitzis* and *tefillin* in the Garden of Eden, but not sandals!

They go and ask the Angel Michael [the Heavenly defender of the Jewish people], who tells them that this merchandise belongs to him. Then he explains, "All of this comes from the Jews who dance with the Torah," and begins to count the sandals, saying, "These are from Kaminka, these are from Medzhibuzh . . ."

And with this, the Angel Michael boasts to the Angel Metat, who weaves crowns for his Maker from the prayers of the Jewish people,[2] that he—Michael—could make a better crown from the torn sandals of Simchas Torah[3] (*Sefer HaSichos* 5701, p. 31, cited in *Kesser Shem Tov, Hosafos*, 114).

---

1. *Chullin* 91b, citing *Iyov* 38:7.

2. *Zohar* III, 33a. According to rabbinic tradition, names of angels should not be pronounced unless they are also commonly used for people, as well; thus, "Metat" is not the full name of this angel.

3. On Chasidic dancing, also see *Likkutei Moharan* I, 10:1, II:24; *Chayei Moharan* I:19, II:9. See *Ta'amei HaMinhagim*, p. 497 (note), citing the Ari z"l.

Once, at the conclusion of Yom Kippur, the Baal Shem Tov and his disciples were unable to recite *Kiddush HaLevanah* (the Sanctification of the Moon), because the moon was not visible. With his *ruach hakodesh*, the Baal Shem Tov saw that if they did not perform this *mitzvah*, a tragedy would immediately befall the Jewish people, God forbid. He was greatly distressed and endeavored to cause the moon to appear by entering a state of *mochin d'gadlus* (expanded consciousness). Time and again he asked, "Has the moon come out?" But to his disappointment, the heavens remained cloudy. There seemed to be no hope for the moon to appear that night.

The Baal Shem Tov's Chasidim had no idea how important it was for them to recite *Kiddush HaLevanah* specifically on this *motza'ei* Yom Kippur. It was always their custom to rejoice upon the completion of their Yom Kippur prayers and those of their master, the Baal Shem Tov, whose Divine service on the holy day was like that of the *Kohen Gadol*. This time, as well, they began to celebrate with dancing and holy fervor. At first, they danced in the outer section of the Baal Shem Tov's house; then, as their joy increased, they dared to enter the Baal Shem Tov's private chamber. Since their fervor had inspired them to joyously dance in the Baal Shem Tov's room, they also mustered up the courage to invite the Baal Shem Tov to join them. Thus, they drew their master into the circle of dancers.

In the midst of this holy festivity, someone called out, "The moon has appeared!" And they all ran out to recite the *Kiddush HaLevanah* prayer that very night. Later, the Baal Shem Tov said, "What I could not accomplish through lofty levels of Divine service, the Chasidim accomplished with simple joy alone."

From this we may see how one must trust in God and rejoice in performing His *mitzvos*. Even at a time of distress (may they never befall us) one can bring about Heavenly deliverance by remaining joyous (*Divrei David—Tchortkov*, cited in *Meir Einei Yisrael*).

The Baal Shem Tov once remarked: Dancing brings joy to the Supernal Family [the Creator and the Ministering Angels] and blessings to the Jewish people, together with happiness, mercy, and great kindness (*Zera Baruch, Hosafos*).

Once, on Simchas Torah, the Baal Shem Tov's disciples were re-joicing, dancing, and drinking wine from the Baal Shem Tov's cellar. The Baal Shem Tov's wife [Rebbetzin Chana] approached him and said, "Tell them to stop drinking and dancing, or there won't be any wine left for *Kiddush* and *Havdalah*!"

The Baal Shem Tov jestingly replied, "Well said! Tell them to stop and go home!"

When she opened the door, they were dancing in a circle, and she beheld a brilliant light surrounding them like a canopy. She then went to the cellar and brought them even more wine.

Afterward, the Baal Shem Tov asked her, "Did you tell them to go?"

She answered, "You should have told them yourself" (*Shiv'chei Baal Shem Tov* 36).

Desires

If a worldly desire enters a person's thoughts, he should dismiss it completely. One should scorn all worldly desires until they become thoroughly despicable to him. [As our Sages state,] one must incite the Good Inclination against the Evil Inclination and its passions and in this way overcome them.[1]

A person should not feel the least bit depressed because he has not fulfilled his desires. On the contrary, he should greatly rejoice in that he has merited to subdue them for the sake of God's glory. Thus, our Sages state, "Of those who rejoice in their afflictions it is written, 'May those who love Him be as the rising of the sun in its might.'"[2] Since one does not follow his desires—even in thought—but despises them, he is able to greatly subdue the *klippos* (evil husks).

"Who may ascend God's mountain? One with clean hands and a pure heart . . ."[3] The *Zohar* explains, "'A pure heart' refers to one who does not allow his will and heart to be drawn after the Other Side."[4] [A person can only experience Godliness to the extent that he has overcome his physical passions] (*Tzava'as HaRivash* 9).

One must attach his thoughts Above and never eat or drink to excess but only in order to preserve his health. One should pay no attention at all to [the blandishments of] this world but regard them as utterly worthless. In this way, one can detach himself from physicality. [However,] by fixing one's attention on worldly things, one makes himself [all the more] corporeal. Our Sages taught that seeing brings to mind [one's lower nature] and physical passions.[5] Thus, it states that the Tree of Knowledge was "desirable to behold and good for food."[6] That is, simply gazing upon [the Tree of Knowledge] aroused desire (*Tzava'as HaRivash* 5).

---

1. *Berachos* 5a.
2. *Shabbos* 88b.
3. *Tehillim* 24:3–4.
4. *Zohar* I, *Bereishis*, 10a.
5. *Menachos* 43b.
6. *Bereishis* 3:6.

One must realize that everything—whether in the Celestial World, the World of Angels, or the World of the Divine Throne—is as naught compared to God, may He be blessed. Everything exists within the void produced by the constriction of the Infinite Light, when God constricted Himself [so to speak, at the beginning of creation]—and everything was brought into being with one Divine utterance.[7] Therefore, why should one be drawn after any desire for anything that exists in these worlds, when everything is merely [part of] one utterance from Him? It would be better to attach oneself Above to the Supernal World—to the Creator, may He be blessed—which is the essential reality, and not to that which is secondary.

This is what the *Zohar* means [when it states], "Meritorious are those *tzaddikim* who know what is of true value. Their heart's desire is directed to the Supernal King and not toward this world and its worthless passions."[8] For the destiny of all the worlds is destruction. [Instead], one should always cleave to the Creator, may He be blessed, with a love that is absolute. One should love Him more than anything in the world, for every good thing that exists is included in its Source, which is God (*Tzava'as HaRivash* 84, section 3).

One should refrain from gazing with desire upon material things—beautiful women in particular. This sort of gazing is self-serving and is therefore like idol worship. Rather, if one suddenly sees a beautiful woman, he should think, "What makes her beautiful if not the Godly life force within her? And if this Godly life force is the source of her beauty, why should I be drawn after a small part of it? Instead, I should attach myself to the Source and Essence of all the worlds, where all beauty may be found."[9]

Likewise, when one gazes upon a material object, such as a beautiful vessel, he should think, "From where does this vessel derive its beauty [if not the Creator]?" The physical aspect of the object is unim-

---

7. See Ramban's *Peirush al HaTorah*, *Bereishis* 1:1.
8. *Zohar* II, 134b.
9. See *Likkutei Moharan* I:60, with the commentary of *Biur HaLikkutim*, ad loc.

portant. Its beauty and design, however, reflect its spirituality and life force. [This inner aspect of the object] is also a portion of God Above.

Also, when one eats he should realize that the taste and pleasantness of the food comes from its inner life force and the delight of the Supernal World. Even inanimate objects are imbued with life force, which may be deduced from the very fact of their existence. Thus, the Divine life force is everywhere.[10]

If one will gaze in this manner—and one's gazing is for the sake of the Infinite One, blessed be He—it will greatly help him to overcome unholy thoughts (*Tzava'as HaRivash* 90, *section* 1).

"Turn away from evil and do good, seek peace and pursue it" (*Tehillim* 34:15). The Baal Shem Tov taught: In every physical thing permitted by the Torah there is good and evil. The material aspect is evil, and the Godly life force which animates the object is good. The person who uses a physical object must "turn away from evil" and not desire the pleasure which it provides. Rather, he must "do good" by deriving sustenance and help from the Godly life force within the object. "Seek peace and pursue it." One who "turns away from evil and does good" must endeavor to make peace between the physical aspect and the Godly life force which animates it. [This is achieved by using it in a holy manner and not for the sake of physical pleasure.] Indeed, this is the ultimate purpose of man's creation and descent to this physical world: he must elevate the physical to the spiritual (*Sefer HaMa'amarim: Yiddish*, p. 76).

Rabbi Dov Ber, the Maggid of Mezeritch, taught [in the name of the Baal Shem Tov]: While having marital relations, one must completely nullify his ego. [Thus, our Sages said,] "Rabba would drive away the flies before having marital relations, in order not to do so in the presence of any living creature."[11] [In other words,] he would drive away the least trace of self-importance, analogous to that of a fly.

---

10. See *Tzetel Kattan* 1. Concerning the concept that even inanimate things possess a soul, see *Eitz Chaim, Sha'ar Mayim Nukvin u'Mayim Duchrin*, Chapter 3, which is further discussed in *Sefer HaTanya, Sha'ar HaYichud V'HaEmunah*, Chapter 1.

11. See Rashi on *Niddah* 17a.

One should think of himself as an instrument [in the hand] of an artisan. When an artisan strikes a stone with a hammer, this reflects his will. It is not the desire of the hammer that causes it to strike the stone, for if so, the hammer would be independent of the one who wields it. Similarly, when the Primordial Mind expressed itself through vessels [i.e., the *sefiros*, they were nullified to the light they received].

All of one's limbs are mere vessels. One must eat—and it is impossible to do so without the necessary physical apparatus. However, one must not do so for the sake of his physical desire, nor should one love anything but God and His *mitzvos*. In the same sense, the purpose of marital relations is the preservation of humanity, which requires the union of male and female. One should think of himself and his wife as mere vessels and not cohabit for the sake of physical pleasure, nor love anything but God and His *mitzvos* . . .

Rabbi Yisrael Baal Shem Tov also once said: Why is [sexuality] such a great passion? One also experiences pleasure in eating and in other physical things. [However,] man is born as a result of sexual desire. [Therefore,] all pleasures are secondary to it and are included within it. That is why it is the greatest passion. This being the case, [all physical desires] are all rooted in something insignificant. Instead, one should cleave to the Holy One, Blessed be He.[12] (*Likkutei Amarim of Rabbi Menachem Mendel of Vitebsk* 40; *Tzava'as HaRivash* 101).

"The path of the *tzaddikim* is like a shining light, growing ever brighter until the noon" (*Mishlei* 4:18). The sun itself shines constantly, whether in the morning or the middle of the day. The problem is the earth which stands between people and the sun. This is why the light does not spread out so much at the beginning of the day, but only a little at a time, until it has spread across the earth. The same is true of the *tzaddik*. He himself always shines. The problem is only with those who receive [his light]. Because people are sunken in worldly desires, they cannot receive the light of the *tzaddik* . . .

Consider another example: a small coin, if held before your eyes, will prevent you from seeing a large mountain. Even though the moun-

---

12. Concerning the primacy of sexual desire, see *Zohar* I, 170b; ibid. II, 203a; *Likkutei Moharan* I, 19:3.

tain is thousands of times bigger than the coin, nevertheless, because the coin stands in front of your eyes, it blocks the vision so that a much larger object cannot be seen.

Similarly, when the time comes for a person to enter this world, he becomes sunken in its vanities and thinks that nothing could be better. This world, although small and insignificant, prevents him from seeing the great light of the Torah . . . However, if one were to remove the small obstruction in front of his eyes—if one could divert his gaze from [physicality], and, instead, lift up his head, raise his eyes, and gaze above the mundane pursuits which intervene—he would merit to see the great light of the Torah and the *tzaddikim*. In truth, their light is thousands and myriads of times greater than this world and its futilities . . .

Thus did the Baal Shem Tov exclaim: "Alas! The world is full of wondrous and awesome lights and mysteries, but a small hand stands in front of the eyes, preventing them from seeing these great lights" (*Likkutei Moharan* I:133, abridged).

Deveykus

The Baal Shem Tov taught: One must realize that essentially he, too, is Godliness—then, when he considers that the "self" is really nothing, Godliness will rest upon him.

[Given this, one might wonder why it is necessary to do anything at all to serve God.] Take the example of a diver who explores the depths of the sea looking for pearls and precious stones. First, he must be careful not to drown when he holds his breath. Also, he must hasten to search and gather pearls. If he sits and does nothing, all his effort [in entering the sea] will be in vain.

This example may be applied to Divine service. The verse states that "those who go down to the sea in ships . . . saw the acts of God and His wonders in the deep."[1] The Holy One, blessed be He, created the Fifty Gates of Understanding (*binah*) [an expansive state of mind], which is like the ocean. These Fifty Gates are also related to the sea because the numerical value of the word *yam* (sea) is fifty. The souls of the Jewish people enter physical bodies like "those who go down to the sea in ships." But the ultimate purpose of creation is for the Jewish people to gather "pearls and precious stones" [or, in this verse, "His wonders in the deep"]. These are the letters of Torah and *mitzvos* and the [holy sparks] which we elevate from the inanimate, vegetative, animal and human realms by eating in a holy manner, etc.

[According to the Kabbalah, each "gate" or level of *binah* entails a greater degree of self-nullification. Holding one's breath therefore represents nullification in the sea of Godliness, which is *binah*. However, absolute self-nullification, the Fiftieth Gate, may not be attained while one still remains alive.[2] Therefore, Moshe, "the humblest of men," only reached the Forty-Ninth Gate before he passed away.[3] The Baal Shem Tov also stresses that it is necessary to explore the treasures of the inner sea by engaging in the various acts of Divine service. This comprises the positive aspect of creation and the reason for the soul's descent to this lowly physical world.]

---

1. *Tehillim* 106:23–24.
2. See *Sefer HaLikkutim of the Ari z"l, Bamidbar* 3:26.
3. *Rosh Hashanah* 21b.

Thus, it is written, "He who dwells in the secret places of the Most High . . ." This refers to the Infinite Light [which, from the perspective of creation, is "secret"]. When a person is about to perform a *mitzvah* or to engage in prayer or Torah study, he must realize that everything is really subsumed in the light of Godliness. Then he will merit to "abide in the shadow of the Almighty."[4] He will be able to gather pearls, which are holy words, knowing that he, the speaker, is really nothing but the Godly life force which animates him and speaks through him.

[This entire spiritual task may be accomplished through the act of prayer.] When one utters the letters [of prayer] such as "*Baruch Atah* . . ." ("Blessed are You"), the *kavanah* (intention) is that each word is a Divine name. Then he continues, "*Hagadol, hagibor, v'hanora* . . ." ("great, powerful and awesome"), which are Divine attributes, corresponding to the *sefiros*. [Each word of prayer should be recited with its particular *kavanah* and feeling, such as love or awe of God, etc. This is the "gathering of pearls and precious stones" mentioned above.] In this way, one will accomplish the unification of all the worlds—for man contains all the worlds within himself (*Ohr HaGanuz L'Tzaddikim, Mattos*).

"And if you will seek the Lord, your God, from there, you will find Him . . ." (*Devarim* 4:29). The Baal Shem Tov pointed out that the verse states "from there." No matter what a person's circumstances may be, there he may find God and cleave to Him (*Me'or Einaim, Likkutim*).

"Enter . . . the ark (*teivah*) . . ." (*Bereishis* 7:1). The Baal Shem Tov's teaching on this verse is well-known: the soul descends to this world, and a person becomes preoccupied with life's necessities, providing for his family by the labor of his hands. He becomes encompassed by work and the anxieties of earning a living—and it is then that he can, God forbid, drown. The best advice is to "enter the *teivah* (word) . . ." Attach yourself to the words of the prayers you recite and the Torah you study. In the merit of this *deveykus* to the holy words of prayer and Torah, said the Baal Shem Tov, "you and your wife and your sons and your sons' wives"[5] will be assisted by God in all of their needs.

---

4. *Tehillim* 91:1.
5. *Bereishis* 7:16.

According to the Baal Shem Tov, *deveykus* to the words of prayer and Torah is one of the greatest means to attain the highest spiritual levels. "*Deveykus*," said the Baal Shem Tov, "is the key that opens all locks." And this [advice]—to attach yourself to the words of prayer and Torah—applies to everyone. For every Jew, even the most common Jew, can come to experience the loftiest *deveykus*.

The Baal Shem Tov taught that the true simple faith with which an ordinary Jewish man or woman recites *Tehillim* is the highest level of *deveykus*. The soul is the same for everyone. However, for the educated and for Torah scholars, *deveykus* opens the gates of perception in Torah. For common folk who cannot study, this does not apply. But *deveykus* to the holy words of prayer awakens Divine mercy and brings about the deliverance of whoever recites them. In this, the ordinary Jewish man and woman are equal to the greatest Torah sage (Letter of Rabbi Yosef Yitzchak of Lubavitch, cited in *Kesser Shem Tov, Hosafos, Noach*, 10).

When a person can read the Torah and see the lights in the letters, even though he does not recite them with their proper musical cantillations (*tropp*), since he is reading with great love and enthusiasm, God does not pay attention to the fact that he may not be reading correctly. This may be compared to a child who is greatly loved by his father. Even though the child cannot speak well, his father derives great joy from his efforts. The same is true when a person recites words of Torah with love. God loves him very much and pays no attention to the fact that he does not read correctly[6] (*Likkutim Yekarim* 3).

One has divested himself of physicality when he no longer perceives any bodily sensation or worldly appearance but only the forms of the Supernal Worlds, such as angels and Seraphim. Then, when one enters the World of Emanation (*Atzilus*), he experiences only the subtlest reality, which is the emanation of Godliness. There he can know the future. At times, the future can be known in the lower worlds as well, for the *Keruvim* announce [Heaven's decrees].

---

6. A similar teaching may be found in *Sefer Chasidim*, section 18, as discussed in R. Avraham Tzeinvirt's *Chayei Moreinu HaRav Chaim Vital, Even Bochen* 6:1, p. 116.

Rabbi Yisrael Baal Shem said concerning this, "When I attach my thoughts to the Creator, I allow my mouth to say whatever it will, because my words are bound to their Supernal Source—the Creator, may He be blessed. For everything has a root Above, in the *sefiros* . . ." (*Kesser Shem Tov* 199).

[Literally,] the Gemara says that a person should attach himself within God's attributes (*b'midosav*), not to His attributes (*l'midosav*) (*Sotah* 14a). The Baal Shem Tov explained [this as follows:] A man's main task is to attach himself to the inner aspect, which is the vital force within the various Divine attributes, and not to cleave to their outer aspect. If, for example, one attaches himself to the outer aspect of Kindness (*chesed*), he cannot also be attached to Severity (*gevurah*), because, outwardly, they are two distinct Divine attributes. If one is kind, he is not severe. However, concerning the inner aspect, the verse states, "I am God, I do not change."[7] [God] encompasses everything that exists. Therefore, one who wishes to serve God must attach himself to the inner aspect, the vital force within the various Divine attributes which encompasses them all. This vital force is the Infinite One, blessed be He. Thus, in truth, Kindness is part of Severity, and Severity is part of Kindness (*Ginzei Yosef, Devarim Nechmadim*).

"Why did the Torah begin with the account of creation? Because [the verse states], 'The power of His acts He has declared unto His people . . .'" (Rashi on *Bereishis* 1:1, citing *Tehillim* 111:6).

This alludes to the soul within God's acts of creation at every time and moment. The Great Maggid received a path from the holy Baal Shem Tov by which one may perceive in everything the inner soul which gives life to its physical form (Rabbi Yitzchak Isaac of Homil, Letter of Rabbi Rephael Kahan, cited in *Ner Yisrael* IV, p. 237).

---

7. *Malachi* 3:6.

Sometimes when a person cleaves to the Supernal World—to the Creator, may He be blessed—he must be careful not to make any physical gesture, so as not to disrupt his *deveykus* (*Tzava'as HaRivash* 59).

Sometimes a person can only worship God in a manner of smallness; that is, one cannot enter the Supernal Worlds at all. However, he should consider that "the entire universe is filled with His Glory,"[8] and that God is near. At that time, one is like a child whose intelligence is not great but limited. Nevertheless, even though one serves God in a manner of smallness, he is [at the same time] serving Him with great *deveykus* (*Tzava'as HaRivash* 67).

The Baal Shem Tov taught: It is not necessary to "place" oneself in Godliness, but only to realize that everything is subsumed in the Divine light (*Ohr HaGanuz L'Tzaddikim, Vayeira*).

A person on a lofty spiritual level continually realizes that he is [one] with the Creator, Who completely surrounds him. His *deveykus* is so great that he does not have to constantly remind himself that he is with God, for he can see the Creator, may He be blessed, with his mind's eye. [The teaching of our Sages that God is] "the Place of the world"[9] means that He precedes creation, and that the world exists within the Creator. Therefore, it is necessary to cleave to Him to such an extent that one primarily beholds Godliness—not that one primarily sees the world and only secondarily is aware of the Creator . . .

When a person reaches this level, the *klippos* (forces of impurity) will remove themselves from him, for they obscure and obstruct a person's perception of God by closing the eyes of his mind. One should contemplate that the Creator is infinite; He encompasses all the worlds, and He bestows His *shefa* (abundance) by means of the channels which

---

8. *Yeshayahu* 6:3.
9. *Bereishis Rabba* 68:9.

extend from above to below throughout creation. We are always living within Godliness and cannot make the least movement without His *shefa* and life force (*Likkutim Yekarim* 54).

[Even when] one is in a state of constricted consciousness, he is really attached to the *Shechinah*. Then, in an instant, as soon as one thinks of the Supernal World, he finds himself there—for a person is wherever his thoughts are. If one were not [already] in the Supernal World, it would be impossible to conceive it at all (*Tzava'as HaRivash* 69).

Sometimes one can attach himself Above [even] when he is not engaged in prayer. [First,] he should imagine that he is higher than the vault of the firmament; then he can fortify himself to ascend [to the Supernal World].

Also, there are times when even while praying one is unable to ascend Above, and he must worship with a lower level of love and fear of God. Because one [continues to] utter his words in love and fear and cleaves to the Creator, he is empowered to ascend beyond all the firmaments, Heavenly Thrones, and all the various angels and to utter [his prayer] in that sublime world (*Tzava'as HaRivash* 136).

Deveykus means that when one utters a word [of prayer] he draws it out greatly—for due to his cleaving, he does not want to part from the word. Therefore, he draws out its pronunciation[10] (*Tzava'as HaRivash* 70).

Sometimes one must gaze about here and there in order to cleave in thought to the Creator, may He be blessed. This is due to the gross physicality of one's body, which is a barrier to the [light of the] soul (*Tzava'as HaRivash* 80).

---

10. See *Likkutei Moharan* I, 65:2.

Deveykus is possible when nothing else intervenes. The Baal Shem Tov explained this with a parable: If one wishes to combine two pieces of silver, he must scratch out a place for the bond to be strong, i.e., for the two pieces to become one. When some rust or foreign substance intervenes, they cannot cleave properly. Thus, the verse states, "If you will seek [Divine wisdom] like silver . . ."[11] [One must eradicate any other attachments in order to cleave to God] (*Pri Ha'aretz, Ki Sisa*; cited in *Sefer Baal Shem Tov, Ekev* 34).

One should attach himself to the Creator, may He be blessed, and then entreat Him concerning the needs of one's household; or one should do something physical or speak in the midst of his *deveykus*, although there is no pressing need to act or speak. [In this way] he will accustom himself to cleave to God in thought even while engaged in physical activity or common speech. One should experience *deveykus* at those times as well. This is a basic principle [in Divine service] (*Tzava'as HaRivash* 81).

I heard from [Rabbi Yaakov Yosef] of Polonoye that [at one time] the Baal Shem Tov was unable to communicate with people because of his *deveykus*, often saying things irrelevant to the subject. Then his master (Achiyah HaShiloni) instructed him to recite "*Ashrei temimei derech . . .*"[12] every day, as well as certain other psalms, and he showed him a method by which he began to speak with others without losing his state of *deveykus*. [The Baal Shem Tov] used to recite these psalms every day (*Shiv'chei Baal Shem Tov* 70).

In all of one's endeavors, he should think, "I wish to perform God's will in order to gratify Him and to serve Him always." One's thoughts

---

11. *Mishlei* 2:4.
12. *Tehillim* 119.

should always cleave to the Supernal World—to God, may He be blessed. This is what the verse alludes to when it says, "From the holy place he shall not go forth."[13] When compelled to speak of mundane affairs, one should feel that he has descended from the Supernal World like a man who leaves his house, intending to return right away. As he walks along, he wonders when he will be able to go back home. Similarly, one should always think of the Supernal World—which is his true home—even when it is necessary to discuss ordinary matters. Then [as soon as one has concluded his business] he should return to his former state of *deveykus* (*Tzava'as HaRivash* 84, section 4).

"Know Him in all your ways" (*Mishlei* 3:6). This is a fundamental teaching. [Knowledge (*da'as*) implies connection, as in the verse "Adam knew (*yada*) Chava, his wife."[14] Thus,] the word *da'eyhu* ("know Him") may be rendered: Connect (*da*) the letter *hey* with the letter *vav* [which completes the word *da'eyhu*. In Kabbalistic terms, the letters *hey* and *vav* signify the unification of the *Shechinah* and the Holy One, blessed be He.] One should bear this in mind in all of one's actions, even in the most mundane matters (*Tzava'as HaRivash* 94).

"Every intelligent man acts with knowledge (*da'as*) but a fool displays his folly" (*Mishlei* 13:16). A wise man, even when he must attend to his mundane affairs, does so with knowledge; that is, with attachment to God. Knowledge (*da'as*) connotes attachment and *deveykus*, as in the verse, "Adam knew (*yada*) Chava, his wife."[15] Similarly, it states, "Know the God of your father;"[16] i.e., attach yourself and cleave to the God of your father constantly in all your actions.

"But a fool displays (*yifros*) his folly." Even though he may remove himself (*porush*) from the world and study Torah assiduously, since he studies and prays without *deveykus* and attachment to God, it is still foolishness (*Tzava'as HaRivash* 98; *Ohr Torah, Pesukim Melukatim* 369, 95).

---

13. *Vayikra* 21:12.
14. *Bereishis* 4:1.
15. Ibid.
16. I *Divrei HaYomim* 28:9.

"If you will diligently keep all of this commandment . . . and cleave to Him . . ." (*Devarim* 11:22). [On this verse, our Sages remark], "Is it possible to cleave to Him? Is He not 'a consuming fire'? Rather, [the verse means that] one should cleave to His attributes. Just as He is merciful, so should you be merciful . . ."[17]

Cleaving to God means to worship Him with fervor. However, it is not possible to experience this constantly, but only in the manner of "reaching and not reaching."[18] This may be compared to a flame. If one blows on it, at first the flame will be diminished, but afterward it will become even larger. Just as a flame goes up and down and flickers, so one's fervor [in Divine service] is an aspect of "reaching and not reaching"—for perpetual delight is not [discernible as] delight.[19]

Thus, our Sages ask, "Is He not 'a consuming fire'?" In other words, one's fervor must be taken away from him [lest he be burned]. This is the aspect of "reaching and not reaching." And how is it possible still to cleave to Him? By cleaving to His attributes, i.e., His garments, which are the letters [of Torah]. The Torah is God's garment, so to speak.[20] And it is possible for a person to keep the letters of Torah in mind continually. [Therefore,] even when one [cannot study but] converses with others, he should remain aware of the letters [that make up the words he speaks,] for they, too, are derived from the twenty-two letters of Torah (*Tzava'as HaRivash* 111).

---

17. *Kesubos* 111b; *Rashi* on *Shabbos* 133b.
18. See *Eitz Chaim, Sha'ar* 7.
19. See *Likkutei Moharan* 1:24.
20. *Tikkunei Zohar, Tikkun* 30.

Divine Assistance

Once the Baal Shem Tov's daughter, Udel, became involved in a heated discussion with her father's disciples about the prayer we recite at the conclusion of the holy Shabbos, "May God open for us the Gates of Light, the Gates of Long Life," etc. They disagreed about which gate was the best, each person asserting his own opinion. Udel said that the Gate of Divine Assistance was the greatest, for the rest are included within it. Then the Baal Shem Tov remarked, "Her words are correct. For when a person grasps a certain gate—whether it is the Gate of Torah, the Gate of Wisdom, or the Gate of Repentance, or even in physical matters, the Gate of Sustenance or the Gate of Livelihood—all this is only because of Divine Assistance. In this gate all other gates are included, because without the help of God it is impossible to make even the smallest gesture. Even the realization that none of one's actions are truly his own comes from God, Who has graced us with such knowledge" (*Shulchan HaTahor, Mevo She'arim,* Chapter 7).

"Teach me, O God, Your way (*derech*) . . ." (*Tehillim* 27:11). It is known that the term *derech* refers to a paved path, whereas [the similar term] *orach* refers to an unpaved path.[1] [On the latter] one can sometimes stray and come to a dangerous place. This is not true of a paved path, which does not allow one to stray.

These two categories also apply to man. There is a paved path in serving the Creator, which, if one follows it, will certainly keep a person from going astray: he may remove himself from all [mundane] things and only engage in Torah and *mitzvos* day and night, speaking no more than is absolutely necessary. And there is another path which is not paved, an *orach*: a person may at times enter into discussion with others, but his words are entirely for the sake of Heaven. That is, his words contain *mussar* (moral instruction) or love of God or fear of God, etc. Or this person may know how to [mystically] elevate his words Above in holiness, as is known of many [*tzaddikim*]. It is surely permissible to speak words such as these. However, there is a danger in [the latter

---

1. *Zohar* III, 88a.

35

approach]: perhaps one will stray from the good path and begin to speak of empty matters, too, like the ignorant masses. One must pray and entreat God to help him when he wants to go on this way, for without Divine assistance one might easily go astray. Therefore, one must fortify himself with prayer so that he should not stumble into transgression, God forbid.

This is the meaning of the verse, "Teach me, O God, Your way (derech) . . ." In other words, teach me to recognize the paved path, and then I shall be able to follow it myself. [The verse continues:] "And lead me on a level path (orach) . . ." because on an orach, one can go astray. I beg You to favor me with Your help and guidance and support, that I may proceed on level ground and not by a tortuous route; for without Your assistance, I could go astray.

This is also implied by the verse, "Know Him in all your ways (d'rachecha) . . ."[2] In all the paved paths one takes, he himself must know how to travel and how to conduct himself upon them. [On a derech] it is possible for a person himself to know what to do. [The verse concludes]: "And He will direct your paths (orchosecha)." [The Holy One] blessed be He, will direct you. Even [when you follow] paths which are not paved, He will help and support you, so that you do not go astray (Likkutim Yekarim 217; Tzava'as HaRivash 140).

---

2. Mishlei 3:6.

Divine Justice

The holy Maggid of Mezeritch once asked his master, the Baal Shem Tov, for the Kabbalistic meaning of the verse, "And these are the judgments . . ."[1]

"I will demonstrate Heavenly justice to you," said the Baal Shem Tov. "Go to such-and-such a forest on such-and-such a day. When you find a tree under which flows a spring, hide yourself nearby and observe what happens."

The Maggid followed his instructions carefully and concealed himself near the spring. The first person to pass was a rider who stopped to refresh himself by the spring. He ate, drank, and then rode off, leaving his money pouch behind. Along came another fellow who spied the pouch, picked it up, and went on his way. Then a third man, a beggar, appeared. He, too, sat down beside the spring, refreshed himself from its cool waters, and lay down to rest. Suddenly, the horseman returned and attacked the beggar, accusing him of stealing his money pouch. Although the beggar protested his innocence, the first man continued beating him until he was covered with blood. Having witnessed all this, the Maggid left his hiding place and returned to ask his *rebbe* for an explanation.

"Mortal man cannot understand Heaven's accounts," the Baal Shem Tov began. "You were surely confused by the seeming injustice of what you saw. But there is truly no injustice on earth. The horseman was a reincarnation of a man who owed the second person money. In a former lifetime, these two had appeared before a judge, who had ruled in favor of the first man without properly investigating the case. In the scene you just witnessed, the first man repaid his debtor what he rightfully owed. The beggar was a reincarnation of the judge, who also received what he deserved: a thorough beating. This is but a small example of Heavenly justice" (*Devarim Areivim*).

"And you shall love your neighbor as yourself (*kamocha*); I am God" (*Vayikra* 19:18). That is, if you relate to your neighbor with love and cooperation, then, "*Kamocha*—as you [conduct yourself], so do I, God."

---

1. *Shemos* 21:1.

Our holy master, the Baal Shem Tov, also taught that this is the deeper meaning of the verse, "God is your shadow . . ."[2] When a person treats his fellow man in this lowly world with love and virtuous behavior, the Supernal King treats him the same way—like a shadow. Whenever a person moves, so does his shadow. This is also how God relates toward man. Thus, the verse states, "And you shall love your neighbor as yourself . . ." [Then it concludes,] "As you [show love to others,] so do I, God," bestow love and favor upon you (*Otzar HaChaim, Kedoshim*, cited in *Sefer Baal Shem Tov, Kedoshim* 21).

"And retribution is exacted from a person with his knowledge and without his knowledge" (*Avos* 3:16).

[Rabbi Nachman of Breslev taught] in the name of the Baal Shem Tov: Before any Heavenly decree is passed against the world, God forbid, the whole world is gathered together [and asked] to endorse that judgment. Even the person against whom the judgment has been decreed, God forbid, is asked whether he concurs. Then the judgment is concluded.

If one were openly asked about himself, he would certainly protest and say that the judgment is not [correct]. However, they mislead him and ask him about a similar case. He passes judgment, and then they render their verdict [concerning him].

This is like what we find in connection with David HaMelech, of blessed memory, when Nosson HaNavi came to him and told him the story of the guest. [David HaMelech] declared, "As God lives, the man that has done this deserves to die. And he shall restore the lamb fourfold . . ."[3] Then judgment was rendered against David according to his pronouncement.[4]

Thus [the Mishnah states:] "And retribution is exacted from a person with his (*da'as*) knowledge . . ." That is, they ask him his *da'as* (opinion). And, nevertheless, it is "without his knowledge," for he does not know that the judgment is against himself.

The subject of how they ask every person is very deep. In all the conversations and stories one hears, high and lofty matters may be found.

---

2. *Tehillim* 121:4.
3. *II Shmuel* 12:1–6.
4. See *Rashi*, ad loc.

[Therefore,] one must be very careful not to pass judgment until he has reviewed [the facts] a second and third time, for it may be a matter of life and death (*Likkutei Moharan* I:113).

I heard from my master (the Baal Shem Tov) that a person's *nefesh,* *ruach,* and *neshamah* [the three levels of the soul that can dwell within the body] correspond to the faculties of thought, speech, and action . . .

If one's actions are improper, he is punished through his servants or livestock, which are aspects of the *nefesh* (vital soul). If he misuses the power of speech, for example, by committing the sin of *lashon hara* (harmful gossip), then others will afflict him verbally. Also, speech is a euphemism for marital relations, as our Sages state in *Kesubos* 13a. Therefore, one's wife corresponds to *ruach* (spirit) and the faculty of speech. "If one is worthy, she will help him; if not, she will oppose him."[5] The *neshamah* (higher soul) dwells within the brain, where the process of physical conception actually begins.[6] If one transgresses in thought, this causes him to suffer because of his children (*Toldos Yaakov Yosef, Lech Lecha*).

I heard from my master (the Baal Shem Tov) that the fear of Divine retribution is an external aspect of the fear of God; it relates to God's hand, which is "outstretched to receive penitents."[7] Through this one may awaken the inner aspect of fear, which is really love, in order to accept [everything one experiences] with love. Then one may let go of the external aspect of fear (*Kesser Shem Tov* 177).

"From all my transgressions deliver me; a disgrace in the sight of the immoral do not make me" (*Tehillim* 39:9).

The Baal Shem Tov taught: When one sees an evil person commit an immoral act, a severe transgression, he should [nevertheless] judge him favorably. [One should think that] he acted only because of the prompting of the Evil Inclination burning within him and due to the

---

5. *Yevamos* 63a.

6. See R. Shneur Zalman of Liadi, *Likkutei Amarim (Tanya)*, chapter 2.

7. *Machzor, Yom Kippur, Ne'ilah.*

lowliness of his coarse physical nature; perhaps he did not realize the severity of the prohibition, etc. Thus, one may also save himself from judgment. In truth, since one perceived something unseemly in his fellow, he must possess a trace of the same thing within himself, for which he, too, is being judged and accused. When he finds merit in his fellow, he will also be [considered] meritorious.

Also, when one does not judge the transgressor but instead assumes that the fiery Evil Inclination compelled him to commit this wicked deed, he fulfills [the Divine commandment], "Do not pervert the judgment of the poor in his struggle . . ."[8] For this [transgressor] is going through trials and struggles in the waters of strife, which are evil and stormy waters indeed. Rather, one should find all sorts of excuses for him.

This is really a great test. For we have received a tradition that no Heavenly decree is issued against a person until he himself has uttered the same judgment. Since one would not indict himself, he is shown another person committing a transgression similar to his own. One renders judgment against the other fellow and thus seals his own fate (*Otzar HaChaim, Mishpatim*, p. 133b, cited in *Sefer Baal Shem Tov, Kedoshim* 2).

---

8. *Shemos* 33:6.

Divine Providence

A Jew is never alone: Wherever he goes and wherever he speaks, God is with him (*Likkutei Dibburim* IV, p. 980).

The Baal Shem Tov taught that when a piece of straw falls from a wagon loaded with straw, this event has been decreed by Heaven. Similarly, when a leaf falls from a tree, it is because Heaven has decreed that this particular leaf at this particular moment would fall upon this particular spot.

Once the Baal Shem Tov showed his disciples a certain leaf as it fell to the ground and told them to pick it up. They did so and saw that a worm was underneath it. The Baal Shem Tov explained that the worm had been suffering due to the heat, so this leaf had fallen to give it shade (*Sha'ar HaOsios, Hashgachah Pratis*).

A fundamental principle is contained in the verse, "Ascribe your doings unto God, and your thoughts will be established" (*Mishlei* 16:3). That is, one should realize that whatever happens comes from God, may He be blessed.

One must entreat God to always prepare for him that which He knows to be for one's true benefit—and not that which appears to be good to mortal men, according to their limited minds. Perhaps what looks good is actually bad for him. Rather, one should cast everything, all of his needs and concerns, upon God, as it is written, "Cast your burden upon God, and He shall sustain you"[1] (*Tzava'as HaRivash* 4).

The Baal Shem Tov taught that every single created thing has its own worth Above, each according to its essence. That which is *domem* (inanimate) is different from *tzome'ach* (vegetative); this in turn is different from *chai* (animal); and this in turn is different from *medaber* (human). Within the realm of *medaber*, the people of Israel are "the

---

1. *Tehillim* 55:23.

people closest to Him." Divine Providence applies to even the smallest detail; however, the degree to which Divine Providence applies to "the people closest to Him" cannot be imagined. For if Divine Providence determines something as minute as whether a leaf or a straw will remain in their present place or be moved elsewhere, the Divine Providence which determines what will happen to one of His people is altogether beyond our understanding (*Likkutei Dibburim* I, 4:3).

One should realize that everything in the world is filled with God-liness, as the verse states, "I fill the heavens and the earth."[2] And all that is produced by human thoughts and schemes, even the smallest things that happen in the world, is really brought about by Divine Providence. It should make no difference to a person whether or not his endeavors go according to his wishes, for everything comes from the Creator, may He be blessed; and He knows that it is [sometimes] better that things do not happen as one had intended (*Tzava'as HaRivash* 84, section 2).

The *Zohar* states: "Why is the *sefirah* of *binah* (understanding) called 'the World of Freedom'? Because even a slave [who reaches this spiritual level] becomes a free man."[3]

The Baal Shem Tov explained this as follows: All things are an expression of the Holy One, blessed be He, through His Divine attributes of love and fear, as is known. However, the Divine attribute of love is in exile, disguised in [one's attraction to] physical things, such as a woman or food. When one takes to heart [the knowledge] that this love is a garment for God—and now one has deprived Him of His garment, God forbid—he will tremble in fear at the evil thing he has done. He will be deeply ashamed and say, "If I am attracted to this woman, it is merely [a reflection of] the love that fell after the Shattering of the Vessels [at the beginning of creation] and is now disguised in this lower form. How much more should I love God Himself."

Similarly, with regard to fear, if one is afraid of a heathen or the sword, he should tell himself, "Why am I afraid of this mortal like my-

---

2. *Yirmiyahu* 23:24.
3. *Zohar* I, 95b and 124b; ibid. II, 183a; ibid. III, 290b.

self? Surely the Creator is disguised within this person. It is the Creator Whom I should fear." Thus should one proceed with the trait of glorification [which is derived from the *sefirah* of *tiferes*] and the rest [of the Divine attributes and their corresponding human traits].

Also, if one is praying and hears another person's voice, he should say, "Why did God bring about this disturbance while I am trying to pray? This is happening by Divine Providence. Speech is actually the *Shechinah*—and now the *Shechinah* has clothed itself in the speech of this person in order to provoke me to worship God, so badly do I need to strengthen myself in prayer." This is particularly true if the speaker is an idolater or a child [who is hardly aware of God's existence]; then the *Shechinah* must constrict itself to an even greater degree. [Since this is all for one's spiritual benefit,] it is only right that one should exert himself [to pray with intense concentration] (*Tzava'as HaRivash* 120).

Once, when the Baal Shem Tov was in the holy community of Nemirov, he was going from a large room into a smaller room and mistakenly went to the cellar. He said, "Since I made a mistake and went to the cellar, there must be something to it." He asked them to examine the *mezuzos*, and they found that one was *pasul* (unfit).

A certain man asked him, "If a person makes a mistake, should he immediately attach some meaning to it? Perhaps it was just an accident."

The Baal Shem Tov replied, "That's what you say. But to me, nothing is accidental. I know that everything, however great or small, is overseen by Heaven. Therefore, one must think about the meaning of everything that happens."

Thus, one should believe that everything happens according to Divine Providence and not ascribe anything to chance, God forbid (*Shiv'chei Baal Shem Tov* 150).

The Baal Shem Tov taught: Whatever a person sees or hears contains a lesson in Divine service. This is the gist of Divine service: to realize how to serve God in all things[4] (*HaYom Yom*, p. 52, cited in *Kesser Shem Tov, Hosafos*, 128).

---

4. See *Likkutei Moharan* I, 1:1; ibid., 54:2.

Dreams

If one [refrains from gazing upon all worldly pleasures] throughout the day, he will merit to see in his dreams the vital force concealed within the physical things he encountered while awake. [This is the mystical meaning of the teaching of our Sages]: "Whatever one thinks about during the day will come to mind at night in one's dreams."[1] During the day one can only see physicality, even though he may understand that the spiritual is enclothed within the physical. But in a dream, one can experience spirituality divested of any garment.

Thus, the word *chalom* (dream) is related to the word *chalim* (healthy), as in the phrase, "sometimes healthy, sometimes insane."[2] During the day, a person's inner life force is weak, for it is bound to the body; hence, one cannot see the vital force within physical objects. However, at night, the vital force spreads throughout one's limbs, and then it is strong. Therefore, it is possible to experience the vital force itself.

In this way one may actually attain the level of prophecy, as the verse states concerning all prophets, "In a dream I shall speak with him."[3] However, Moshe Rabbeinu was able to see the vital force within physical things even while awake.

David HaMelech said, "In righteousness I will behold Your face; when I awaken, I will be sated with Your likeness."[4] This [experience] was mainly at night; for the word *echezeh* ("I will behold") is related to *chezyon layla* ("a vision of the night"). And what is the cause [of this vision]? "When I awaken, I will be sated with Your likeness." The likeness of a thing refers to its spiritual form. In other words, when I gaze at a physical object, I not only observe its material aspect, but I gaze [with the knowledge] that its likeness—its spiritual form and inner life force—belongs to You and is [merely] garbed within this physical thing (*Tzava'as HaRivash* 90, section 2).

---

1. *Berachos* 55b.
2. *Rosh Hashanah* 28a.
3. *Bamidbar* 12:6.
4. *Tehillim* 17:15.

Eating

"Hungry and thirsty, their soul fainted within them" (*Tehillim* 107:5).
A great and awesome mystery is contained here. Why did the Holy One,
blessed be He, create the various sorts of food and drink that man craves?
The reason is because there are actually sparks of Adam hidden in inanimate things (*domem*), vegetative life (*tzome'ach*), the animal kingdom
(*chai*) and mankind (*medaber*). They long to attach themselves to holiness, [which in Kabbalistic doctrine is called] "the awakening of the
Feminine Waters." Concerning this mystery it has been taught, "No drop
descends from above unless two corresponding drops ascend from
below."[1] All of the food and drink a person consumes contain sparks
which actually belong to him, and which he must rectify.

Thus, the verse states, "Hungry and thirsty"—when people crave
after food and drink, what happens? "Their soul fainted within them"—
[the holy sparks remain] in exile, in alien garments. For all the things
one uses are actually his children, held in captivity [in these forms]
(*Rimzei Yisrael; Sefer Katan*).

The Baal Shem Tov taught: The purpose of eating is to rectify [the
holy sparks within the food]. This is accomplished from one level to the
next: from vegetative life (*tzome'ach*) to the animal kingdom (*chai*), from
animal (*chai*) to man (*medaber*), up to [the level implied by the verse]:
"Man does not live by bread alone, but by all that proceeds from the
mouth of God does man live" (*Devarim* 8:3). This is explained in the
writings of the Ari z"l.[2] One might ask: Since it is the way of that which
is passive to be drawn after that which is active, why doesn't food pursue the one who wishes to eat? The answer is that it dreads going into a
mouth full of corruption, God forbid[3] (*Ohr HaEmes* 33b).

---

1. *Taanis* 25b; *Zohar* III, *Pinchas*, 247b.
2. *Sha'ar HaMitzvos, Ekev.*
3. See *Likkutei Moharan* II:16.

The words of Torah spoken at one's table constitute the soul of the physical things served. [Therefore, the Baal Shem Tov] would always say words of Torah during his meals, both on weekdays and certainly on Shabbos (*Ner Mitzvah* 8:2).

"If three people ate together at one table and did not speak words of Torah, it is as if they partook of slaughter to the dead" (*Avos* 3:4). Basing himself on a teaching of the Baal Shem Tov, the Maggid of Mezeritch once said: [Souls of] the deceased are [sometimes] reincarnated in food and drink, so that a person will speak words of Torah and give them life. However, if one does not say words of Torah, he "slaughters the dead" who had been thus reincarnated and casts them back to the inanimate realm (*Be'er Mayim, Haggadah Shel Pesach*).

"All the days of the poor are evil . . ." (*Mishlei* 15:15). This may be understood in the light of the teaching of our Sages, "One is only poor when he lacks knowledge."[4] When one lacks spiritual knowledge, his days are evil. His prayer and Torah study are of little worth before God, for they surely lack love and awe, and [thus] do not blossom forth Above.[5]

[Our Sages discuss this verse in *Kesubos* 110b. There] the Gemara contends, "Do their evil days also include Shabbos and Yom Tov?" In other words, on these days every Jew surely experiences an awakening from Above and prays with *kavanah*. [Then the Gemara answers its own question:] "Changing times bring on intestinal sickness." That is, even though one now prays with [greater] *kavanah*, he watches himself doing so—and for this reason begins to feel self-important. He sees himself ascending to a lofty spiritual level. Therefore, even these days have become evil. [The reference to] intestinal sickness suggests [the *Zohar*'s remark] that the Evil Inclination overcomes a person only through [improper] eating and drinking.[6] This, in turn, brings one to pride and all of its consequences (*Tzava'as HaRivash* 131).

---

4. *Nedarim* 41a.
5. See *Tikkunei Zohar, Tikkun* 10.
6. *Zohar* I, *Midrash Ne'elam, Vayera* 110a; *Likkutei Moharan* I, 60:6.

Equanimity

"I have placed (*shivisi*) God before myself continually" (*Tehillim* 16:8).
"I have placed (*shivisi*)" is related to the word *hishtavus*—equanimity.[1]
Whatever happens to a person should be the same to him, whether others praise or disparage him; and this rule applies to all things. When it comes to eating, it should make no difference whether one eats tasty foods or otherwise. Everything should be the same to him, since the Evil Inclination has been completely renounced. In all circumstances one should say, "Does this not come from Him, may He be blessed? And if this is meet and proper in His eyes, [should it not be acceptable to me?]" One's efforts should be entirely for the sake of Heaven; but [whatever happens] should make no difference from one's own standpoint. This is a very high spiritual level (*Tzuva'as HaRivash* 2).

---

1. This subject is also discussed in *Chovos HaLevavos, Sha'ar Yichud HaMa'aseh*, Chapter 4 and elsewhere; R. Yitzchak of Acco's *Mei'ras Einaim, Ekev*, p. 281; *Reishis Chochmah, Sha'ar Ahavah*, Chapters 3–4; *Sha'arei Kedushah*, IV:15a; *Maggid Mesharim, Beshalach*. In other Chasidic works, see *Maggid Devarav L'Yaacov* 159; *Ner Yisrael* I, *Tehillim*, p. 192; *Sefer HaTanya, Igeres HaKodesh*, Chapter 11; *Likkutei Moharan* I, 4:1, 33:1, 65:3, 251; *Sichos HaRan* 51; *Likkutei Dibburim* I, 2:14, 4b:2 ("*atzmi*").

Some scholars have questioned the origin of this concept, since the term "*hishtavus*" is not used in the Talmud. However, R. Aryeh Kaplan points out in his "Meditation and Kabbalah" (Aronson 1995) that the masters of the Talmud used the expression "to overcome one's natural tendencies" (*l'ma'avir al midosav*) in a similar sense. Thus, the great mystic Rabbi Nechunia Ben HaKana said that this was one of the main traits responsible for his accomplishments (*Megilla* 28a). Elsewhere, the Talmud ascribes the immediacy with which a certain individual's prayer was answered to the fact that he had "overcome his natural tendencies" (*Taanis* 25a). Eliyahu HaNavi only reveals himself to such a person (*Mesechta Kallah Rabbasi*, Chapter 5). And this is one of the preconditions for one to be taught the Divine Name of Forty-Two Letters (*Kiddushin* 71a).

R. Kaplan further states that, according to the Talmud, one who has attained this trait is able to radiate spiritually. He cites the following passage from *Yoma* 23a:

"Regarding those who are insulted but do not insult, who hear themselves scorned, but do not respond, who serve [God] with love and rejoice in suffering, it is written: 'Those who love [God] shall be like the sun when it shines forth with [all] its strength'" (*Shoftim* 5:31).

The Baal Shem Tov stressed the great importance of equanimity (*hishtavus*). That is, it should make no difference whether one is taken to be an ignoramus or an accomplished Torah scholar. This may be attained by continually cleaving to the Creator—for due to his *deveykus*, there is no possibility for a person to consider [what other people think]. Rather, he should continually endeavor to attach himself Above to God, may He be blessed (*Tzava'as HaRivash* 10).

One should think of himself as belonging to the Upper World; then all those who dwell in this lower world will make no impression upon him. For this whole world is like a mustard seed in comparison to the Upper World. The love or hatred of others should be the same to him, for it amounts to nothing.

Likewise, one should not heed in the least the desires of one's impure body, which the *Tikkunei Zohar* compares to the leprous skin of a snake[2] (*Tzava'as HaRivash* 6).

One should make himself as if he does not exist, as the Gemara states, "Rabbi Yochanan taught: The words of Torah cannot be fulfilled except by one who makes himself as if he does not exist. Thus the verse states, 'And wisdom—from where (*ayin*) does it come?'[3] [Or, alternatively, 'And wisdom comes from Nothingness (*ayin*).']"[4]

This means that one should think that he does not exist in this world at all—so what difference does it make if he is important in the eyes of others? (*Tzava'as HaRivash* 53).

---

2. *Tikkun* 21 (48b) explains that Moshe was born in holiness and Pharaoh's daughter was not. Her leprosy was cured when she touched Moshe, who in turn became thus afflicted until God cured him at the Burning Bush. Pharaoh's daughter represents the spiritual impurity of the body—"the leprous skin of the snake"—which the *tzaddik* must rectify in himself and in others.

3. *Iyov* 28:12.

4. *Sotah* 21b.

When one speaks words of Torah with others, he should first bind himself in thought to the Creator, may He be blessed. [He should also contemplate that] the soul of his fellow is similarly bound to the Creator, for all men live only because of the *shefa* (abundance) which God imparts to all creatures.

One should think, "I am speaking only before the Creator, may He be blessed, in order to gratify Him. I am not performing for my fellow men—for what difference does their praise or blame make to me?" (*Tzava'as HaRivash* 93).

In everything one does, his only purpose should be to gratify the Creator, and not to serve himself in the least. Even the desire to experience delight in the act of Divine service is a form of serving oneself[5] (*Tzava'as HaRivash* 11).

"Many attempted to conduct themselves like Rabbi Shimon bar Yochai but were not successful" (*Berachos* 35b). This means to say that they wanted to mortify themselves in order to reach the spiritual level of Rabbi Shimon bar Yochai—and that is why they were not successful. One's only intent in Divine service should be to gratify the Creator alone, not to attain a lofty spiritual level (*Tzava'as HaRivash* 47).

---

5. See *Likkutei Moharan* I, 15:5. Also R. Shalom Dov Ber of Lubavitch discusses this point in his *Kuntres HaAvodah*, Chapter 5, and in the discourse *Padah V'Shalom* (5675).

Faith

[We begin to address the Creator in our prayers with the words], "Our God and God of our fathers . . ." (*Siddur, Shemoneh Esrei*). The reason for this is that there are two types of people who believe in God. One believes because his fathers taught him to do so; nevertheless, his faith is strong. The other believes as a result of his own search for truth.

There is a difference between these two individuals. The first has an advantage in that he cannot be tempted, even when confronted by philosophical arguments contrary to his beliefs. His faith is strong, for he received it from his fathers, and also because he never questioned it in his life. On the other hand, this person has a disadvantage: his faith was imposed upon him by others. It has become a matter of habit, without reason or insight.

The second one also has an advantage in that he recognizes the Creator as a result of his great searching. Therefore, his faith is complete, and his love of God is very deep. But he, too, has a disadvantage. [Since he acquired his belief through reason], he can be influenced by philosophical arguments to question his own faith, God forbid.

However, a person who possesses both qualities has every advantage. He strongly relies upon the faith of his forebears, and he also believes in God as a result of his own search for truth. Thus, he has the best and most complete faith. That is why we say, "Our God and God of our fathers . . ." We refer to our own search for truth, and we acknowledge the tradition we have received (*Kesser Shem Tov* 206).

The Baal Shem Tov taught: By crying out to God from the depths of one's heart, one attains lofty perceptions and his faith is strengthened. Faith depends upon the mouth, as it is written, "I shall make known Your faithfulness with my mouth."[1] [Therefore,] when a person falls from faith, God forbid, he should [nevertheless] verbally declare that he believes in God. In this way, he will clear his mind with faith, for "the last in deed is first in thought."[2] One should keep far away from philosophy

---

1. *Tehillim* 89:2.
2. R. Shlomo Alkabetz, "*L'cha Dodi.*"

to the utmost degree, lest one forfeit Eternity in an instant. Philosophical inquiry causes the power of [spiritual] forgetfulness to overcome that of memory and weakens one's faith, God forbid. [But] faith draws forth *shefa*, blessing, and success.[3] (*Minchas Yehudah, Emes v'Emunah*, cited in *Meiras Einaim, Emunah*).

The great principle in Divine service and its main point is faith. My grandfather (the Baal Shem Tov) stressed this, for faith is the root of the entire Torah[4] (*Degel Machaneh Ephraim, Ekev*).

The Baal Shem Tov told his disciples always to say: "*Ko'ach haPoel b'nifal*—The power of the Creator is in the creation" (*Shomer Emunim, Ma'amar Emunah*, cited in *Meir Einei Yisrael, Emunah*).

Rabbi Zusha of Annipola heard from the *tzaddik* Rabbi Shmer'l of Vochivke that the Baal Shem Tov predicted: "Before Moshiach comes there will be no more signs and wonders and open miracles, nor will there be outstanding spiritual leaders to attract and inspire others to serve God. The only way for the Jewish people to persevere will be to cling to faith"[5] (*Eretz HaChaim*, 180, cited in *Meir Einei Yisrael, Emunah*).

The Baal Shem Tov taught: The power of faith is so great that even if a person believes in a physical impossibility, faith can accomplish miracles.

Concerning the *tzaddik* of the generation, the verse states, "And they believed in God and in Moshe, His servant."[6] [When this faith is present] the *tzaddik* can perform wonders and acts of great kindness to

3. See *Likkutei Moharan* II:44
4. *Mishneh Torah, Yesodei HaTorah* 1:1.
5. See *Sichos HaRan* 35, 126, 220.
6. *Shemos* 14:31.

satisfy all of one's needs, whether concerning children, health or sustenance. But if a person does not believe in the *tzaddik* of the generation,
it is impossible for him to receive help, and there is no remedy for his
ailment[7] (*Minchas Yehudah, Emes v'Emunah*, 31, cited in *Meir Einei Yisrael,
Emunah*).

Once, during a *Melave Malka*, the Baal Shem Tov spoke at length
about the need to remain strong in one's faith, without any trace of doubt,
God forbid. "Doubt is in the heart," he remarked. "*Hasafek* (doubt) contains the same letters as *hefsek* (interruption). Thus, [lack of faith] can
cut off the channel of Divine sustenance, God forbid" (*Be'er Yaacov
Chaim, Beshalach*, cited in *Meir Einei Yisrael, Emunah*).

The Baal Shem Tov once said, "An idolatrous non-Jew has more
hope of receiving a *tikkun* (spiritual rectification) than an atheist."
[Rabbi Menachem Mendel of Lubavitch, known as the "*Tzemach
Tzedek*," explained:] It is written, "And then I will turn the nations to a
pure speech . . ."[8] and, "All the nations will flow into [the Holy Temple]
. . ."[9] [This will take place] because they believed in the Oneness of God,
but, due to the "leprous skin of the snake," their nature was more physical, and it seemed to them that everything was determined by astrological forces. But of the Ultimate Future, the verse states, "All flesh shall
see [Godliness] together,"[10] for this will be after the final rectification.
However, an atheist will not be spiritually elevated even in the Ultimate
Future. [Since he does not possess even a trace of truth there is nothing
to elevate.] Rather, his destruction will be his rectification (*Derech
Mitzvosecha* II, p. 592).

"For with my staff I passed over this Jordan . . ." (*Bereishis* 32:11).
Concerning this verse, [Rabbi Moshe Chaim Ephraim of Sudylkov]
states: "Once my grandfather (the Baal Shem Tov) crossed the Dneister

---

7. See *Sichos HaRan* 63; *Likkutei Moharan* I, 22:3.
8. *Tzephania* 3:9.
9. *Yeshayahu* 2:2.
10. Ibid. 40:5.

River without using any Divine name. He simply put his *gartel* (sash) upon the water and crossed the river upon it."[11]

Our master, Rabbi [Dov] of Leovo, asked: Why did the author state that [the Baal Shem Tov] put his *gartel* [over the water]? How did his *gartel* help? There is something deeper to be learned here.

The *gartel* is related to faith, as it is written, "He girded himself with faith."[12] Thus, the author suggests that the Baal Shem Tov [reasoned]: The One "Who spoke and the world came into being" created the land to be walked upon—and so, too, did He create the water. Therefore, if necessary, one may walk on water just as one walks on dry land. It was this faith which the Baal Shem Tov stretched upon the Dneister and walked across (*Ner Yisrael* I, *Vayishlach*, p. 44).

I heard this parable from my grandfather (the Baal Shem Tov): A musician was once playing his instrument very beautifully, with the greatest sweetness. The music was so moving that all those who heard it could not contain themselves, and they began to dance until they felt as if their delight would carry them up to the ceiling. Whoever was closer (or who brought himself closer) to the musician experienced even more pleasure and danced even more joyously.

In the middle of all this, a deaf man arrived who could not hear the musician's sweet melody. He only saw the people dancing in ecstasy, and, to him, they looked like they were mad. "What are these people so happy about?" he wondered.

In truth, if the deaf man had been wise, he would have deduced that the excitement was due to the beautiful music, and he would have joined the dance, as well. The parallel is obvious (*Degel Machaneh Ephraim*, *Yisro*).

Faith itself is *deveykus*[13] (*Kesser Shem Tov* 310).

The Baal Shem Tov once remarked, "After all my lofty perceptions, I am but a fool and a simple believer" (*Beis Avraham*, *Shemini Atzeres*).

---

11. *Degel Machaneh Ephraim*, *Vayishlach*.
12. *Yeshayahu* 11:5.
13. See *Sichos HaRan* 47.

Fasting

When a person wants to fast, he should not refrain from doing so—even though he realizes that it is best to serve God with joy and not with self-mortification. These [ascetic practices] can lead to depression. Nevertheless, every person knows within himself that he must fast, for he still has not attained the complete rectification of his soul.

Similarly, there are many things about which one should be stringent upon himself in order to benefit his soul and others about which he need not be so strict (*Tzava'as HaRivash* 56).

When a person fasts from one Shabbos to the next, he should do so without any trace of pride. He might think that he is doing something very great by afflicting himself so much, and that he will become very pure because of this fast. But such a fast belongs to the realm of unholiness. Rather, one should think, "What are my deeds when compared to the way the angels serve God, who worship Him continually—whereas I am 'born of a putrid drop' and my destiny is dust"[1] (*Likkutim Yekarim* 188).

Sometimes in the middle of a weeklong fast, the Evil Inclination overtakes a person and makes him experience great difficulties in his fast, telling him that he cannot bear to continue anymore. One must realize that the Evil Inclination is jealous and does not want him to attain a higher spiritual level. [Therefore], it attacks him fiercely.

If one will think wisely and fortify himself against the Evil Inclination, he will accomplish something very great in the Supernal World at that hour. Thus, the *Zohar* states, "It is more precious to the Holy One, blessed be He, when the realm of unholiness is overcome as a result of great effort."[2] The Evil Inclination adamantly wanted him to stop fasting. But he fortified himself against it and vanquished the realm of unholiness (*Tzava'as HaRivash* 78).

---

1. *Avos* 3:1.
2. *Zohar* II, 128b; 184a.

Sometimes the Accuser is given permission to cause a person great suffering in order to test him as to whether or not he will hold his ground and overcome the Evil Inclination. If one is wise, he will beseech God with tears and words of supplication to give him enough strength to prevail. As our Sages taught, "When one comes to purify himself, he is helped . . ."[3] Afterwards, when one concludes the fast, he will not even remember the pain he endured at that hour.

One must also beg the Creator for mercy, that he be given the strength not to harm himself by fasting (*Likkutei Amarim of Rabbi Menachem Mendel of Vitebsk*, 31; *Tzava'as HaRivash* 79).

The essential point of *teshuvah* is to turn away from one's evil ways [and not the specific penitential acts one takes upon himself].[4] One should never pride himself [about fasting], for "a fast over which one takes pride is given to the dogs [i.e., the forces of impurity]."[5]

Even if only one person [truly] repents, the entire world is forgiven.[6] And since one rejoices in the afflictions of the fast, which is an act of self-sacrifice, he has certainly accomplished something of great value.

One [who fasts for an extended period] should sleep during the daytime for the first three days in order to strengthen his mental faculties, but he should not sleep a great deal. He should sit for awhile in one place and then in another. Afterwards, it is good to walk a bit and then lie down briefly in order to reduce one's discomfort. One may study Torah in thought alone, without speaking, so as to avoid taxing himself.

Sometimes one's lips become dry and bitter, and the Evil Inclination makes him imagine that his head hurts so much that it is unbearable. But if one trusts in the kindness of the Creator, his strength will return, and he will not experience any more pain at all.

One should intend to gratify the Creator by fasting and to reduce the sufferings of the *Shechinah* by taking affliction upon himself. [Therefore], one should serve God with joy, bearing in mind that the *Shechinah*

---

3. *Shabbos* 104a; *Yoma* 38b.
4. See Rambam, *Mishneh Torah, Hilchos Teshuvah* 2:2.
5. *Tikkunei Zohar, Tikkun* 18, 33b; also note *Talmud Yerushalmi, Chagiga* 3:2.
6. *Yoma* 86b.

supports him, just as She supports the rest of the sick,[7] and God will help him (*Likkutei Amarim of Rabbi Menachem Mendel of Vitebsk*, 29; *Tzava'as HaRivash* 43, version 2).

It states in *Tanna D'vei Eliyahu* that anyone who fasts and separates himself from all worldly pleasures for forty days in a row—even a slave or a maidservant—will be granted a revelation of Eliyahu HaNavi. [Concerning this the Baal Shem Tov once remarked], "One may have a revelation of Eliyahu—but not a revelation of the soul" (*Sefer HaSichos* 5704, p. 98, cited in *Kesser Shem Tov, Hosafos*, 99).

---

7. *Shabbos* 12b.

God

"Our God and the God of our fathers—the God of Avraham, the God of Yitzchak, and the God of Yaakov . . ." (*Siddur, Shemoneh Esrei*). The Baal Shem Tov explained: The reason we mention God's name in conjunction with each of the Patriarchs is to show that one should not merely rely upon the search for God and manner of Divine service of his father. Thus, Yitzchak and Yaakov did not rely upon the search for God and the Divine service of Avraham; rather, they each discovered the Oneness of the Creator and served Him in their own way (*Korban HeAni, Bechukosai*).

The viewpoint of our master, the Baal Shem Tov, is one teaching that may be expressed in two ways: Godliness is everything, and everything is Godliness (*Likkutei Dibburim* IV, 36).

"Hear, O Israel, the Lord, our God, the Lord is One" (*Devarim* 6:6). When, during this part of the prayer service, a person recites the word "One," he should contemplate that the Holy One, blessed be He, is all that truly exists in the universe, for "the entire earth is filled with His glory."[1] One must realize is that he is nothing, for the essence of a person is his soul, and the soul is a "portion of God Above."[2] Therefore, nothing truly exists except the Holy One, blessed be He[3] (*Likkutim Yekarim* 161).

"And you shall turn aside and serve other gods . . ." (*Devarim* 11:16). As soon as one turns aside from *deveykus*, God forbid, he comes

---

1. *Yeshayahu* 6:3.

2. *Shefa Tal* 1a.

3. See Maharal of Prague, *Haggadah, Shabbos HaGadol D'rasha* (citing *Devarim* 4:39); *Sefer HaTanya, Sha'ar HaYichud V'haEmunah*, Chapter 6.

to serve "other gods," [i.e., to think that things exist independently of the Creator] (*Likkutei Amarim of Rabbi Menachem Mendel of Vitebsk*, 28a; also see *Me'or Einaim, Shemos, Vayigash*, and *R'ei*).

"And I will surely hide (*haster astir*) My face . . ." (*Devarim* 31:18). The Baal Shem Tov taught: As soon as one realizes that the Holy One, blessed be He, is hidden, there is no longer any concealment, and all negativity disappears. Thus, the verse uses a double expression of concealment—*haster astir*. The Holy One, blessed be He, will also obscure the knowledge that He is present in the midst of His hiddenness (*Toldos Yaakov Yosef, Bereishis*).

The Creator is present in every movement, for it is impossible to make any gesture or to utter any word without His power. This is the meaning of the verse, "His glory fills the entire world"[4] (*Kesser Shem Tov* 273).

The Baal Shem Tov taught: If a person grasps a "part" of Oneness, he grasps the whole; and the opposite is also true[5] (*Kesser Shem Tov* 65).

It is written, "Forever, O God, Your word stands in the heavens" (*Tehillim* 119:89). The Baal Shem Tov, of blessed memory, explained that "Your word" which You uttered [in saying], "Let there be a firmament in the midst of the waters . . ."[6]—these very words and letters stand and are established forever in the firmament of heaven and are enclothed within all the firmaments forever to give them life. [Thus] it is written, "The word of our God shall stand forever,"[7] and, "His words live and

---

4. *Yeshayahu* 6:3.

5. A similar concept may be found in *Sefer Chareidim*, as cited in *Shemiras HaLashon of the Chofetz Chaim, Chasimas HaSefer*, 3.

6. *Bereishis* 1:6.

7. *Yeshayahu* 40:8.

stand forever . . ."[8] For if the letters were to depart for even a moment, God forbid, and return to their Source, all the heavens would revert to naught and absolute nothingness, and it would be as if they had never existed all, as before the Divine utterance, "Let there be a firmament . . ."[9] This applies to all created things in all the upper and lower worlds—even this physical earth and the inanimate realm (*domem*). If the letters of the Ten Divine Utterances by which the world was created during the Six Days of Creation were to depart for an instant, God forbid, [everything] would return to naught and absolute nothingness, exactly as before the Six Days of Creation (*Sefer HaTanya, Sha'ar HaYichud V'haEmunah*, 1).

"How great is the goodness You have hidden for those who revere You . . ." (*Tehillim* 31.20). That is, You hide and conceal Yourself from those who revere You, which causes them to fall into constricted consciousness. [However,] since this is a "descent for the sake of a later ascent," it is actually very good.

This may be compared to a father who wishes to teach his child to walk. When the child is about to reach him, the father steps back a bit, so that the child may come closer to him on his own (*Toldos Yitzchak*).

When a person realizes that the Master of the Universe is actually present in his every word and gesture, however great or small, all the spiritual confusions disperse that obscure the light of Essential Mind (*Nesiv Mitzvosecha*, cited in *Sefer Baal Shem Tov, Vayeilech*, note 6).

One should continually occupy his thoughts with the *Shechinah*. He should think about his love for the *Shechinah* unceasingly in order that it should cleave to him. He should always ask himself, "When will I merit to have the light of the *Shechinah* dwell with me?" (*Tzava'as HaRivash* 8).

---

8. *Siddur, Shacharis.*
9. Ibid.

I heard in the name of the Baal Shem Tov: "I, I am the One Who consoles you . . ." (*Yeshayahu* 51:12). When one realizes that the true "I" is God, and nothing exists beside Him, then [the Divine promise is fulfilled that] "I am the One Who consoles you" (*T'shuos Chein, Tzav,* cited in *Meiras Einaim, Emunah*).

First and foremost, one must of his own free will choose [the good]. Then, after having chosen, one must make his heart and his mouth one in believing with perfect faith that "the whole world is full of His glory,"[10] and that everything derives its life force from Him. Therefore, every manifestation of love and fear and all other human emotions really come from Him—even the evil that exists in the world.

Thus, it is not right to love or to fear or to praise anything but God. When considering something one loves or fears, he should think, "Where does this feeling come from? Does not everything come from God, Who puts love and fear into even evil creatures such as savage beasts as a result of the Shattering of the Vessels [at the beginning of creation]? Thus, there is nothing to fear but God. Why should I fear this single spark of Godliness which has fallen into an evil form? It would be better to bind myself to a higher fear."

One should proceed this way with love and the rest of his feelings in order to extract the spark [of Godliness] from its fallen state and to raise it up to its Source. For this is our main spiritual task: to elevate [the holy sparks that fell during] the Shattering of the Vessels to their Source.

Also, while speaking, one should not think that his "I" is the speaker. Rather, the life force within him—which is the Creator, may He be blessed—speaks through him. In this way he will elevate speech to its Source. The trait of equanimity is also [attained in this way]. The faculty of speech belongs to the next person as well as oneself. [Therefore, the "true" self is not the personal self]; everything comes from God.

Likewise, while eating, one's intent should be to bring forth the life force within [the food] in order to raise it up to the Creator. In everything one does, his only intent should be to bind himself Above (*Tzava'as HaRivash* 127).

---

10. *Yeshayahu* 6:3.

God's Name

"*Toras Hashem temimah* (God's Torah is complete) . . ." (*Tehillim* 19:8). The Baal Shem Tov rendered this literally: The Torah in its entirety spells the name of God[1] (*Toldos Aharon, Beshalach*).

"The Lord (YHVH) is Your name forever" (*Tehillim* 135:13). The Divine name YHVH is called the Essential Name, because it denotes that He brings all existence into being. Nevertheless, God's greatness and splendor is far loftier than even His Essential Name. For who imbues these four letters with existence? Does not everything come from Him?

Thus, Eliyahu HaNavi declared, "You have no name by which You can be known, for You permeate all names. You are the perfection of them all. And when You remove Yourself from them, all names remain as a body without a soul."[2]

This is the meaning of the verse, "The Lord (YHVH) is Your name forever (*l'olam*)." [The word *l'olam* can also mean "for the world."] Even when we use the Essential Name, YHVH, it is only for the sake of the world. In this way, we may call upon God and bring His Providence to bear upon ourselves. However, in truth, He is far beyond all names.

I later heard that this teaching had been said in the name of the Baal Shem Tov[3] (*Ohr HaMeir, Shoftim*).

---

1. Also see *Zohar* III, 35b, 265b, 298b.

2. *Tikkunei Zohar, Hakdamah* II.

3. Also see *Ohr Ne'erav* VI:1; *Sichos HaRan* 95; *Likkutei Moharan* I, 15:5 with commentary of *Mai HaNachal*, ad loc.; *Likkutei Halachos, Yoreh De'ah, Hilchos Ribis* 5:31–32; ibid., *Hilchos Birkas HaRei'ach* 5:17; *Derech Mitzvosecha, Mitzvas Ha'amanas Elokus*, Chapter 1.

Good and Evil

"Who is a sage? One who learns from every man, as the verse states, 'From all my teachers I gained wisdom'" (*Avos* 4:1, citing *Tehillim* 119:99). [The Mishnah] should have said, "One who learns from every teacher." [Rather,] it means that one must learn from every person— one must learn a good character trait even from an evil-doer (*Sefer HaSichos* 5700, cited in *Kesser Shem Tov, Hosafos*, 90).

"Turn from evil and do good" (*Tehillim* 34:15). That is, transform evil into goodness[1] (*Kesser Shem* Tov 69).

"There are four types of people who go to the House of Study. One who goes but does nothing will be rewarded for going. One who studies but does not go will be rewarded for studying. One who goes and studies is pious. One who does not go and does not study is wicked" (*Avos* 5:14)

The Baal Shem Tov asked: How can one who does not go and does not study be counted among those who attend the House of Study? [This may be understood according to the principle] that evil causes the good to be discerned. If there were no evil, then good would not be recognized. This is what is meant by "the advantage of light which emerges from darkness."[2] Therefore, even the wicked and foolish person is counted among those who attend the House of Study. From [the example of] this fool, the benefit of wisdom may be appreciated.

Our master also said that since evil serves a purpose in the world, one might think that it, too, may be elevated. But the verse states, "'Though you make your nest as high as the eagle, from there I will cast you down,' says God"[3] (*Notzer Chesed* on *Avos* 5:14).

---

1. Note *Chayei Moharan* 447.
2. *Zohar* I, 32b; ibid. II, 187a; ibid. III, 37b.
3. *Yirmiyahu* 49:16.

One might wonder at the Torah's declaration, "Behold, I have set before you this day life and good, death and evil . . ." (*Devarim* 30:15). In the account of creation, it repeatedly states that everything was good [in God's eyes].[4] Where did [man's potential to do] evil come from? However, evil [in its spiritual source] is not actual evil; this [potential] evil is also good. It is just on a lower level than absolute good. [Therefore, it can manifest itself as actual evil, depending on man's freedom of choice.] The *Zohar* alludes to this [with the phrase] "from above or below."[5] [The word "below" in Aramaic is *ra*, which in Hebrew means "evil." This suggests that in their source, good and evil are one; evil only manifests itself as such below, in this world.]

Thus, when one does good [the potential for] evil also becomes good. But when one sins, God forbid, actual evil comes into existence. This is like a broom with which a person sweeps his house in order to make it clean. The broom is good, albeit on an inferior level. However, when it is used to strike a child who has misbehaved, the broom becomes a vehicle for evil (*Tzava'as HaRivash* 130).

I received the following from my teacher [the Baal Shem Tov]: When evil results in good, it [retroactively] becomes a throne for the good—and everything is transformed to complete good. Thus, in the Ultimate Future, the Evil Husks (*klippos*) will become subsumed in the Divine Nothingness[6] (*Toldos Yaakov Yosef, Bo*).

---

4. *Bereishis* 1:1–31.

5. *Zohar* I, 49b.

6. Thus the Gemara states that through penitence one's transgressions can actually become meritorious deeds; see *Yoma* 86b. Also note *Degel Machaneh Ephraim, Tzav*; *Likkutei Moharan* I, 22:11; and at length in *Likkutei Halachos, Orach Chaim, Hilchos Minchah* 7, especially subsection 32.

Guests

"Receiving guests is even greater than greeting the *Shechinah* (Divine Presence)" (*Shabbos* 127a). My master (the Baal Shem Tov) once remarked, "One might have thought otherwise, for sometimes receiving guests leads a person to neglect the study of Torah or to relate *lashon hara* (harmful gossip), etc. Nevertheless, receiving guests is greater" (*Toldos Yaakov Yosef, Devarim Sheshamati MiMori* 24).

Rabbi Yisrael of Vizhnitz elaborated [upon the teaching cited above]: The Baal Shem Tov's remark needs to be understood [in context of the *Gemara*]. If one performs any *mitzvah* with love and fear of God, this itself will enable him to "greet the *Shechinah*." Why, then, is receiving guests greater than greeting the *Shechinah*? By performing this *mitzvah*, one also should be able to greet the *Shechinah*. However, receiving guests sometimes leads to speaking *lashon hara* (harmful gossip), one of the sins for which one will not merit to greet the *Shechinah*,[1] as well as neglecting the study of Torah. Therefore, [the Baal Shem Tov said,] "Nevertheless, receiving guests is greater" (*Kuntres Ohr Yisrael*).

I heard from my master (the Baal Shem Tov): When a guest arrives, he brings his host Torah insights; for the Torah insights the host receives from Above correspond to the nature of his guests[2] (*Degel Machaneh Ephraim, Vayeira*).

---

1. *Sanhedrin* 103a.
2. The Baal Shem Tov also taught that "*orei'ach*," the Hebrew word for guest, may be divided into the words "*ohr ches*"—"the light of the eighth." The eighth *sefirah* in ascending order is *binah* (understanding), which corresponds to the Supernal Torah and the Godly perception of the World to Come. Relative to this world, such a lofty perception comes from without, like a guest. Thus, by opening his home to another, the host actually receives more than he gives: an illumination of this sublime light (see *Toldos Yitzchak, Likkutei HaShas*, cited in *Sefer Baal Shem Tov, Vayeira*, 4).

The Baal Shem Tov once said: "Just as everyone joyously exclaims when a guest arrives, so do [the angels] joyously exclaim Above"[3] (*Imrei Pinchas*, p. 215).

---

3. See *Tikkunei Zohar, Tikkun* 6, 23b.

Healing

The Baal Shem Tov taught: When the body is sick, the soul is sick and cannot pray properly, even if it is pure and without sin. Therefore, one must be very careful to safeguard his health[1] (*Tzava'as HaRivash* 106).

The Baal Shem Tov taught: When a person knows the sickness of his heart, realizing that his true sickness consists in that the soul has fallen into a low spiritual state, this knowledge itself is his healing. However, when a person lacks such knowledge—as the verse states, "I will surely hide My face . . ."[2]—and doesn't know that he is spiritually sick, there can be no true healing for his physical ailment[3] (*Kesser Shem Tov* 25).

The Baal Shem Tov said that all remedies, according to their names in the seventy primary languages, [are hidden] in the Biblical passage that enumerates the twenty-four types of impure birds (*Vayikra* 11:13–21). I seem to remember that it was the *Rebbe* [Rabbi Nachman of Breslev] who attributed this to the Baal Shem Tov [his great-grandfather] (*Chayei Moharan*, 557).

Rabbi Nachman of Kolomaye told Rabbi Moshe of Ziditchov that his great-grandfather once met the Baal Shem Tov. At that time, the Baal Shem Tov was first beginning to heal the sick, and his teachings had not yet been publicized.

"Where did you acquire your remedies?" Rabbi Nachman's great-grandfather asked. "I, too, would like to learn them."

"From *Sefer Vayikra* (Leviticus)," the Baal Shem Tov replied. "One can find all remedies in the Order of Sacrifices" (*Ayalah Sh'luchah* 167).

---

1. See *Mishneh Torah, Hilchos De'os* 4:1.
2. *Devarim* 31:18.
3. See *Likkutei Moharan* I:268.

I heard from my grandfather, the Baal Shem Tov: Why are most medicines very bitter? Because the physical world contains inanimate things (*domem*), vegetative life (*tzome'ach*), animals (*chai*) and mankind (*medaber*). Each one elevates [that which is inferior to itself]. Animals are supposed to raise up the holy sparks which exist in bitter plants. However, if they refrain from doing so because the plants are too bitter, it is decreed that people must become ill. Then, due to their illness, they must eat or drink bitter [remedies made from plants] in order to elevate [these holy sparks] to their source[4] (*Sharsheres Zahav* 27).

There are several versions of how the Maggid (Rabbi Dov Ber of Mezeritch) came to the Baal Shem Tov. However, I heard that his relatives pressed him to do so. When he arrived, he found the Baal Shem Tov sitting on his bed, studying *Gemara*. After offering his greetings, the Maggid asked the Baal Shem Tov to heal him.

The Baal Shem Tov scolded him and said, "My horses do not eat *matzos*."[5]

The Maggid began to sweat from illness, so he went outside and sat down to rest on the step in front of the house. Seeing a young man, he called him over and said, "Please go and ask the Baal Shem Tov why he does not fulfill the verse: 'Therefore shall you love the stranger.'"[6]

The young man was Rabbi Yaakov of Annipola. He felt sorry for the Maggid, so he went to the Baal Shem Tov. Too intimidated to speak openly, he pretended to busy himself at the far end of the house. Then, on his way out, he said, "There's an unhappy man sitting on the front step who told me to ask my master why he has not fulfilled the verse: 'Therefore shall you love the stranger.'" With this, he left the house.

The Baal Shem Tov immediately gathered ten men and went to the Maggid to ask his forgiveness. He attempted to heal him with words. I heard from Rabbi Gershon of Pavlysh that for a period of two weeks the Baal Shem Tov came to the Maggid and sat beside him, reciting Psalms. Afterwards, the Baal Shem Tov said, "If you had so desired, I might have cured you with words alone, for this is a lasting remedy. But now I will

---

4. See *Likkutei Moharan* I, 27:7.

5. This unclear retort probably implies the Baal Shem Tov's disapproval of the Maggid's stringent ascetic practices.

6. *Devarim* 10:19.

have to cure you with medication." The Baal Shem Tov gave him an apartment and twelve golden coins every week for his expenses. At first, the Maggid was too weak to visit the Baal Shem Tov. But after a short time he began to recover and would join the Baal Shem Tov at his table (*Shivchei Baal Shem Tov* 37).

Once a famous doctor came to the duchess of the town. She praised the Baal Shem Tov highly, saying that he was a great man who also was knowledgeable in medicine.

The doctor said, "Tell him to come here."

She replied, "It would be rude unless we sent a carriage for him, as one does for the nobility, for he is a great man."

She sent for the Baal Shem Tov, and he appeared before them.

The doctor asked the rabbi if it was true that he was knowledgeable in medicine.

He answered, "It is true."

"Where did you study and with which expert?" the doctor inquired.

"God taught me," he replied.

At this, the doctor began to laugh. Then he asked if the Baal Shem Tov understood pulse-diagnosis. The latter said, "I have a deficiency. You take my pulse, and then I will take your pulse."

When the doctor took the rabbi's pulse, he knew that something was amiss, but could not identify it. In truth, the Baal Shem Tov was lovesick for God, and this was beyond the doctor's understanding.

Then the rabbi took the doctor's pulse. He turned to the duchess and asked her, "Were such-and-such objects stolen from you?"

"Yes," she replied. "It has been several years since the theft, and I still don't know where they are."

The rabbi said, "Send someone to the doctor's room at the inn and open his trunk. There you will find everything that is missing."

A person was dispatched immediately, and the valuables were found, in accordance with the Baal Shem Tov's holy words. The doctor left in disgrace and contempt[7] (*Shivchei Baal Shem Tov* 209).

---

7. Concerning pulse-diagnosis in Kabbalistic thought, see *Tikkunei Zohar, Tikkun* 69 (108a); *Sha'ar Ruach HaKodesh*, p. 3; *Likkutei Torah of the Ari* z"l, *Vayeira* 2; *Likkutei Moharan* I, 56:9; ibid. II:24; *Sichos HaRan* 273; *Sippurei Ma'asios, Ma'aseh* 13, section 6. Much of this material is translated and discussed in "The Wings of the Sun" by Avraham Greenbaum (Breslov Research Inst. 1995).

His Aura

Rabbi David, the Maggid of Kolomiya, traveled about collecting alms for Chanukah. He once lost his way and arrived at the Baal Shem Tov's house just before the time of lighting the candles. [Since this was before the Baal Shem Tov revealed himself to the world, Rabbi David took his host for an unlettered rustic.]

In the middle of the night, the Baal Shem Tov arose. (I heard that he usually slept no more than two hours.) He sat quietly at the foot of the oven and did whatever he did without making any noise.

The Maggid, Rabbi David, woke up and saw a great light beneath the oven. He thought that the logs above the oven had been kindled and were burning. [Therefore,] he took the chamber-pot with the waste-water and went to put out the fire. When the Maggid came to the oven, he saw the Baal Shem Tov sitting there, surrounded with light—and he fainted at the sight. [Later,] he personally told me that the Baal Shem Tov's aura was like a rainbow[1] (*Shiv'chei Baal Shem Tov* 15).

---

1. In Kabbalistic thought, the *Shechinah* is identified with the rainbow. See *Zohar* III, *Pinchas*, 215a, which is discussed in *Likkutei Moharan* I:42.

His Passing

I heard from the Rav of our community [Rabbi Gedaliah of Linitz,] who heard from Rabbi Yosef of Kaminka that the Baal Shem Tov had hoped to ascend to Heaven in a storm wind, like Eliyahu HaNavi. But after his wife passed away, he continued to grieve exceedingly. His disciples assumed that he was suffering because of his great loss. Since it was unlike [their master] to act this way, they broached the subject with him. The Baal Shem Tov explained that he was distressed because of the higher consciousness (*mochin*) which must descend to the grave.

"I thought I would ascend in a storm wind," he said. "But [without my wife] I am but half a body, and it is impossible. That is why I am suffering" (*Shiv'chei Baal Shem Tov* 107; for another version, see "The Land of Israel").

As the time of his death drew near, the holy Baal Shem Tov said: "Now I know the reason why I was created and the purpose of my existence" (*Hilula D'Rashbi*, p. 113).

The Baal Shem Tov, of blessed memory, once said that because of the episode of Shabbsai Tzvi, may his name be blotted out, two holes were made in his heart, and this brought about his death (*Likkutei Moharan* I:207; *Shiv'chei Baal Shem Tov* 20, 211).

Before he passed away, the Baal Shem Tov said that it was within his power to ascend to heaven in a storm wind like Eliyahu HaNavi. But he did not wish to forego the verse, "For you are dust, and to dust you shall return"[1] (*Likkutei Dibburim* I, 4:15).

---

1. Also note the explanation of this remark in *Toras Shmuel*, p.46. Both teachings are cited in *Kesser Shem Tov, Hosafos*, 268, and note 277, p.114.

[The Baal Shem Tov] predicted that when he passed away, the two clocks [in his house] would stop. [On the last day of his life,] as he washed his hands, the big clock stopped. His followers stood in front of the clock so that he should not see it.

"I know the clock stopped," he told them. "But I am not worried about myself. I know clearly that as soon as I leave [this room,] I will immediately enter [the next]."

He sat up in bed and asked those present to gather around him. He said words of Torah about the Column through which one ascends from the Lower Garden of Eden to the Upper Garden of Eden, and thus from world to world. [The Baal Shem Tov described] what it is like in the World of Souls. He then explained the order of Divine service, instructing them to recite, "Let the pleasantness of the Lord, our God, be upon us . . ."[2] He sat up and lay down several times. He concentrated on the *kavanos* (specific Kabbalistic meditations) until those present could not distinguish the syllables. He told them to cover him with a sheet and began to tremble, as when he prayed the *Shemoneh Esrei*. Then slowly he became still. They saw that the small clock had also stopped. After waiting for a long time, they held a feather under his nose and realized that he had passed away.

I heard all this from Rabbi Yaakov of the holy community of Medzhibuzh (who passed away in the Holy Land). He said that Rabbi Leib Kessler saw the Baal Shem Tov's soul depart as a blue flame (*Shiv'chei Baal Shem Tov* 211).

I heard that [before his death] the Baal Shem Tov said, "If Moshiach does not come within sixty years, I will have to return to this world."

When I asked Rabbi Aharon of Medzhibuzh [about this], he told me, "[The Baal Shem Tov] said, 'Certainly, I will be reincarnated and return to this world—but I will not be as I am today.'" However, the meaning of his words is unknown; for [as Rabbi Aharon] added, "Who can fathom the explanation of this matter?" (*Shiv'chei Baal Shem Tov* 108 and 109).

---

2. *Tehillim* 90:17.

Before he passed away, our master, the Baal Shem Tov, declared, "Let not the foot of pride overtake me . . ." (*Tehillim* 36:12).

[He then elaborated, homiletically interpreting one of the Scriptural verses of reproof:] "And there you shall sell yourselves to your enemy . . ." You should always suspect that you have sold yourselves to your enemy, the Evil Inclination. "To be slaves and bondmaids . . ." for all your deeds have been for the sake of personal gain, which is the spiritual aspect of a slave or bondmaid. You have not really begun to perform the will of the Creator. Then, when your heart has been subdued and broken, [the conclusion of the verse will be fulfilled:] "And none shall buy."[3] No evil will be able to rule over you, nor will there be any [Heavenly] accusation against you, and you will cleave to the Source of Life.

With these words, his soul departed. This took place before the morning prayers on the first day of Shavuos in the year 5520 (1760 C.E.).[4] (*Heichal HaBracha, Ki Seitzei,* 129b).

---

3. *Devarim* 28:68.

4. In support of the view that the Baal Shem Tov passed away on the first day of Shavuos, also see *Sefer Baal Shem Tov, Ki Savo, Mekor Mayim Chaim,* note 12; *Likkutei Dibburim* III, p.1054, cited in *Kesser Shem Tov, Hosafos,* 270; *Siddur of R. Avraham Shimshon of Raszkov,* p. 298; *Darkei Chaim V'Shalom, Hilchos Yom Tov,* 527.

Humility

The Baal Shem Tov taught: If not for his ego, a person would be able to apprehend [Godliness] like the Tannaim and Amoraim.

[Rabbi Aharon of Karlin explained:] Depression is also a form of egotism. One thinks to himself, "I am a superior person. Therefore, I should feel inspired with awe [while praying]." However the main thing is to concentrate on the simple meaning of the words, each person to the best of his ability, and not to be preoccupied with oneself (*Beis Aharon, Seder HaYom*).

The Baal Shem Tov taught: If a person is completely unconcerned with himself, such that everything is the same to him, he will surely reach the highest spiritual levels—for humility is loftier than all other spiritual attainments[1] (*Hanhagos Yesharos*, 14b, cited in *Sefer Baal Shem Tov, Metzora* 12).

"'Can a man hide in secret places and I not see him?' declares God" (*Yirmiyahu* 23:24). The Baal Shem Tov rendered this interpretively: A person can hide in secret places—but as long as he is an "I" in his own perception, God will not look at him (so to speak) (*Likkutei Sichos* IV, p. 1033).

One must not think that he is better than his fellow because he experiences *deveykus* to a greater extent. In truth, he is no different than any other creature, since all things were brought into being in order to serve God. Just as God bestowed consciousness upon one person, so did He bestow consciousness upon the next.

---

1. See *Likkutei Moharan* II:70.

What makes a human being better than a worm? A worm serves
the Creator with all of his intelligence and ability; and man, too, is comparable to a worm or a maggot, as the verse states, "I am a worm and
not a man."[2] If God had not given one [a greater] intellect, he would
only be able to serve him like a worm. In this sense, one is of no greater
worth in the eyes of Heaven than a worm.

One should consider himself and the worm and all small creatures
as comrades in the universe. For we are all created beings, whose abilities are God-given. This should always remain in one's thoughts[3]
(*Tzava'as HaRivash* 12).

"And Moshe and Aharon said unto all the children of Israel . . . 'In
the morning you shall see the glory of God, inasmuch as He has heard
your murmurings against God—for what (*mah*) are we, that you mur-
mur against us?'" (*Shemos* 16:6–7). Our Sages taught: "The words
ascribed to Moshe are greater than those of our forefather, Avraham.
Avraham declared, 'And I am but dust and ashes,'[4] whereas Moshe said,
'What (*mah*) are we . . .'"

Our master, the holy Rabbi Yisrael Baal Shem Tov, of blessed
memory, explained that the spiritual level of Moshe Rabbeinu was
greater, therefore his self-effacement [indicated by the term *mah*] was
greater[5] (*Noam Megadim, Korach*).

The Baal Shem Tov also pointed out the difference between the two
statements [cited above]. Moshe did not use the term "I," as did Avraham,
but instead included himself with others when he asked, "What are we?"
(*T'shuos Chein, Shemos; Sifsei Tzaddikim, Ki Sisa*).

2. *Tehillim* 22:7.

3. A similar analogy is given in *Sefer HaKuzari* 5:20, *Hakdamah* 3.

4. *Bereishis* 18:27.

5. See *Bamidbar* 12:3. The self-nullification of Moshe Rabbeinu is elaborated upon
in *Kedushas Levi, R'ei*, and *Likkutei Moharan* II:72. Also note the general explanation of
this concept in *Likkutei Moharan* II:82 and *Likkutei Eitzos, Mach'shavos v'Hirhurim* 18;
Likkutei Halachos, Hilchos Tefillin 6, especially subsection 8.

When a person always serves God in every moment, there is no possibility for him to become self-important or to be attracted to pride or other evil traits (*Tzava'as HaRivash* 52).

Self-importance—even the least thought of it—is a great obstacle. All biased judgment stems from pride. Since each thought is "a small world," [a proud thought] can cause great harm Above; it "pushes against the very feet of the Divine Presence."[6] Thus, the verse states, "Anyone with a proud heart is an abomination unto God"[7] (*Tzava'as HaRivash* 92).

The *Zohar* states that one should perform the will of God like a poor man (*Zohar* III, 195a). Like a poor man, one should always address God with humble words of supplication (*Tzava'as HaRivash* 7).

I heard in the name of the Baal Shem Tov that he would behave warmly even toward transgressors, as long as they were not brazen. However, he would distance himself [even] from Torah scholars who were not transgressors if they were haughty. He once explained that if a person is a sinner and knows it, he will have a low opinion of himself. Therefore, God is with him, for "He dwells with them in the midst of their impurity." This other fellow may not be a sinner, but since he is full of conceit, God is not with him; for "he and I cannot dwell together"[8] (*Pri Chaim, Avos* 4:4).

At times one must appear to be great in front of others, for this will enhance God's glory. As our Sages taught, "A Torah scholar must

---

6. *Berachos* 43b.
7. *Mishlei* 16:5.
8. *Sotah* 5a.

have an eighth of an eighth part of conceit."[9] However, at that moment one must remain intensely aware of his own lowliness. In his heart he should say, "The truth is that I am quite inferior, and this show of importance is really only for the glory of the Creator, may He be blessed. As for myself, I deserve no honor at all. 'I am but a worm and not a man.'[10] For what do I deserve any honor?" (*Tzava'as HaRivash* 91).

"Better is one of little esteem who is a servant than a man who is glorified but lacks bread" (*Mishlei* 12:9). It is a sure sign that one serves God when he has no esteem in his own eyes. Then he has attained a high level and can truly serve God. [However], "a man who is glorified"— in his own eyes—"lacks bread," i.e., spiritual sustenance (*Tzava'as HaRivash* 114).

"They have made Yerushalayim into a heap of ruins. They have given the corpses of Your servants as food to the birds of the sky [and] the flesh of Your pious ones to the beasts of the earth" (*Tehillim* 79:1–2).

The Baal Shem Tov taught: Exile has come to the world because "they have made Yerushalayim into a heap of ruins." Our Sages state that "Yerushalayim" is composed of the words *yirah* (awe or reverence) and *shaleim* (completeness or perfection.)[11] As soon as a person experiences *yirah* (awe) or properly performs a *mitzvah*, he may begin to feel self-important. Thus, the verse states, "They have made *yirah* into a heap of ruins." Their Divine service is but rubble. Similarly, if one accomplishes something—for example, in Torah or prayer—he does so "for the lyre and the harp," that is, one does not act with love and awe of God, but like [a performer] who plays music on the lyre and the harp. This causes his Divine service to enter the realm of the *klippos* (forces of impurity). "As food to the birds of the sky . . ." This refers to the *klippos*, which are compared to predatory birds[12] (*Tzava'as HaRivash* 124).

---

9. *Sotah* 5a.
10. *Tehillim* 22:7.
11. *Bereshis Rabba, Vayeira* 56.
12. *Zohar I, Bereishis,* 34b.

A soul is taught the Torah by the Holy One, blessed be He, in the Heavenly Academy. Then it is sent down to this world—not only to study Torah but also to transform the *ani* ("I") to *ayin* ("nothingness"). [In Hebrew, the words *ayin* and *ani* are composed of the same letters.] Even a person who is truly an *ani* in Torah and *mitzvos* must nevertheless make his *ani* into *ayin*, until he feels [that all his accomplishments are] truly nothing compared to the artless simplicity of an ordinary Jew (*Sefer HaZichronos* I, p. 345, cited in *Kesser Shem Tov, Hosafos,* 132).

I heard in the name of my grandfather (the Baal Shem Tov): Our Sages state that whoever renounces idolatry is called a Jew (*Megilla* 13a). Self-importance is a form of idolatry.[13] Thus, whoever renounces self-importance is called a Jew[14] (*Degel Machaneh Ephraim, Purim*).

---

13. *Sotah* 5a.

14. Humility as the essential Jewish trait is discussed in *Chullin* 89a. However, the subject is dealt with at length throughout rabbinic literature. For further study, see R. Bachya ibn Pekudah's *Chovos HaLevavos* ("Duties of the Heart"), *Sha'ar HaK'niah;* R. Avraham Ben HaRambam's *Sefer HaMaspik L'Ovdei HaShem, Perek al Arichus Apayim, Perek al HaAnavah;* Maharal's *Nesivos Olam, Nesiv HaAnavah;* R. Eliyahu DeVidas' *Reishis Chochmah, Sha'ar HaAnavah;* R. Chaim Vital's *Sha'arei Kedushah* II:4; R. Moshe Chaim Luzzatto's *Mesilas Yesharim* ("The Path of the Just"), Chapters 22–23.

Journeys

I heard in the name of my master (the Baal Shem Tov) that during his journey [to the land of Israel,] his master [Achiyah HaShiloni] declared, "This place was alluded to by the name of such-and-such a journey when the Children of Israel traveled through the wilderness. In fact, all of a person's journeys are indirectly mentioned in the Torah."

Similarly, when [the Baal Shem Tov] was shipwrecked and became depressed, his master appeared to him and was amazed [to find him in such a state]. He showed [the Baal Shem Tov] the effect of his actions in the Supernal Worlds. Then he was able to fortify himself and to sweeten all the forces of severe judgment in their Source (*Toldos Yaakov Yosef, Likkutim*).

I heard in the name of my grandfather (the Baal Shem Tov): The forty-two journeys [of the Children of Israel in the wilderness] are a paradigm for all journeys. This applies to every person, from the day of his birth until he returns to the World of Truth.[1]

For example, the day of one's birth and emergence from his mother's womb is like the exodus from Egypt, as is known.[2] From then on, a person takes one journey after another until he reaches the supernal Land of the Living. Thus, the verse states, "By the word of God they camped, and by the word of God they journeyed forth."[3] For throughout life, one must experience many highs and lows (*Degel Machaneh Ephraim, Mas'ei*).

"The steps of man are prepared by God, and He favors his path" (*Tehillim* 37:23). The Baal Shem Tov taught: This verse refers to those who travel to distant lands for business or other similar reasons. [However], God's thoughts are not like their thoughts.[4] They think they are

---

1. See *Likkutei Moharan* II:62.
2. See *Midrash Shochar Tov, Tehillim* 114.
3. *Bamidbar* 9:20.
4. *Yeshayahu* 55:8.

going to a certain distant land in order to increase their gold and silver through business transactions, and for this purpose they expend their strength. But, in truth, God's plan is otherwise, for He knows how to accomplish His purpose better than man.

Sometimes a person receives a piece of bread in a distant land, which is related to [the root of his soul]. Therefore, it comes about that he must eat this particular piece of bread in this place and at this time, or drink a mouthful of water in a certain spot. For this reason "the steps of man are prepared," and to this end did he exert himself to travel so far. By eating this bread or by drinking this water, however much or little, one [elevates the holy sparks contained therein, and in so doing] perfects his soul.

Thus, the verse states, "The steps of man are prepared by God." A person travels to a distant place; but everything is Divinely determined to enable this individual to perfect his soul by something that God, according to His wisdom, brings about. The nature of man is otherwise, and his heart does not think this way. Nevertheless, "[God] desires his path," to travel and to engage in business, etc. (*Ohr HaMeir, Tzav*).

Each person must serve God with all of his various abilities. This is necessary, for God desires that man serve Him in every way. At times, a person must go and speak with others, and then he cannot study Torah. [Nevertheless,] he must continue to remain attached to God and to effect mystical unifications. Similarly, when one travels on the road and finds himself unable to pray and study, he must serve God in other ways.

One should not grieve over this, for God desires that one serve Him in all things—at times in one way and at times in another. Therefore, [He causes] one to embark upon a journey or enter into discussion with people in order to serve Him in other ways[5] (*Tzava'as HaRivash* 3).

---

5. See *Likkutei Moharan* II:76, 78.

Joy

My master (the Baal Shem Tov) once discussed the subject of beginning a Torah dissertation with a humorous remark.[1] The verse states, "The Living Angels advanced and retreated."[2] This alludes to two states of mind: smallness and greatness. By means of joy and a humorous remark, one leaves the state of "smallness" and enters the state of "greatness." Then one can cleave to God through the study of Torah (*Ben Poras Yosef*, 49b, cited in *Meir Einei Yisrael*).

I received a teaching from our master, the Baal Shem Tov, that holy joy and gladness help one to attain *ruach hakodesh* (Divine inspiration).[3] Our Sages also refer to this, as the *Gemara* states, "One should only arise to pray while feeling the joy of performing a *mitzvah*."[4] This is so that one may reach a degree of holy fervor, as is known to the wise (*Damesek Eliezer, Hakdamah*, 67).

Weeping is a great evil, for one must serve God with joy. But if one cries because of joy and attachment to God, then it is very good[5] (*Tzava'as HaRivash* 48).

One's Torah study should be conducted with enthusiasm and joy; this [itself] will cause one to experience fewer alien thoughts (*Tzava'as HaRivash* 51).

---

1. See *Shabbos* 30b.
2. *Yechezkel* 1:14.
3. See *Likkutei Moharan* I:24.
4. *Berachos* 31a.
5. See *Likkutei Moharan* I:175.

A prayer recited in great joy is surely more acceptable to God than one recited in sadness and tears. This may be explained with a parable. When a poor man tearfully begs and implores and entreats before the king, he usually receives next to nothing for his troubles. But when a nobleman presents himself before the king with praises and in a joyous spirit and then makes his request, the king grants him the finest gifts in keeping with his princely station (*Tzava'as HaRivash* 107).

One should serve God with both awe and joy—they are "two friends who never part"[6]—for awe without joy leads to depression.[7] One should not [even] aggrieve himself about matters of Divine service, but always remain joyous. It is necessary to serve God in the present—there is no time to brood [about the past][8] (*Tzava'as HaRivash* 110).

I heard from my master, the Baal Shem Tov: When the leaders of the generation are joyous, this awakens joy throughout the world (*Divras Shlomo*).

Rabbi Noach of Lechovitch once said, "The Baal Shem Tov came to the world in order to implant true humility and true joy into the hearts of the Jewish people. And the opposite of these qualities are sadness, despair and levity" (*Toras Avos, Simchah V'Hischazkus*).

---

6. *Zohar* III, 4a.
7. See *Berachos* 30b.
8. See *Likkutei Moharan* II:24; *Sichos HaRan* 20.

The Land of Israel

Our Sages taught that all Torah authorities in Babylonia were called *rav*, whereas those in the land of Israel were called *rabbi*. My master (the Baal Shem Tov) explained: The aspects of wisdom (*chochmah*) and understanding (*binah*) spread through all the world. This is symbolized by the letter *reish* (of the word *rav*), as in the phrase, "The beginning (*reishis*) is wisdom (*chochmah*)."[1] The next letter, *beis*, indicates *binah* (understanding). [Hence, the word *rav*.]

All of the characteristics and events that make up this world contain mystical unifications and combinations. However, [outside of the Holy Land] they do not flow. This flowing forth from the Infinite One is symbolized by the letter *yud*. [The letter *yud* is represented by a mere point; therefore it symbolizes the quality of smallness and self-nullification. Also, since every Hebrew letter is derived from the letter *yud*, it symbolizes essentiality.] When there is [a flowing forth from the Infinite One], the *yud* is added to the letters *reish* and *beis* (*rav*), and the word *rabbi* is formed. [Thus, this title may only be applied to the Torah authorities of] the land of Israel (*Toldos Yaakov Yosef, Chukas*).

"Whoever dwells in the land of Israel is comparable to one who has a God; whoever lives in the outside of the land of Israel is comparable to one who does not have a God" (*Kesubos* 110b).

The Baal Shem Tov taught: This may be understood in light of the Mishnah which contrasts the disciples of Avraham with those of the evil Bilaam.[2] [The former are humble and constantly strive to improve themselves, whereas the latter are filled with pride about their few, meager accomplishments.] If one is a disciple of Avraham and diligently exerts himself in the study of Torah and Divine service all day long, he is called "one who dwells in the land of Israel." But when he [chooses to] desist from Torah study and prayer, he dwells "outside of the land of Israel." Then he is like one who does not have a God (*Ben Poras Yosef, Vayeishev; Mikeitz;* also see *Sefer Baal Shem Tov, Lech Lecha,* 36, footnote 50).

---

1. *Tehillim* 111:10.
2. *Avos* 5:19.

The holy Rabbi Nachman of Breslev said that the Baal Shem Tov had once appeared in a vision and told him: "When people are disrespectful toward the land of Israel, they go into exile. An allusion to this may be found in the verse, 'And from there the Shepherd, the Stone of Israel . . .'"[3] [Rabbi Nachman] then asked us to offer an explanation of this vision, but we did not know what to say[4] (*Chayei Moharan* I:3).

The holy Baal Shem Tov shed tears as a result of his own suffering three times in his life: when [the Heavenly Court] took away his spiritual attainments; when his daughter, Adel, fell into the sea [on their journey to the Land of Israel]; and when his wife passed away. He said, "I waited and yearned to be buried in the Land of Israel. But now that I am but 'half a body' left in the Diaspora, I see that this half must remain here, too"[5] (*Ner Yisrael* II, *Eretz Yisrael*, p. 134).

---

3. *Bereishis* 49:24.

4. A reference to this vision and its meaning may be found in *Likkutei Moharan* I:9, which contrasts the land of Israel, the paradigm of prayer and the revelation of miracles, with Egypt, the paradigm of idolatry and belief in the autonomy of nature. R. Nachman's interpretation is based upon a verse describing the drowning of Pharaoh's armies during the Exodus: "The deep covered them; they sank into the depths like a stone" (*Shemos* 15:5):

"The deep covered them." This refers to those who cover up miracles and try to show that everything follows the natural order.

"They sank into the depths like a stone (*even*)." [This is related to the verse] ". . . from there the Shepherd, the Stone (*even*) of Israel." Onkelos treats "*even*" as [a compound word] *av'han u'vinin*—"a father and sons" (ad loc.). [Thus, the phrase suggests the descent of a father and his sons.]

[In other words, those who cover up miracles go into exile like an "*even*," i.e., like] Yaakov and his sons, who embody the aspect of prayer, miracles, and the land of Israel. To whatever extent people fall and to whatever extent people blemish prayer, faith, and the land of Israel, they must descend into the depths of Egyptian exile, just as Yaakov and his sons descended to Egypt because Avraham had asked [God], "How will I know?" concerning his inheritance of the Holy Land.

5. Also, see a variant of this tradition in "His Passing."

Levity

My master (the Baal Shem Tov) taught: If one wants to know if he is attached to the World of Life or the World of Death, he should examine his own desires. If one is attracted to *lashon hara* (harmful gossip) and levity, this indicates that he is attached to the World of Death. And, on the contrary, if one is attracted to Torah and good deeds, he is attached to the World of Life (*K'sones Pasim, Tazriah*).

The Baal Shem Tov often told his disciples that even non-Jews know that one should never scorn any person. As the folk adage goes, "Take a good look at what you have done, and at another's expense you won't have fun"[1] (*Luchos Erez,* 59).

---

1. See *Avodah Zarah* 18b; R. Moshe Cordovero's *Tomer Devorah*, Chapter 2; Maharal's *Nesivos Olam, Inyan Leitzanus*.

A Light Unto the Nations

I heard in the name of Rabbi Yisrael Baal Shem Tov that when the Seven Universal Commandments were given to the descendants of Noach, the [souls of the] Jewish people agreed to become guarantors for the rest of the world[1] (*Rav Yeivi, Vayeishev*).

I heard this story from Rabbi Moshe, son-in-law of the rabbi of Polonoye's sister. [R. Moshe] heard it himself from the Baal Shem Tov when he addressed the villagers in the holy community of Nemirov.

"Once I dreamed that I was walking in a field, and in the distance I saw something like a mist. I went on until I came to the [edge] of the mist. The sun was shining on one side, including the road; the other side was dark and cloudy. There was a long slope, which I followed to the bottom of the valley.

"For several years I had retained a non-Jewish servant, who eventually left me. I saw him walking there with a heavy load of wood on his back. Upon seeing me, he dropped the wood and fell at my feet and said, 'When I served you, sir, I kept the Shabbos. But when I left you I served a certain Jewish innkeeper who made me work on Shabbos. He used to send me to the forest to fetch wood on the Shabbos day. Now both of us are dead, and every Shabbos I have to bring wood to *Gehenna* until there is enough to burn the innkeeper for a whole week. Therefore, I beg you to wait for us until I come back, and I will show you, sir, where you can

---

1. The Seven Universal Commandments are: to establish courts of justice; to respect and therefore refrain from blaspheming God; not to practice idolatry; not to commit murder, suicide, or atrocities during war; not to steal—whether money, property, or persons; not to engage in sexual immorality; not to tear a limb from or consume the flesh of a living creature, but rather to treat all animals humanely. See *Sanhedrin 56b*; *Tosefta Avodah Zarah 9:4*; *Bereishis Rabba 16:9*; *Devarim Rabba 2:17*; *Shir HaShirim Rabba 1:16*; *Zohar I, 35b*; *Mishneh Torah, Hilchos Melachim 9:1*. Concerning the obligation of the Jews to teach these precepts to the world, see *Yeshayahu 42:6–70*; ibid., 49:6; *Vayikra Rabba 6:5*; *Tanchuma, Devarim, 2*; *Tanna D'vei Eliyahu 6:17*; *Mishneh Torah, Hilchos Melachim 8:10*; *Likkutei Moharan 62:3*; *Likkutei Halachos, Even Ha'ezer, Hilchos Kiddushin 3:1*; *Toras Chaim, Shemos, 335b*, citing *Pesachim 87b*; Hirsch, *Haftoros, Yirmiyahu 1:5*; *Likkutei Sichos, Beshalach, 5743*.

ask them to release me from my sentence—for in this world you are very important. I cannot show it to you now because of the attendants who are walking behind me.'

"I said to him, 'If I am important in this world, put down the wood, come along with me right away, and show me the place.'

"He went with me and pointed out a certain castle. I entered it and interceded for him, and they released him from the sentence. When I pleaded for the gentile, I pleaded for the Jew, as well, and they also released him from his sentence" (*Shiv'chei Baal Shem Tov* 129).

Meditation

In these generations, when our spiritual awareness is on an extremely low level, it is necessary to strengthen oneself by meditating upon God in a state of awe. Even in the midst of studying Torah, it is good to pause from time to time in order to meditate. Although this will cause one to neglect his studies slightly [it is proper to do so], "for study is not the main thing, but practice"[1] (*Kesser Shem Tov* 167).

How can one merit to cleave to God? By secluding oneself (*hisbodedus*) from one's fellow men,[2] by writing the mysteries of the Torah,[3] and by meditating upon the Kabbalistic unifications of the Ari z"l, as is known [to the initiated].

When one engages in such unifications, he should remain aware of God's greatness [and not be distracted by the techniques themselves] to the best of his ability (*Tzava'as HaRivash* 82).

One who engages in [Kabbalistic] meditation should have a companion with him, for to do so alone is dangerous. Both people should stay in one room, and each one should meditate upon the Creator by himself.

---

1. *Avos* 1:17.

2. Rabbi Avraham, son of the Rambam, stresses the primacy of secluded meditation in his *Sefer HaMaspik L'Ovdei Hashem, Perek Al HaHisbodedus*. Also see R. Yitzchak of Acco, *Meiras Einaim, Ekev*, pp. 281–282.

3. This possibly alludes to the Kabbalistic meditative techniques of Rabbi Avraham Abulafia, which involve the writing of complex letter combinations and Divine names. According to tradition, the Baal Shem Tov learned such techniques from the *Sefer HaTzoref*. A handwritten copy of this text remained with the Chasidic dynasty of Karlin until the Holocaust, when it was hidden together with other precious manuscripts. Although their location is known, these writings have not yet been recovered. In a general sense, the *Zohar* states that through contemplating the Torah's mysteries one can come to experience *deveykus*. See *Zohar* II:213b.

Sometimes, when one cleaves to God, he is able to meditate even in a house full of people[4] (*Tzava'as HaRivash* 63).

The holy Rabbi Nachman of Breslev taught: No matter how small or great one may be, it is impossible to truly refine oneself except through meditation (*hisbodedus*). He mentioned many celebrated *tzaddikim*, and said that they all attained their spiritual levels only through *hisbodedus*. Indicating a simple fellow who was one of the Baal Shem Tov's descendants, he said, "This man, too, tearfully pours out his heart to God all the time. The Baal Shem Tov was especially accustomed to do this, for he came from the lineage of David HaMelech. And this practice was David HaMelech's main preoccupation: he always used to break his heart exceedingly before God. This is the foundation of his *Sefer Tehillim* (Book of Psalms)" (*Likkutei Moharan* II:100).

It is written that when one designates a special place for Torah study, he causes the *sefirah* of *tiferes* (harmony) to dwell within *malchus* (majesty), which is [metaphorically compared to] a house. Thus, when a person simply sits in his house in the place he has set aside for Torah study and Divine service, this effects a unification between the last two letters of the Divine Name YHVH. [The letter *vav* corresponds to *tiferes* and the last letter *hey* to *malchus*.]

[Moreover,] when one turns to God in a spirit of *teshuvah*, this corresponds to *binah* (understanding). [*Binah* is represented by the upper *hey* in the Divine Name YHVH.] And when he studies Torah, this corresponds to *chochmah* (wisdom), [which is represented by the *yud* in the Divine Name YHVH]. In this way, he effects a unification between the first two letters in the Divine Name YHVH.

---

4. See Rabbi Eliezer Rokeach's *Peirush al HaSefer Yetzirah*, 15b, *Emek HaMelech* 9c, and R. Yosef Tzayach's *Even HaShoham* 1b-2a for similar warnings about Kabbalistic meditation. An interesting tale describes how the son of a hidden mystic named Rabbi Adam once persuaded the Baal Shem Tov to engage in such meditations, with tragic results. See *Shiv'chei Baal Shem Tov* 3 (last section).

Thus, by setting aside a place to seclude oneself in *teshuvah* and Torah study, one binds together the four letters of the Divine Name YHVH. This is the aspect of "be secluded with your God."[5] [By this practice], one may cleave to God, which unites the four letters of the Divine Name YHVH. Even during the week, when one is involved in the "thirty-nine categories of labor"[6] and the millstone is around his neck, he should still seclude himself for at least one hour every day to effect this unification, and this will benefit him forever[7] (*Ben Poras Yosef, Hakdama*).

---

5. *Michah* 6:8.

6. *Shabbos* 73a.

7. A similar practice of secluded personal prayer is discussed in *Likkutei Moharan* 1:52; ibid. II:11, 25, 96, 97; *Sichos HaRan* 47, 68, 227, 274, 275. Also see R. Eliezer Azkari's *Sefer Chareidim, Teshuvah* 3; *Midbar Kadmos of the Ari* z"l 5:13; *Beis Aharon* (Karlin), *Seder HaYom* 3.

Melody

"And it came to pass that when the musician played (*k'nagen hamenagen*), the hand of God came upon him" (II *Melachim* 3:15). Although a musician may look good while he is playing, he bears many selfish motives within himself, such as to receive acclaim for his music, etc. However, the instrument he uses has no such motivation. Thus, *k'nagen hamenagen* [can also be rendered,] "The musician is like an instrument." If he can play without ego, like a mere instrument, then "the hand of God will rest upon him" (*Eitz HaDaas Tov*, cited in *Doresh Tov*).

Rabbi Yitzchak of Neshchiz once said that from the melody a musician played, the Baal Shem Tov knew everything he had done since the day of his birth (*Zichron Tov*, 11:2).

The Baal Shem Tov could hear words in the sounds of a musical instrument, for he [had truly attained the level of man and therefore] could transform inarticulate sounds [the animal level] to words of holiness (*Likkutei Moharan*, I:225).

When Rabbi Shneur Zalman of Liadi came to Mezeritch, the Maggid told him in the name of the Baal Shem Tov that melody is one of the paths of Divine service according to the teachings of Chasidism (*Sefer HaSichos* 5702).[1]

---

1. Although singing and dancing play a unique role in Chasidic life and teachings, they have always been a significant part of Judaism. The ancient prophets of Israel used music to induce the prophetic state (cf. I *Shmuel*, Chapter 10; II *Melachim* 3:15; I *Divrei HaYomim* 25:1; *Mishneh Torah*, *Yesodei HaTorah*, 7:4). David HaMelech, the "sweet singer of Israel," is described as dancing before the Ark of the Covenant (cf. II *Shmuel*, Chapter 6). The Levites composed and performed music to accompany the various rites in the *Beis HaMikdash* (Holy Temple). And the *Gemara* describes the ecstatic dancing of the Sages of Israel during the festival of Succos (cf. *Sukkah* 51a). The medieval Jewish philosopher-poet, R. Yehudah HaLevi, explains that the intent of such dancing and music-making is spiritual: "Just as the performance of a *mitzvah* requires thought and

Before the Baal Shem Tov would deliver a Torah discourse to his disciples, they would sing a melody together[2] (*Mevo She'arim*, 43:1).

Before he passed away, the Baal Shem Tov asked those present to sing the melody known as *His'orerus Rachamim Rabbim* composed by the *tzaddik*, Rabbi Michel of Zlotchov. When they were finished singing, the Baal Shem Tov said, "I promise you and the generations to come that whenever anyone sings the melody *His'orerus Rachamim Rabbim* with a thought of *teshuvah*, in whatever Heavenly Palace I may be, I will hear it and sing along with him and awaken Divine mercy on behalf of that penitent singer" (*Sefer HaSichos* 5703).

---

kavanah, so does the joy in its performance. One rejoices in the *mitzvah* itself, out of love for the One who commanded it for our benefit. . . . And if one's joy leads to singing and dancing, this, too, is a form of Divine service and *deveykus*." (*Kuzari, Ma'amar Sheini*, 50).

2. According to Chasidism, this singing is not only preparatory but reaches to the source from which the forthcoming teaching is drawn. R. Nachman of Breslev taught that melody is the highest form of wisdom and the source of whatever may be expressed through the intellect. See *Likkutei Moharan* I:3, I:64.

Mitzvos

The Torah and *mitzvos* were emanated from God's very Essence, which is the true Oneness. Therefore, when a person performs any *mitzvah* properly and with love—which is *deveykus*—he grasps Oneness. [By performing this *mitzvah*] it is as if he has fulfilled them all; for they are all bound together in a common structure that expresses God's Oneness (*Ner Mitzvah*, 13a).

"One *mitzvah* leads to another *mitzvah* . . ." (*Avos* 4:2). The word *mitzvah* is related to the word *tzavsa*, which denotes *deveykus* and unification. Thus [the Mishnah may be rendered,] "One *mitzvah*," one experience of attachment to God, "leads to another *mitzvah*," an even higher state of *deveykus* (*Degel Machaneh Ephraim, Korach*).

"The wise-hearted will acquire *mitzvos* . . ." (*Mishlei* 10:8). The Baal Shem Tov asked: Why does this verse not state the word *mitzvah* in the singular? Because [every *mitzvah* has two aspects] which we must bind together. The physical performance of the *mitzvah* is called the "lower *mitzvah*," and the thought and intent of the *mitzvah* is called the "higher *mitzvah*." Thus, when [we recite a blessing prior to performing a single *mitzvah*] we say, "Blessed art Thou . . . Who has sanctified us with His *mitzvos* . . ." using the plural form. (*Ohr HaGanuz L'Tzaddikim, Vayeira*).

Whenever one studies Torah or performs a *mitzvah*, he should realize that the agent of his actions is not really himself but the *Shechinah*[1] (*Tzafnas Paneach* 21b).

---

1. See *Avodas Yisrael, Lech Lecha*, p. 37.

In reference to the mystery of God's Oneness, the Baal Shem Tov said that wherever a person grasps a "part" of Oneness, he grasps the whole. The Torah and *mitzvos* were emanated from His Essence, which is the true Oneness. Therefore, when a person fulfills a *mitzvah* properly and with love, he binds himself to Him; with this *mitzvah* he grasps a part of Oneness; and in so doing, he grasps the whole. It is as if he had fulfilled all of the *mitzvos*, which together comprise God's Oneness. [Particularly,] when one experiences joy, he should bind himself to the supernal joy, which is the root of everything (*Kesser Shem Tov* 111).

"I was foolish and ignorant; I was like a beast before You. Yet I am with You continually . . ." (*Tehillim* 73:22–23). The Baal Shem Tov taught: A Jew must be extremely humble, [considering himself] a total fool in his apprehension of Godliness. He must fulfill the *mitzvos* in a spirit of *kabbalas ol*—acceptance of the yoke of Heaven—not because he understands them. Since God commanded them, they are decrees of the Omnipotent King. Only in this manner can one reach the level of "I am with You continually . . ." Then he will be bound to God and His *mitzvos* with all the fibers of his soul. By virtue of this powerful bond, a person will eventually begin to understand that which had previously been hidden from his intellect. Thus, when the Torah was given, the Jewish people declared, "We will do, and we will understand . . ."[2] First, there had to be an actual deed; then it was also possible to comprehend. (*Sippurei Chasidim*, cited in *Meir Einei Yisrael, Emunah*)

Our master, Rabbi Yisrael Baal Shem Tov, taught that a person's way of serving God should be characterized by simplicity and inner unity. The main thing is not to forget the words [of Torah,] but to study works of ethics and self-improvement (*mussar*) every day, however much or little. One must always endeavor to bind himself to good character traits and to conduct himself in an upright manner. And one should never let a day go by without performing some *mitzvah*, whether great or small.

---

2. *Shemos* 24:7.

[This is the meaning of the teaching,] "Be as careful with a *mitzvah* of minor importance as with a major one."[3] The Hebrew word for "careful" (*zahir*) also suggests luminosity, as in the verse, "And those who are wise shall shine (*yazhiru*) . . ."[4] Thus, the soul of man can shine and be luminous from the performance of a minor *mitzvah* just as from a major one—for "the Merciful One desires the heart"[5] (*Tzava'as HaRivash* 1).

If one ardently desires to perform a certain *mitzvah*, he should see to it that he does so. He must not let the Evil Inclination tell him that the deed is so great that it might lead to a public display of piety. Even if this seems to be true, one should not desist. However, one should be extremely careful that if he begins to experience pride in the midst of the act, he thrusts away this temptation forcefully and vigorously. In the end, he will surely perform the *mitzvah* for its own sake, in truth, and without any ostentation, for "through [serving God] with selfish motives, one comes to do so with pure motives."[6]

One should perform as many *mitzvos* as possible, and the Holy One, blessed be He, will help him to do so without any trace of ego. However, he must exert himself as much as possible (*Tzava'as HaRivash* 55).

The Baal Shem Tov taught: "Yissaschar is a big-boned donkey (*chamor garem*)" (*Bereishis* 49:14). [Yissaschar can also be read as] *yesh s'char*—"there is recompense." And this [recompense] is caused (*garam*) by physicality (*chomer*). [The word *chamor* (donkey) contains the same letters as the word *chomer* (physicality). The very things of this physical world, with which a person must struggle all his days, ultimately bring about the greatest spiritual illuminations] (*Tzava'as HaRivash* 100).

---

3. *Avos* 2:1.
4. *Daniel* 12:3.
5. *Sanhedrin* 106b.
6. *Pesachim* 50b.

"The reward of a *mitzvah* is not given in this world" (*Kiddushin* 39b). According to the Baal Shem Tov, the reason for this is that this world is unable to receive the light of even one *mitzvah* or good deed. [This light is emanated] from the Infinite One, blessed be He, and even a spark of it [qualitatively] contains the whole. [Thus, the reward for each *mitzvah* is infinite, whereas] this is a world of limitations (*Meor Einayim, Beshalach*, cited in *Sefer Baal Shem Tov, Va'eschanan* 86).

Money

"And Yaakov dreamed and, behold, a ladder (*sulam*) stood on the earth, and its head reached the heavens; and, behold, angels of God were ascending and descending upon it" (*Bereishis* 28:12).

It was taught in the name of the holy Rabbi Yisrael Baal Shem Tov: The word *sulam* (ladder) has the same numerical value as the word *mamon* (money). Thus, money "stands on the earth," for it represents materialism and physicality; but "its head reaches the heavens," which alludes to the eternal reward [reserved for those who use money in a beneficial and holy manner]. "And behold, the angels of God were ascending and descending upon it." Some people are elevated because of money, while it causes others to fall into the abyss (*Turei Zahav, Vayeitzei*).

"Everything is given [by the Creator] on collateral, and a net is spread (*p'rusah*) over all the living . . ." (*Avos* 3:16). The word *p'rusah* (spread) is similar to the word *p'ras* (portion), as in the Mishnah, "Do not be like servants who serve their master for the sake of receiving their portion (*p'ras*) . . ."[1] In this context, *p'ras* refers to one's livelihood. Thus, [the former teaching likewise alludes to] the net of earning a living, which is everyone's lot. A person can become so busy seeking his livelihood that there is no room left in his heart to search for God[2] (*Bas Ayin, Bamidbar*).

I heard from our master, the holy Rabbi Gedaliah of Linitz, that there was once a *Sefer* Torah in which scribal errors were repeatedly found. Although they corrected the *Sefer* Torah again and again, new mistakes always appeared. Finally, they showed it to the Baal Shem Tov. He explained, "This *Sefer* Torah was donated by a man who paid for it

---

1. *Avos* 5:3.
2. See *Sichos HaRan* 51; *Likkutei Halachos, Hilchos Kiddushin, Halacha* 3.

with money obtained by operating a gambling establishment. No matter how many times you fix it, this Sefer Torah will always remain *pasul* (ritually unfit)" (*Shiv'chei Baal Shem Tov* 110).

Involvement in business can also be a form of Divine service and Torah study, for there are many laws about commerce. If a person studies Torah for the sake of the Creator—for example, if he studies the Mishnah which begins, "If one exchanged a cow for a donkey [which had been borrowed] . . ."[3]—this is very precious to the Holy One, blessed be He. However, it is even greater if one actually exchanged the cow for a donkey [and subsequently divided the value of its offspring] in conformance with Torah law.[4]

"All that the Holy One, blessed be He, created in His world, He created only for His glory . . ."[5] [The Jewish people must deal with] everything that exists, whether great or small, according to the Torah's laws, unlike the nations of the world who conduct themselves according to astrological influences. One may serve God with anything and discern therein the wonders of the Creator and the Supernal Intellect [that imbues it with life].

This applies to the simplest matters. If one lives according to the dictates of Torah, with "a righteous weight and a righteous measure," he also performs a *mitzvah*. Thus our Sages taught: "If one refrains from a transgression, [he is rewarded as if he had performed a *mitzvah*] . . ."[6] When one lives this way, he will always be involved in Torah, even while he is preoccupied in business matters (*Me'or Einaim, Masechtas Shabbos*).

"Save me from bloodshed (*damim*), God . . ." (*Tehillim* 51:16). The Baal Shem Tov interpreted this to mean: "Save me from money (*damim*), that I should not make it my God" (*Imrei Tzaddikim* 16:2).

---

3. *Bava Metziah* 100a.
4. See *Likkutei Moharan* I:280.
5. *Avos* 6:11.
6. *Kiddushin* 39b.

"The Torah has pity on the money of the Jewish people" (*Yoma* 39a). Why is this so? [The answer is based upon] the principle that whatever one wears or eats or uses as a vessel [exists by virtue of an inner life force]—and it is this life force that causes one gratification. Without this spiritual aspect, the object could not exist. [Moreover], everything contains holy sparks which are related to the root of a person's soul. That is why one person loves a certain object and another person dislikes it and is attracted to something else.

When one uses the vessel or eats the food in his possession [according to the Torah's dictates]—even if he eats to satisfy his physical needs—he rectifies those holy sparks. For subsequently the benefit he derives from that garment or food or other object enables him to serve God. Thus, [the holy sparks therein] attain their spiritual rectification.

That is why possessions often change hands. Once the holy sparks related to the root of the owner's soul have been spiritually rectified, God takes the object away from that person and gives it to someone else. The sparks remaining within it belong to a different sublime root.

The Baal Shem Tov taught that people eat and dwell together and make use of their various possessions because of the holy sparks contained in everything. Therefore, ["the Torah has pity on the money of the Jewish people." This teaches us that] one must have pity upon all his possessions, for by doing so one has pity upon the holy sparks (*Tzava'as HaRivash* 109).

Moshiach

Whenever one prays properly, binding his thoughts to his words, the aspect of Moshiach is perfected. [In Kabbalistic and Chasidic literature, Jewish souls are identified with letters and words of the Holy Tongue.[1]] When our righteous Moshiach comes, the unification of everything will be final and complete, and all the thoughts and letters of speech will be elevated. This aspect of Moshiach is perfected by every person during prayer or Torah study. Thus, the Baal Shem Tov taught that the soul of every Jew contains a part of Moshiach which he must perfect and prepare.

As is known, the word *adam* (man) is an acrostic of Adam, David, Moshiach. The form of Adam HaRishon (the first man) encompassed the entire universe, for the souls of all Jews were included within him. After the first sin, his form was diminished. Similarly, the form of Moshiach will encompass all 600,000 [primary] Jewish souls, just as when they were part of Adam HaRishon, before the first sin. Therefore, every Jew must prepare the portion of Moshiach which his soul contains, until the entire structure has been completed and prepared. Then the ultimate and eternal unification will be accomplished—may it be speedily, in our days (*Me'or Einaim, Pinchos*).

I received this tradition from [Rabbi Yaakov Yosef HaKohen of Polonoye] in the name of the Baal Shem Tov: When Moshiach comes (may it be speedily in our days) he will explain the entire Torah from beginning to end, according to all the letter combinations within each word. Then he will combine the entire Torah into one word, which will contain letter combinations beyond calculation. [Moshiach] will explain them all, as well[2] (*T'shuos Chein, Tazria*).

---

1. *Zohar Chadash, Shir HaShirim,* 74b; *Sichos HaRan* 91; also see *Likkutei Moharan* I, 2:6, 14:3, 273.
2. Also see *Zohar* III, 265b; *Bris Menuchah, Hakdamah; Likkutei Moharan* II, 8:6.

My master (the Baal Shem Tov) was told in a Heavenly vision that the coming of Moshiach is delayed because we do not prolong the recitation of *Ahavah Rabbah* [the prayer which describes the mutual love between God and the Jewish people] (*Toldos Yaakov Yosef, Va'eira*).

Once, on *erev* Shabbos before the afternoon prayer service, [the Baal Shem Tov] asked his disciple, Rabbi Leib, the Maggid of Polonoye, to accompany him on a journey. They boarded a wagon and traveled a great distance, past forests and fields, until they came to an isolated house. [The Baal Shem Tov accomplished this by *k'fitzas haderech*, a miraculous contraction of time and space.]

The Baal Shem Tov ordered the wagon to halt. Then a man with a most striking appearance came out of the house and warmly greeted the Baal Shem Tov. He returned the man's greeting with great joy. Then the man asked the Baal Shem Tov to remain with him for the holy Shabbos, but he declined. Rabbi Leib observed everything with amazement but asked no questions.

Later, the Baal Shem Tov said, "Do you know who that is? He is the Moshiach of our generation." For our holy books state that the soul of Moshiach is present in every generation, and when the time comes, he will be revealed to the entire world in all his virtue and beauty.[3]

This was a great wonder to Rabbi Leib, who then asked, "If so, why didn't the *Rebbe* accept his invitation and spend the holy Shabbos with him?"

The Baal Shem Tov replied, "Heaven has decreed that this holy man who bears the soul of Moshiach will pass away on this Shabbos, due to the sins of the generation. How could I eat [the Shabbos meals] and witness the death of the God of Yaakov's anointed one?" (*Likkutei Divrei Torah* 9, cited in *Meir Einei Yisrael, Moshiach*).

"Grace is false and beauty is vain . . ." (*Mishlei* 31:30). The holy Baal Shem Tov once remarked: Before Moshiach comes, falsehood will possess grace and vanity will seem beautiful. (*Ohr HaNer* 16b, cited in *Siddur T'zlosa D'Yisrael*; attributed to Rabbi Shlomo of Karlin in *Shema Shlomo* I, p. 108).

---

3. *Arba Meos Shekel Kessef*, 68b.

Piety

"Know what is above you . . ." (*Avos* 2:1). Know that whatever is Above [depends upon] you[1] (*Tzava'as HaRivash* 142).

It is necessary for one to conceal his actions so that he does not appear to be pious in the eyes of others. However, when one has not yet attained a high level, he must openly behave [in a devout manner]. If one were to behave in public like everyone else and only wished to be devout privately, he might [eventually] be seduced by the world; thus, "by acting with proper motives, one may come to act with improper motives"[2] (*Tzava'as HaRivash* 65).

"Yerushalayim was destroyed only because they rendered their judgments according to the strict interpretation of the law . . ." (*Bava Metziah* 30b). "Yerushalayim" alludes to the fear of Heaven (*yiras Shomayim*). Thus, conducting oneself only according to the letter of the law destroys one's fear of Heaven. [However], going beyond the minimal requirement of the law strengthens one's fear of Heaven (*Sefer HaZichronos* I, p. 345).

---

1. R. Chaim of Volozhin offers a similar interpretation in *Nefesh HaChaim* 1:4 (note). It is also ascribed to the Maggid of Mezeritch in *Ohr Torah* (*Al Aggados HaShas*) 112b. A probable source for this concept may be found in *Zohar* III, Emor, 92a-92b.

2. A wordplay on *Pesachim* 50b.

Prayer

There are some people who sing their way through the prayer service, one section with one melody and the next with another, thinking that in this way they will attain ecstasy and gratify the Creator. However, this is foolishness; their [approach to] Divine service is totally mistaken, and they walk in darkness, far from the truth.

Rather, this is the right path: During prayer one must divest himself of all physical desires until it is as if he no longer exists in this world. He should recite [the prayers] simply and audibly, fixing his attention upon the holy letters, while contemplating the plain meaning of the words. Then, of its own accord, his heart will burst into flame with love and fear of God. This is the inner path of Divine service leading to enlightenment that I heard and received from my master, Rabbi [Levi Yitzchak of Berditchev], who received it from his master, the Maggid [of Mezeritch], who received it from his master, the Baal Shem Tov, who received it from his [angelic mentor], Achiyah HaShiloni (*Geulas Yisrael, Pisgamin Kaddishin*, 17a, citing Rabbi Aharon of Zhitomir).

I heard from my master (the Baal Shem Tov) that sometimes a person prays for one thing, and he is given something else. Sometimes his prayer only has an effect in the Supernal Worlds. [But prayer is always beneficial] (*Degel Machaneh Ephraim, Ekev*).

It is said in the name of the Baal Shem Tov that if a person merits to pray properly [even] one time, he can raise up all the unworthy prayers that have remained below for so many years. Together, these prayers will also achieve perfection and be favorably received Above (*Tiferes Shlomo, Shabbos Teshuvah*).

As soon as one says, "May God open my lips [that my mouth may utter Your praise,"] the *Shechinah* enclothes itself within him and speaks through him. When one truly believes that it is the *Shechinah* speaking, he will be overcome by awe; then the Holy One, blessed be He, will constrict Himself and rest upon him[1] (*Kesser Shem Tov* 198).

"Who can recount God's *gevuros* (mighty deeds) and make known all His praise?" (*Tehillim* 106:2). The Baal Shem Tov rendered this interpretively: "Who can recount (*y'malel*)" alludes to breaking, as in the phrase, "You may break off the ears of grain (*m'lilos*) . . . "[2] (*Devarim* 23:26). And who can "break" God's *gevuros* (stringencies)? How can one break and nullify Heaven's decrees? [The verse itself offers a solution:] "Make known all His praise (*tehilaso*)." Recite the entire *Sefer Tehillim* (Book of Psalms) (*Likkutei Sichos* IV, p. 1310).

"In those days . . . the transgression of Israel shall be sought, but it shall not exist; and the sin of Yehudah shall not be found" (*Yirmiyahu* 50:20).

My master, the Baal Shem Tov, asked: Why search for it? Do the Jewish people need transgressions?

In a related vein, he also remarked: When Moshiach comes, all the afflictions about which we pray will no longer exist. Is it possible that prayer, which is a "limb of the *Shechinah*," will become obsolete?

He then explained: There are four types of prayer. First, one must grieve because God's Glory is profaned among the nations of the world and pray [that it be elevated and revealed]. Second, [one must pray for the forgiveness] of transgression. Affliction is actually the transgression itself. Also, sin is worse than death. Death atones for transgression and cleanses [the soul], whereas sin brings about many forms of severe punishment and death. Third, one must pray for livelihood. And fourth, one must pray for life itself.

The *Shechinah* is bound up with these four types of distress. When one prays about them, he extracts the sparks of the *Shechinah* hidden

---

1. In Kabbalistic literature, the *Shechinah* is identified with the *sephirah* of *Malchus* and the voice of the Jew during prayer, etc. See *Zohar* III:230a, 281b; *Tikkunei Zohar, Tikkun* 18, 38b; *Likkutei Moharan* I:42, 48, 78; ibid., II:84.

2. *Devarim* 23:26.

within the physical and elevates them Above. Without distress, a person would not know what to pray for.

Thus the verse states, "The transgression of Israel shall be sought," so that we may pray for it—"but it shall not exist; and the sins of Yehudah shall not be found." The other forms of distress will not exist, either; hence, we will have nothing to pray for. [Therefore,] prayer will consist solely of spiritual unifications (*Kesser Shem Tov* 81).

"There are things which stand in the heights of the universe that people nevertheless take lightly" (*Berachos* 6b). The Baal Shem Tov explained that the results of prayer are often manifest "in the heights of the universe" and not in the world below. Therefore, prayer is "taken lightly by people." They think that it is ineffective, but they are mistaken[3] (*Kesser Shem Tov* 138).

There is a revolving sword that guards the path to the Tree of Life [in the Garden of Eden] (*Bereishis* 3:24). When a person endeavors to attach his thoughts to the Supernal Worlds—to the Creator, may He be blessed—the *klippos* [forces of impurity] do not allow him to do so.

Despite this, he should force himself [to concentrate] over and over again with all his strength during the same prayer until he cleaves to the Creator and enters the Supernal Worlds. He should believe with complete faith that "the entire universe is filled with His Glory,"[4]—and then he [will realize that he already] is in the Supernal World. Thus, the verse states, "The *tzaddik* lives by his faith."[5]

Similarly, if one falls from his level [of *deveykus*] during prayer, he should continue to recite the words with a lesser degree of concentration, according to his ability. Then he should fortify himself to regain his previous level, even if this happens many times during the same prayer. First he should utter the body of the word; then he should give it a soul [by binding his mind to it].

---

3. See *Likkutei Eitzos, Tefilah,* 3.
4. *Yeshayahu* 6:3.
5. *Chavakuk* 2:4. In other words, by virtue of one's faith in the omnipresence of the Creator, it is possible to reach the "Tree of Life," i.e., the experience of *deveykus*.

[This reflects a basic principle.] At first, one must exert all his strength to awaken his body [from its heaviness and lethargy], so that the light of the soul may illuminate it. Thus, the *Zohar* states, "If a wooden beam does not catch fire, strike it until it ignites."[6] Afterward, one will be able to serve God in thought alone, without any bodily movement at all[7] (*Tzava'as HaRivash* 58).

It is impossible to pray with intense concentration except by exerting oneself. [Before beginning to pray,] one must beg God for His help and assistance[8] (*Tzava'as HaRivash* 60).

One should consider himself fortunate if God helps him to concentrate intensely for more than half of the prayer service. As for the latter portion, when one is tired and no longer experiences *deveykus*, what should one do? He should just pray according to the best of his ability, with a lesser degree of concentration, until the end of *Aleinu* [the last prayer] (*Tzava'as HaRivash* 61).

"If I am not for myself, who will be for me? But if I am only for myself, what am I? And if not now, when?" (*Avos* 1:14).

During prayer, it must be as if one is divested from physicality. Thus, the [Mishnah] states, "If I am not for myself . . ." in reference to the time when one is divested from physicality and does not sense that he exists in this world. In other words, "When I reach the level at which I no longer know or feel that I exist 'for myself' in this world—then I will have no fear of [unholy] thoughts. For no alien thought can approach me while I am removed from this world." [The Mishnah continues:] "Who will be for me?" as if to say, "Which alien thought will come to me?" However, "when I am only for myself . . ." When I take myself to be an autonomous entity within the phenomena of this world, then, on the contrary, my existence is worthless. Thus, it states, "What am I?" What am I worth, and of what worth is my Divine service before God,

---

6. *Zohar* III, 168a.
7. See *Likkutei Moharan* I:279.
8. See ibid. I:9.

may He be blessed? For then alien thoughts confuse me, and I am really comparable to one who does not exist in the world. Essentially man was created in this world in order to serve God, but now I am unable to serve Him because of the alien thoughts which confuse me. [Therefore, when one feels that he exists as a separate entity, he does not really exist. Only when one does not cling to his personal existence does he exist in truth[9]] (*Tzava'as HaRivash* 62).

My grandfather (the Baal Shem Tov) taught: What is it in a person that feels pleasure or pain if not the soul? The soul is the life force. Thus, when it departs, one no longer feels anything. This life force is actually one with the Source of all life and all creatures: the Holy One, blessed be He. When one realizes this, he binds his mind to its Source, which is the *Shechinah*. Then, by praying for the sake of the *Shechinah*, he brings about the unification [of all creation]. "*Tzaddikim* are the emissaries of the Divine Queen." That is, [the *tzaddik*,] by means of his own suffering and privation, knows how to pray for the needs of the holy *Shechinah* (*Degel Machaneh Ephraim, Bechukosai*).

If, at times, one is unable to pray [with *deveykus*,] he should not feel that he will be unable to pray for the rest of the day. On the contrary, the more one fortifies himself, the more he will experience awe [of the Creator].[10] This may be illustrated by a parable. Once a king went to war dressed so that no one would recognize him. The wise men who were familiar with the King's manner of walking and his other bodily movements recognized him by those gestures. However, those who were not so wise recognized the King by inferring that only in the most fortified and well-guarded place might he be found. Similarly, when one is unable to pray with *kavanah* (concentration), he should realize that the

---

9. Concerning self-nullification through prayer, see *Maggid Devarav L'Yaacov* 96, 97, 159; *Likkutei Moharan* I, 22:10; ibid., I:52; ibid., II:103. A lucid description of self-nullification through confession in the presence of a *tzaddik* is given in *Likkutei Moharan* I, 4:9, which the commentary of *Parparaos L'Chochma* also relates to confessional prayer at the gravesites of *tzaddikim* (ad loc.). Also note *Otzar HaYirah* (*Likkutei Eitzos HaMeshulosh*) vol. I, *Hasagas Elokus*.

10. See *Sichos HaRan* 12.

area surrounding the King is heavily guarded. The King is there—but one cannot approach due to the guards who surround Him. Therefore, one should strengthen himself with awe [of the Creator] and exert himself to concentrate in order to come closer to God and to pray before Him. Then one will be able to pray with even more *kavanah* [than he would have otherwise experienced] (*Tzava'as HaRivash* 72).

[Our Sages state that] one should arise to pray with "a heavy head" (*Berachos* 30b). This means that you should not pray for that which you lack, for then your prayer will not be accepted. Rather, when you wish to pray, do so for the "heaviness" which is in the Head (i.e., the *Shechinah*)—for whatever you lack, the *Shechinah* also lacks. Since [the soul of] man is "a portion of God Above,"[11] whatever is missing in the part is missing in the whole. [And certainly] the whole feels what the part lacks. Therefore, let your prayer be for needs of the whole. This is the meaning of the teaching that one should pray with "a heavy head"— for the *Shechinah* rests upon the head[12] (*Tzava'as HaRivash* 73).

Once, during a severe drought, the Baal Shem Tov observed a simple Jew crying out in prayer, "He has shut up (*v'atzar*) the heavens, and there will be no rain!"[13] However, the Baal Shem Tov did not criticize him [for his apparent misunderstanding of the verse], for he saw that his prayer had been favorably received. After the rain began to fall, he called the man aside and asked him, "What did you mean when you recited that verse?" The man replied, "He has wrung out (*v'atzar*) the heavens, and there will be no more rain—above—because it will all have fallen below!" And, in fact, Targum Onkelos (*Bereishis* 40:11) translates the word *va'eschat* ("and I squeezed") as *v'atzaris* [like the word *v'atzar* in the verse cited by the simple Jew, whose prayer was accepted nevertheless] (*Kesser Shem Tov* 385).

---

11. *Shefa Tal* 1a, citing *Iyov* 31:2.
12. Also see *Zohar* III, 123b and 142b; *Sefer HaTanya*, Chapter 52.
13. *Devarim* 11:17.

[When one begins to pray,] he should imagine that he is in the World of Action (*Asiyah*). Afterwards, he should imagine that he is in the World of Formation (*Yetzirah*), the world of angels. Then he should imagine that he is in the World of Creation (*B'riah*), until he imagines that he has soared to the heights of the World of Emanation (*Atzilus*). Like a person who walks from one room to another, he should mentally depict himself traveling through the Supernal Worlds.

One must be careful not to fall from this lofty state of mind, [when he senses that he has reached] the Supernal Worlds. He should exert all of his strength to remain Above, controlling his thoughts as if with a bridle and reins to prevent himself from falling.

When one wants to do this in order to experience *deveykus* at a time other than during prayer, it is necessary that no one else be present. Even the chirping of birds can disrupt his state of mind—even another person's thoughts can interfere[14] (*Kesser Shem Tov* 216).

One must proceed from one level to the next in prayer and not expend all of one's strength at the very beginning. Rather, one should begin slowly and, in the middle of his prayers, cleave to God enough to utter the words with intense concentration, strengthening himself by degrees until God helps him to pray with great *deveykus* (*Tzava'as HaRivash* 32).

One must study—and one must accustom himself to pray, even the psalms—with a gentle voice and to cry out in a whisper. He should utter the words of the psalms or Torah with all of his strength, as the

---

14. For a similar meditative practice, see Rabbi Chaim Vital's *Sha'arei Kedushah* III:8. Aside from its great merits as both a pietistic work and an introduction to Kabbalah, *Sha'arei Kedushah* outlines this basic meditative technique. An extended version may be found in Rabbi Pinchos Eliyahu of Vilna's *Sefer HaBris*, Part II, *Eichus HaNevuah* 8:6; ibid., *Sod Ruach HaKodesh*, 11:7. The recently published Section IV of *Sha'arei Kedushah* (*K'savim Chadashim L'Rabbeinu Chaim Vital*, Machon Ahavat Shalom, Jerusalem 1988) is a compendium of meditative and mystical techniques from various pre-Lurianic schools.

verse states, "All my bones shall declare . . ."[15] [Nevertheless], the scream produced by *deveykus* should be in a whisper (*Tzava'as HaRivash* 33).

Each word [of prayer] is a complete structure. It must contain all of one's strength; for if not, it is [like a body] lacking a limb (*Tzava'as HaRivash* 34).

It is a great favor from God that [the *tzaddik*] still remains alive after praying. According to the laws of nature, he should have expired from expending his strength in prayer, such effort did he put into the great *kavanos* (mystical intentions) upon which he concentrated (*Tzava'as HaRivash* 35).

Even if a person prays with all the *kavanos* (mystical intentions) known to him, his consciousness is limited by his knowledge. But when one pronounces each word with deep attachment, all *kavanos* automatically become included in his words.

Every letter is a complete universe. When one pronounces a word with deep attachment, he surely arouses the Supernal Worlds and accomplishes great things. Therefore, one must be careful to pray with attachment and intense fervor. Certainly, this will have great consequences in the Supernal Worlds, for each letter effects an awakening Above (*Tzava'as HaRivash* 118).

Sometimes one can recite one's prayers with great speed. Since one's heart is aflame with the love of God, the words come out of his mouth automatically[16] (*Tzava'as HaRivash* 36).

---

15. *Tehillim* 35:10.
16. See *Likkutei Moharan* I, 4:9.

Sometimes, one can pray with love and awe of God, with great fervor—yet with no outer display of emotion. Another person might think that he is reciting the words of prayer without any *deveykus* at all. This is how one can serve God with his soul alone, with a great and profound love. This sort of Divine service is carried out more quickly and with a greater degree of *deveykus* than that which makes itself visible through one's bodily gestures. The forces of impurity (*klippah*) cannot touch such a prayer, for it is entirely inward (*Tzava'as HaRivash* 104).

During the silent [*Shemoneh Esrei*] prayer, when one attaches himself Above, he may ascend to an even higher spiritual level. This is in accordance with the teaching of our Sages, "When one comes to purify himself, he is helped . . ."[17] By means of this prayer, he merits to attach himself Above. He may then attain such a lofty spiritual level that even when he is not praying he will remain in a state of *deveykus* (*Tzava'as HaRivash* 37).

One should not recite many psalms prior to the morning prayers, so as not to weaken the body and thereby come to neglect the main thing: one's daily obligation to recite the *Zemiros* (psalms included in the liturgy), the *Krias Shema* ("Hear, O Israel . . . "), and the [*Shemoneh Esrei*] prayer with intense *deveykus*. [This will not be possible] if one expends all his strength on preliminaries. Instead, one should first recite the main prayers with *deveykus*. Then, if God gives him more strength, he may recite psalms and *Shir HaShirim* with *deveykus*, as well (*Tzava'as HaRivash* 38).

When one is on a lower spiritual level, he should pray from a *siddur* (prayer book), for by seeing the letters a person can pray with greater concentration. However, when one is attached to the Supernal World, it is better to close one's eyes, so that his vision should not disturb his *deveykus* (*Tzava'as HaRivash* 40).

---

17. *Shabbos* 104a.

Prayer is an act of unification with the *Shechinah*. Just as marital relations require physical movements, so must one move his body during prayer because of his spiritual ardor. Then, afterward, one is able to stand still without any physical movement and cleave to the *Shechinah* with intense *deveykus* (*Tzava'as HaRivash* 68).

The Gemara states that Torah study is called *chayei olam* (eternal life), whereas prayer is called *chayei sha'ah* (temporal life) (*Shabbos* 10a). The Baal Shem Tov interpreted this [as follows]: Torah-study is called *chayei olam*, because it teaches a person how to conduct himself in the world (*olam*). However, prayer is *chayei sha'ah*. The word *sha'ah* can also mean "to turn." Prayer teaches a person that he must turn and entreat the Almighty (Letter of Rabbi Yosef Yitzchak of Lubavitch, cited in *Kesser Shem Tov, Hosafos, Masechtas Shabbos* 72).

The soul [of the Baal Shem Tov] told him that it revealed lofty matters to him not because he had studied the *Gemara* and Poskim to such a great extent, but because of prayer. The Baal Shem Tov constantly prayed with intense concentration, and for this reason attained his high spiritual level[18] (*Tzava'as HaRivash* 41).

---

18. Also note *Likkutei Moharan* 1, 8:6–7.

Sacrifices

[*Megillas Esther* describes the feast of King Achashverosh and the refusal of Queen Vashti to appear before him unclothed. Therefore, the King sought the advice of his royal ministers, who are mentioned by name.] "And those close (*v'hakarov*) to him: Carshena, Sheisar, Admasa . . ." (*Esther* 1:14).

Rabbi Levi said: This entire verse alludes to the sacrificial offerings (*korbanos*). [Taking the term "royal minister" as an allusion to the ministering angels, R. Levi rendered the names in the verse interpretively.] "'Carshena'—the Ministering Angels declared before the Holy One, blessed be He, 'Master of the Universe! Did any other nation offer before You yearling lambs (*karim b'nei shanah*) as the Jews have offered before You?' 'Sheisar'—Did any other nation offer before You two turtledoves (*sh'tei torim*) as have the Jews? 'Admasa'—Did any other nation build before You an altar of earth (*adamah*) as have the Jews?" (*Megilla* 12b).

[The relationship between this Talmudic passage and the incident of Vashti may be derived from a teaching of the Baal Shem Tov.] Vashti was asked to appear before the King naked but did not come. Concerning this, the Baal Shem Tov remarked, "The aspect of nakedness still has not come."

[Rabbi Mordechai Yosef Leiner of Izhbitz explained this as follows:] God gave the Jewish people the Torah and *mitzvos*, which are garments by means of which His Essence may be grasped. In this world it is impossible for a human being to apprehend God's Essence except by means of garments. [Thus, Godliness is concealed] within physicality—to the extent that whatever we perceive is through the intermediacy of garments.

In the present state of reality, God pours forth *shefa* by way of the Four Worlds, using whichever *sefirah* is necessary at a given time until the *shefa* reaches this world. All this is so the influx of *shefa* is graspable. Also, the nations of the world are able to receive some of this, for they, too, can grasp the outer garment. However, they misuse this *shefa* by performing all sorts of abominations.

When the Men of the Great Assembly saw that Achashverosh had commanded Vashti to appear before him naked, they understood that God wanted to confer upon the Jewish People a true revelation without any garment, as will be the case in the Ultimate Future. Then the Holy

One, blessed be He, will reveal His light without any garment. [However, as long as man is attached to his lower nature, such a revelation] can only reinforce his physical passions.

Therefore, at this time the Men of the Great Assembly endeavored to uproot the desire for sexual immorality from the heart of humanity.[1] [This would have made this direct revelation equally available to those who had struggled against their desires and those who had pursued them without restraint. That is why] the Ministering Angels protested, "How can the nations of the world be permitted to grasp the aspect of nakedness? Did any other nation offer before You . . ." For even when the light was concealed from them, the Jewish People exerted themselves with all their strength to bring sacrificial offerings and to serve God in order to come closer to the light. [Throughout history, they worked through the barriers of physicality, symbolized by the sacrificial offerings, by striving to live according to the Torah.] Thus, it is fitting that in the Ultimate Future God will reveal His light to them completely, without any intermediary.

It is written, "My soul longs and even expires for the courtyards of God; my heart and my flesh will sing unto the Living God" (Tehillim 84:3). That is, in the present state of reality, since garments are necessary, "my soul longs and even expires for the courtyards of God," for [the physical Holy Temple and the various forms of Divine Service which are] garments of His light. However, "my heart and my flesh will sing unto the Living God." My waiting and hoping is for the revelation of light which will take place in the future, without any garment—a revelation of life in its very simplicity. This is [suggested by the term] "Living God." But the nations of the world, who did not exert themselves in Divine service nor endeavor to draw near to the Divine light— why should they deserve to share this revelation when, at last, struggle and garments will not exist?[2] (Mei HaShiloach, Likkutei HaShas, Megilla, 12).

---

1. Yoma 69b.

2. However, righteous non-Jews will also be granted a portion in the World to Come. See Sanhedrin 105b; Yerushalmi Berachos 9; Bereishis Rabba 26:2; Zohar, Pekudei; Pirkei Rabbi Eliezer 34; Yalkut, II Melachim, 296; Mishneh Torah, Hilchos Melachim, 8:10–11. The Kabbalists also frequently cite the following teaching from Tanna D'vei Eliyahu Rabba (9:1): "I call heaven and earth to witness that anyone—Jew or non-Jew, man or woman, slave or bondmaid—can attain ruach hakodesh (Divine inspiration). Everything is in accordance with one's deeds."

"Thus in the Sanctuary do I behold You . . ." (*Tehillim* 63:3). Paraphrasing this verse, the Baal Shem Tov once remarked, "Would that in the days of the Holy Temple I thus behold You!"

[Rabbi Shneur Zalman of Liadi explained:] In other words, "Would that in the days of the Holy Temple I behold a revelation of Divine Light comparable to that which is elicited by our Divine service during this period of exile." In the time of the Holy Temple, Divine service will involve the mind and the heart, thus bringing about great delight and spiritual joy. However, as long as we are in exile, our Divine service [primarily] consists of "accepting the yoke of the Kingdom of Heaven" and acts of self-sacrifice. During the exile, a Jew must sacrifice himself to study the Torah and observe the *mitzvos*, particularly when there are decrees by which he may be punished for doing so. However, by such self-sacrifice, he draws forth the greatest and most awesome spiritual lights, surpassing even those that will exist in the days of the Holy Temple[3] (*Sefer HaMa'amarim: Kuntreisim* I, p. 106).

---

3. In a sense, this teaching alludes to the Kabbalistic concept of the "superiority of light which emerges from darkness," i.e., the revelation of Divine Oneness which can only be accomplished through limitation and diversity. See *Likkutei Moharan* I:11.

Shabbos

The *Zohar* states, "What is Shabbos? The name of the Holy One, blessed be He" (*Zohar* II:88b). And our Sages taught, "When Shabbos comes, rest comes."[1]

God is called "rest," for movement cannot be attributed to Him. Movement only applies to something which exists in time and space. However, the Holy One, blessed be He, is infinite and does not move from place to place; nor is He limited by time. [Therefore, Shabbos is bound up with God's Infinite Essence, which transcends all change] (*Kesser Shem Tov* 400).

On Shabbos, the Root is revealed, and all the branches yearn for it.

Shabbos is a holy day; for it reveals light from the Source of holiness, which is the Creator, and illuminates all of creation.

The spirituality of everything consists in that it was emanated from the Primordial Thought. This is the life force of everything, as well. Subsequently, when [the universe] was actually created through the chain of cause and effect, this spirituality remained above, hidden within its Source. The life force within creation was extremely limited, for it had to be constricted in order to be clothed in the physical.

If the universe had remained just as it was after the six days of creation, it could not have endured. Therefore, after completing the entire process of creation, God caused a light to shine forth from the Hidden World, from the highest spiritual entities which were created in the Divine Thought. This radiance of His splendor shone from one end of the universe to the other, throughout all of creation. To man in particular, who is the focal point of creation, God shone forth this light from its hidden source within the Divine Thought.

Thus, our Sages taught that [before the first Shabbos], the world lacked rest.[2] This "rest" refers to God Himself [as stated above]. "When Shabbos comes, rest comes." This is the hidden light which was ema-

---

1. Rashi on *Bereishis* 2:2; *Tosafos, Sanhedrin* 38a.
2. *Bereishis Rabba* 10:9.

nated from God's Essence, through which creation comes into existence. Then [on Shabbos] creation is filled with longing and desire for Him.

This is like a baby, who follows its childish ways and forgets about its father. Later, when it sees its father, it throws everything aside because of its desire for him and runs to embrace him; for [the child] is really part of the parent.

Similarly, to the extent that we can express it, when God illuminates the universe with the radiance of His splendor, all creatures will turn to Him with great longing, which is the purpose of creation.

This is the meaning of Shabbos: it is a return (*shavah*) to the Root. The Root shines to the branches, the branches desire and long and yearn for Him, and everything becomes one with God[3] (*Kesser Shem Tov* 401).

To observe Shabbos according to its laws, with all of their details and fine points, [brings about the forgiveness of sin]. The verse states, "You bring (*tashev*) a man (*enosh*) to the point of being crushed and say, 'Return, children of man'" (*Tehillim* 90:3). *Tashev* (bring) is composed of the same Hebrew letters as Shabbos. *Enosh* (man) [suggests the statement of our Sages in *Shabbos* 118b] that even if one had previously worshiped idols like the generation of Enosh, [he will be forgiven for his sins in the merit of observing the holy Shabbos][4] (*Tzava'as HaRivash* 18).

When God created the world, it was like a body without a soul. Just as God breathed the soul into the body of the first man, He brought the peace of Shabbos into the world. Thus, it is written, "On the seventh day He rested and was refreshed (*vayinafash*)" (*Shemos* 31:17). [*Vayinafash* is related to the word *nefesh*, "soul."] For Shabbos is the soul of all creation (*Toldos Yaakov Yosef, Hakdama*, based on a teaching of R. Moshe Alshich).

3. See *Likkutei Moharan* II, 2:5–6.
4. See *Sefer HaTanya, Kuntres Acharon* 9 (end).

"On Shabbos when the time for the *minchah* prayer arrives, the Will of Wills (*Ra'ava d'Ra'avin*) is manifest" (*Zohar* II, 88b). The act of creation revealed the [encompassing] Divine will, which is above any other [particular manifestation of] will. This may be understood from the example of a person who wishes to travel from the Diaspora in order to settle in the Land of Israel. Right now, his wish is to embark upon his journey. However, his true desire, his "will of wills," is to dwell in the Land of Israel. It is in this sense that [the time for the *minchah* prayer on Shabbos] is called the Will of Wills.

Similarly, whenever there is a time of affliction or harsh decrees against the Jewish people, God forbid, this, too, is an expression of God's will. Suffering can bring a person to repent, or it may enable him to reach a higher spiritual level. This also fulfills the ultimate purpose, the Will of Wills.

The Baal Shem Tov taught that when everything ascends to the Will of Wills, all harsh decrees are "sweetened in their Source." God's innermost will is the epitome of goodness and mercy. Therefore, on Shabbos at the time of *minchah*, we pray for God to reveal His Will of Wills, just as it was manifest in the first act of creation (*Ohr HaGanuz L'Tzaddikim, Yisro*).

The holy Baal Shem Tov and his disciples, according to whose words we live, enlightened us and our entire people [by encouraging] Chasidim and sincere Jews to gather together with the leaders of the generation in order to internalize the holiness of Shabbos and faith in God's Oneness—for they are inseparable from one another (*Imrei Chaim*).

Once the Baal Shem Tov spent Shabbos in a little village, together with his disciples. When the time for *Shalosh Seudos* (the mystical third meal) arrived, the most prominent member of the community provided a meal for all the simple folk. He sat together with them, and they ate and drank, singing *zemiros* and holy melodies. The Baal Shem Tov saw that this was favorably received Above. After the repast, he called the man over and asked, "Why did you waste your whole *Shalosh Seudos* this way?" The man answered, "There is a popular saying: 'When my soul departs, may I be among my fellow Jews.' I once heard that on Shabbos every Jew receives an additional soul, which leaves him on *Motza'ei Shabbos*. So I said to myself, 'Let my additional soul, too, depart while I am among my fellow Jews.' That is why it is my custom to gather everyone together [at the end of the holy day]." This explanation gave the Baal Shem Tov great pleasure (*Kesser Shem Tov* 386).

Silence

"The fence for wisdom is silence" (*Avos* 3:13). When one is silent, he is able to bind himself to the World of Thought, which is called "wisdom" (*Kesser Shem Tov* 225).

". . . Whoever increases words brings about sin (*chet*)" (*Avos* 1:17). The Hebrew word for sin (*chet*) means a lack or deficiency.[1] [Thus, the Mishnah implies that] even when one discusses the wisdom of Torah with others, silence would still be better. With silence, one can contemplate the greatness of God and bind oneself to Him more completely than through speech.

At times one may lie in bed and appear to be sleeping, when one is really meditating upon the Creator, may He be blessed (*Tzava'as HaRivash* 133).

If a person is subjected to ridicule because of his manner of prayer or such things, he should not respond, even with pleasant words. In this way, he may avoid both strife and the feeling of self-importance which comes from forgetting about the Creator, may He be blessed. Thus, our Sages taught that a man's silence is greater than his speech, for it brings him to humility[2] (*Tzava'as HaRivash* 49).

One must often serve God with his soul alone—that is, in thought—and the body must remain still, so that it should not become weak from exertion (*Tzava'as HaRivash* 104).

---

1. See Rashi on *Bereishis* 31:39.
2. *Megilla* 18a; also see *Chullin* 89a; *Reishis Chochmah, Sha'ar HaAnavah,* Chapter 3; *Likkutei Moharan* 1:6.

"And it came to pass, when the ark set forward, that Moshe said, 'Rise up, O God, and let Your enemies be dispersed, and let those that hate You flee from Your Presence.' And when it rested, he said, 'Return, O God, to the myriads of thousands of Israel'" (*Bamidbar* 10:35–36).

There is a type of Divine service through movement (*t'nuah*), which includes all the positive *mitzvos*, Torah study, and prayer; and they all entail various mystical unifications. However, there is another type of Divine service by means of resting (*menuchah*). One sits alone in silence and contemplates God's loftiness. This relates to the World of Thought, which is also called the World of Rest; for one enters into a state of stillness. When one wishes to experience *deveykus*, he should sit quietly, with holy thoughts, in a state of awe and attachment to God[3] (*Ohr Ganuz L'Tzaddikim, B'Ha'alosecha*).

---

3. See *Likkutei Moharan* I, 64:3; ibid., I:234; *Likkutei Halachos, Shabbos* 7:43, 39b; *Sefiras HaOmer* 1:2; ibid., *Chezkas Karkaos* 4; ibid., *Reishis HaGez* 3:14; *Likkutei Eitzos, Machshavos V'Hirhurim* 12; *Derech Mitzvosecha Milah*, 7a; ibid., *Kiddush HaChodesh*, 69b; *Likkutei Dibburim* I, 3:18; *Derech HaMelech* (*Piaseczno*), *Inyan Hashkata*.

Sin

If one desires to transgress, God forbid, he should recite the scriptural verse that refers to that sin with its proper cantillation and vowelization, in awe and in love, and then the [forbidden desire] will leave him (*Tzava'as HaRivash* 13).

If one experiences any evil trait, God forbid, he should recite the names of the six nations [that occupied the land of Israel prior to the Jewish people], "The Canaanite, the Hittite," etc., with all his strength and with awe and love. Then it will depart from him.[1]

Also, he should bind this trait to the Holy One, blessed be He. For example, if one experiences an evil love, God forbid, he should direct his feeling of love only to God. All of his striving should be only for this. If one succumbs to anger—which is an evil fear derived from the Divine Attribute of Might (*Gevurah*)—he should use his own [trait of] might to overcome his Evil Inclination. In this manner, the trait itself can become a vehicle for God.

When one hears someone else speak words of Torah in awe and love, he should intensely fix his attention upon the words and become one with the speaker. Then the speaker's words will become his own thoughts, and in this way [any unholy tendencies] will depart from him[2] (*Tzava'as HaRivash* 14).

A person should not be excessively fastidious about everything he does [in serving God], for the Evil Inclination wants to make one afraid that he has not fulfilled this or that detail in order to make him depressed. And depression is one of the greatest obstacles to serving the Creator.

Even if one does transgress, God forbid, he should not become so morose that he can no longer serve God. Rather, one should feel remorse

---

1. There were actually seven nations in the Land of Israel who, in Kabbalistic thought, personified the seven basic evil traits discussed here. According to Rashi, the seventh nation, the Girgashites, left of their own accord. Therefore, they are not mentioned in this verse. Note the explanation of R. Yaakov Tzvi Yalish in *Kehilas Yaakov, Inyan Girgashi*.

2. See *Tzetel Kattan* 5.

for having sinned—and then he should rejoice in the Creator as before, since he regrets his sin completely and does not intend to return to his foolishness again.

Even if one knows with certainty that he has not fulfilled a certain requirement because of various difficulties, he must not become melancholy. He should consider that the Creator searches our hearts, and He knows that one really wanted to perform [His will] properly but could not do so. [Therefore,] he should strengthen himself to rejoice in the Creator, may He be blessed.[3]

The verse states, "It is a time to act for God—they have overturned Your Torah."[4] Sometimes the performance of a certain *mitzvah* may contain a trace of sin.[5] Nevertheless, one should pay no attention to the Evil Inclination, which wants to deter one from performing this *mitzvah*. One should tell the Evil Inclination, "My intent in fulfilling this *mitzvah* is only to gratify the Creator, may He be blessed. If I knew that the Creator did not want this act to be performed, I surely would refrain from it. Rather, I only wish to gratify the will of my Creator with this *mitzvah*." Then, with God's help, the Evil Inclination will depart from him [and he will know what to do]. In every case, one must use one's intelligence as to whether or not he should perform a given *mitzvah* (*Tzava'as HaRivash* 46).

"The words of his mouth are iniquity and deceit; he has ceased using his intellect to do good" (*Tehillim* 36:4). There are two kinds [of transgressors]. One is completely evil; he knows his Master and nevertheless intends to rebel against Him. The other is blinded by the Evil Inclination, which makes him appear to be perfectly righteous in his own eyes and even in the eyes of others. But, in truth, although [the latter] studies Torah constantly and prays and afflicts himself, he strives for naught—for he does not cleave to the Creator, nor does he possess the pure faith [which would enable him] to experience *deveykus* at all times. He does not realize that this is an essential component of Divine ser-

---

3. It is self-understood that this does not obviate the need for *teshuvah* and the rectification of one's misdeeds.
4. *Tehillim* 119:126.
5. See Rashi on *Berachos* 54a, citing this verse.

vice, like studying Torah or praying or performing *mitzvos* for their own sake.

The difference between these two [transgressors] is that the complete evildoer still may be healed from his sickness, for he may experience an awakening of *teshuvah*—[he may] return to God with all his heart and beg Him to show him the path of enlightenment. However, the second fellow is irremediable, for he has sealed his eyes shut from beholding the Creator and His greatness and His proper manner of worship. He is righteous in his own eyes—so how can he ever repent?

This is how the Evil One commonly entices a person to sin: he makes the transgression seem to be a *mitzvah*, so that the sinner will never repent. This is what the verse cited above means when it says, "The words of his mouth are iniquity and deceit. . . ." The Evil Inclination deceives a person by making a sin appear to be a *mitzvah*. And, in this, "he has ceased using his intellect to do good"; that is, he has desisted from ever repenting.

Moreover, [the next verse continues,] "Iniquity he devises upon his bed." In other words, [the Evil Inclination] deceives him even further, and when he falls sick upon his bed, he prays that God should heal him in the merit of the Torah he has studied and the *mitzvos* he has performed. He does not realize that he has mentioned his very transgressions, inasmuch as all [of his seeming virtues] were due to the blandishments of the Evil Inclination [i.e., for self-serving motives and not for the sake of cleaving to God] (*Tzava'as HaRivash* 74).

"There are four principal causes of damage: the ox, the pit, the tooth, and the outbreak of fire" (*Bava Kamma* 2b). [These four categories also correspond to four negative human tendencies.] The word *shor* (ox) is related to the word *ashurenu* ("I see him"). This alludes to the sort of peering and gazing that leads to harm. The word *bor* (pit) is related to *s'dei habor* (a fallow field). This suggests one who does not study Torah but wastes his time in idle pursuits. "Tooth" refers to the passion for eating, and "fire" refers to the fire of anger[6] (*Tzava'as HaRivash* 121).

---

6. Also see *Ta'amei HaMitzvos* of the Ari z"l, *Mishpatim*, 63b; *Likkutei Moharan* I:4, citing *Mishnas Chasidim*.

Speech

Rabbi Yisrael Baal Shem, peace be upon him, taught: "[And God said to Noach . . .] 'You shall make a light (*tzohar*) for the ark (*teivah*)'" (*Bereishis* 6:16). That is, the word (*teivah*) which you utter should be luminous.

For every letter contains worlds and souls and Godliness. And they ascend and combine and unite with one another—with Godliness. Afterward, the letters unite and gather themselves together to form a word, and they effect true unifications in Godliness. One must incorporate his soul within each and every aspect [of these unifications]; then he must unify all the worlds as one. Thus, they will all ascend, bringing about great joy and delight without measure.

The verse continues, "You shall construct it with lower, second, and third [levels]."[1] This alludes to worlds and souls and Godliness, as the *Zohar* states, "There are three worlds . . ."[2]

A person must listen to each word he says, for the *Shechinah*, [which corresponds to] the World of Speech, actually speaks.[3] And when [the word] possesses a light, it comes forth shining and brings gratification to its Maker. This [level of prayer] requires great faith (*emunah*), for the *Shechinah* is called *emunas uman*, "the Work of a Craftsman."[4] But without faith, [one's utterance] is that of "a complainer who separates a Leader."[5] [According to Rashi, the leader to whom this proverb refers is God. Thus, by not attempting to pray with *kavanah* (concentration), one actually estranges himself from the *Shechinah*.]

"And to a cubit (*amah*) you shall finish it upward . . ."[6] [The Hebrew word *amah*] suggests fear or awe (*eimah*). [That is, one must utter each word of prayer in a state of awe, so that it will ascend Above.] Or, alternatively, one could interpret this to mean that once the word leaves his mouth, he need not remember it anymore. We cannot see the lofty place to which it ascends, just as we are unable to gaze at the sun. Thus, the

---

1. Ibid.
2. *Zohar* III, 159a.
3. *Zohar* III, 230a and 281b; *Tikkunei Zohar, Tikkun* 18, 38b. For further elucidation, see *Likkutei Moharan* I:42, 48, 78; ibid., II:84.
4. *Zohar* I, 32a.
5. *Mishlei* 16:28.
6. Ibid.

verse concludes, "You shall finish it upward." [Once it is expressed, it immediately goes upward.] How may this be accomplished? By putting yourself and your whole body into each word [of prayer] (*Tzava'as HaRivash* 75).

Speech is the very life of a person, as the verse states, "He breathed into [Adam's] nostrils a living soul," which the Targum renders, "a spirit that speaks."[7] And life comes only from God. Thus, when a person says a good word, it ascends Above and arouses the Supernal Speech, which, in turn, confers life upon him in even greater measure.

However, when one says an evil word, his vital force leaves him, it does not ascend Above, and he nearly forfeits his life altogether. Thus, it is said in Yiddish, "*Er hot ois-ghiret*"—"He spoke out." [That is, through speech a person can divest himself of his very life force] (*Tzava'as HaRivash* 103).

---

7. *Bereishis* 2:7.

Suffering

The Baal Shem Tov taught: One may attempt to run away from suffering, but it will still pursue him. This may be compared to a pregnant woman who goes to another place in order to escape the pains of childbirth, but they come along with her. The best advice is to pray to God, and He will alleviate one's suffering[1] (*Kesser Shem Tov* 109).

The Baal Shem Tov taught: In every affliction, whether physical or spiritual, a holy spark of Godliness is present. Thus our Sages state: "When a person is in pain, what does the *Shechinah* say? 'Woe to my head! Woe to my arm'!"[2] That is, the *Shechinah* shares the person's sufferings—for a human being is a spark and a branch of the *Shechinah*, albeit in a concealed state. When one realizes that God is together with him, this concealment is removed, and the pain desists[3] (*Ohr HaGanuz L'Tzaddikim, Vayeitzei*).

I heard from my grandfather (the Baal Shem Tov): All the sufferings a person experiences, may the Merciful One spare us, reflect the needs of the *Shechinah*. There is a lack of unity [between the *sefiros* of *tiferes* and *malchus*, which correspond to the Holy One, blessed be He, and the *Shechinah*]. Therefore, God sends a person sufferings so that he will pray for the needs of the *Shechinah*. As the verse states, "I am sick with love [of God]."[4] One must awaken boundless love for God and thus unite the Holy One, blessed be He, and the *Shechinah* in perfect harmony. Then all suffering and adversity will automatically disappear (*Degel Machaneh Ephraim, Beshalach*).

---

1. See *Sichos HaRan* 308.
2. *Chagigah* 15b.
3. *Yeshaya* 63:9; *Megilla* 29a; also note *Likkutei Moharan* II:66.
4. *Shir HaShirim* 2:5.

I heard from my master [the Baal Shem Tov] that he once told a certain man, "Accept whatever happens to you in this world with love, and you will live both here and in the World to Come."

"God must also give a person the ability to accept everything with love," he replied.

"You have spoken the truth," [the Baal Shem Tov] said (*Ben Poras Yosef, Vayechi*).

Teshuvah

"A voice cries out in the wilderness, 'Clear a path for God . . .'" (*Yeshayahu* 40:3). The Baal Shem Tov taught that this refers to the thoughts of *teshuvah* that every Jew experiences when he contemplates the ultimate purpose of his existence (*Pri Tzaddik, Va'eschanan*).

"A Heavenly voice came forth and declared, 'Wayward children, return . . .'" (*Chagigah* 15a, citing *Yirmiyahu* 3:22).

My grandfather, the holy Baal Shem Tov, asked: What is the purpose of this Heavenly voice? The *tzaddikim* do not need it, for they know that they must repent—and the wicked have stopped listening.

The answer is that this Heavenly voice is really the thought of *teshuvah* that enters the heart of the transgressor. The Holy One, blessed be He, yearns for him to repent of his evil path; for He does not desire the death of the wicked. God only wants to awaken him to *teshuvah*, so that "no one shall remain banished from Him"[1] (*Zimras Ha'aretz, Shabbos Teshuvah*).

Concerning [Elisha Ben Avuyah, known as] *Acher* (the "Other"), a Heavenly voice proclaimed, "'Return, O wayward children'—except *Acher*."[2] [Elisha Ben Avuyah was known as *Acher* because he was a Torah scholar who became an apostate.] It was his punishment to be cast aside. However, if he had persisted and repented anyway, his *teshuvah* would have been accepted. [Thus, our Sages taught], "Nothing can stand in the way of *teshuvah*"[3] (*Shiv'chei Baal Shem Tov* 5).

---

1. II *Shmuel* 14:14.
2. *Chagigah* 15a, citing *Yirmiyahu* 3:22.
3. *Yerushalmi Pe'ah* 1:1; *Yerushalmi Sanhedrin* 10:1; *Zohar* II, 106a; also note *Sichos HaRan* 71.

It once happened that a certain man became so sick that even a great physician who had been called in to examine the patient despaired of healing him. The man was not even able to speak. The Baal Shem Tov was also visiting the locality at that time. Therefore, he was asked to see the patient.

Immediately upon arriving, the Baal Shem Tov ordered them to boil some broth with meat. [While the soup was being prepared], the sick man regained his power of speech. After tasting it, he began to feel better, until at last his health was restored completely.

The doctor, who was Jewish, asked the Baal Shem Tov, "How were you able to heal him? The patient's vascular system had deteriorated beyond all hope."

"You saw the patient's physical condition," the Baal Shem Tov explained. "However, I saw his spiritual condition. A man has two hundred, forty-eight limbs, and three hundred, sixty-five veins, which correspond to the two hundred, forty-eight positive *mitzvos*, and the three hundred, sixty-five negative *mitzvos*. When a person does something wrong, God forbid, he damages the part of his body which corresponds to the *mitzvah* transgressed. If one violates many prohibitions, he damages many veins. The blood cannot flow properly, and the person's life is endangered. Therefore, I spoke to this man's *neshamah* (soul), and asked it to undergo certain penances. The soul agreed. Then all of the patient's limbs and veins were repaired, and I was able to heal him" (*Nifla'os HaBaal Shem Tov*, Section III).

"For if you will diligently keep all of this commandment . . . to cleave to Him . . ." (*Devarim* 11:22). On this verse, Rashi comments, "Is it possible to speak thus? Is He not 'a consuming fire'?[4] Rather, it means, 'Cling to the Sages and their disciples, and I will consider it as if you were attached to Him.'" I heard from my master (the Baal Shem Tov) that the rectification of the souls of *baalei teshuvah* is primarily accomplished by the great *tzaddikim* of the generation, who are able to elevate [each one] and bind him to his Source[5] (*Toldos Yaakov Yosef, Korach*).

---

4. *Devarim* 4:24.
5. *Likkutei Moharan* 1, 4:5; *Likkutei Eitzos, Teshuvah* 32; *Sichos HaRan* 111; *Chayei Moharan* 304; *Likkutei Halachos, Betzias HaPas* 5:47; ibid. *Tefillin* 2:11; ibid. *Beis HaKnesses* 5:24; ibid. *Tefillas HaMinchah* 5:3; ibid. *Shabbos* 7:7, 7:45; ibid. *Shechitah* 3:2; ibid. *Nedarim* 4:10; ibid. *Gezeilah* 5:3.

My grandfather [the Baal Shem Tov] said: It is known [from the writings of the Ari z"l] that Adam could rectify his sin only through the holy Patriarchs.[6] Thus, the perfection of *teshuvah* is impossible to attain without the *tzaddik*—only through him is one able to ascend[7] (*Degel Machaneh Ephraim, Sh'mini*).

---

6. *Likkutei HaShas, Avos*, 5.
7. See *Likkutei Moharan* I, 4:5; I:193.

Thoughts

The Baal Shem Tov taught: Wherever a person puts his thoughts, there is the whole man[1] (*Kesser Shem Tov* 56).

Rabbi Yisrael Baal Shem Tov said: When one cleaves to the Creator and suddenly a certain thought occurs to him about a certain matter, it usually proves to be true. This is a minor form of *ruach hakodesh* (Divine Inspiration)[2] (*Kesser Shem Tov* 195).

"Moshe told the people of Israel, 'Remove this evil desire from your hearts, and may you possess one spirit of reverence and one counsel in serving God. Just as He is unique in the universe, so must your worship be uniquely designated to Him . . .'" (*Sifra, Shemini, 6*).

A person must always have but one thought in serving the Creator. Thus, the verse states, "God did [everything] so that one should revere Him" (*Koheles* 3:14). [However, one must exert himself in this matter, as it states,] "God has made man upright; yet they have sought out many schemes (*cheshbonos*)" (*Koheles* 7:29). [The word *cheshbonos* (schemes) is related to *machshavos* (thoughts).] Many thoughts lead to a confused heart (*Tzava'as HaRivash* 84, section 1).

"And you will be destroyed swiftly (*va'avaditem m'heyra*) . . ." (*Devarim* 11:17). The Baal Shem Tov taught that one must always have a calm, settled mind. Thus, [the verse may be rendered interpretively] "*Va'avaditem m'heyra*—You must destroy (*avad*) hurriedness (*m'hirus*)" (*Tz'ror HaChaim* 47).

---

1. See *Likkutei Eitzos, Da'as,* 9.
2. See *Likkutei Moharan* I:138.

"And [the Shunamite woman] said unto her husband, 'Behold, he is a holy man'" (II *Melachim* 4:9). [The *Gemara* explains:] "She knew this because she never saw a fly pass his table . . ."(*Berachos* 10b).

The holy *Zohar* asks: Would this not have been observable to anyone, not only the Shunamite woman?[3]

My master (the Baal Shem Tov) explained the matter in the light of [another Talmudic teaching]: "Hillel had eighty disciples . . . and the greatest of them was Rabbi Yonasan ben Uzziel . . . It was said of Rabbi Yonasan ben Uzziel that while he sat engaged in Torah study, any bird that flew over his head would immediately be consumed by fire."[4]

There are Supernal Worlds that correspond to a person's thoughts. If one's thoughts are holy and spiritual, so are the worlds above him. If one's thoughts are impure, the worlds will be impure. Also, corresponding to one's thoughts and the worlds [they engender] are the pure or impure birds that pass before him in the physical world. This is the rule with all creatures, pure or impure, which pass before a person.

There are three categories [in creation]: the pure, the impure, and the intermediate. Above them all is the World of Intellect, which nothing can grasp. Thus, [the *Gemara*] states, "Any bird which flew over his head was consumed by fire."

This is [similar to what was said concerning Elishah HaNavi], "A fly was never seen on his table." [The Shunamite woman alone understood from this] that he was a holy man, and his thoughts were holy[5] (*Ben Poras Yosef, Vayeitzei*).

If one prays and experiences an alien thought, [this indicates that] the *klippos* (forces of impurity) ride upon his speech, God forbid. The verse states, "To horses for Pharaoh's chariots have I likened you, my beloved."[6] "Horses" represent words.[7] When Pharaoh, that is, the alien thought, rides upon [one's words], then "I have likened you (*d'misich*), my beloved." [The word *d'misich* is homiletically related to the word

3. *Zohar* II, *Beshalach*, 44a.
4. *Succah* 28a.
5. Also see *Sefer HaTanya, Igeres HaKodesh*, 147a, citing *Asarah Ma'amaros* of Rabbi Menachem Azariah of Fano.
6. *Shir HaShirim* 1:9.
7. *Tikkunei Zohar, Tikkun* 47.

d'mamah, "silence," as Rashi explains, *op. cit.*] It would be better to remain silent [and not continue to pray until the alien thought departs].
However, "a word that comes from the heart enters the heart."[8] This
alludes to the Supernal Heart, by means of the heart [i.e., heartfelt prayer][9]
(*Tzava'as HaRivash* 71).

"For My thoughts are not your thoughts, and your ways are not
My ways" (*Yeshayahu* 55:8). The Baal Shem Tov taught: This means that
as soon as a person separates himself from God, he serves false gods.
There is no middle way. Thus, the verse states, "[Take heed, lest your
heart be deceived,] and you turn aside and serve other gods . . ."[10].
However, the *Gemara* explains that if one remains still and does not transgress, it is accounted to him as if he had performed a *mitzvah*.[11] Therefore, [if one imagines that it is harmless to cease thinking of God, he
should realize that "My thoughts are not your thoughts." In truth, this
is a matter of great consequence.[12] But if one desists from action, in order
to avoid transgression, God accounts this as a positive act, as the verse
states,] "Your ways are not My ways" (*Tzava'as HaRivash* 76).

As one prays, he should imagine that he is proceeding from one
Heavenly palace to the next. And when an alien thought enters his mind,
he should banish it—for at every Heavenly palace one is judged before
being admitted [and the presence of an unholy thought indicates one's
unworthiness].

If one cannot pray with fervor, he should force himself to pray,
nevertheless. And when he does pray with fervor, he should observe the
nature of any alien thought that he may experience. For example, if it is

---

8. See Rabbi Moshe Ibn Ezra's *Shiras Yisrael*, 156.

9. In the original text the word "*hevel*" (breath) is found here. This is probably
a typographical error for the word "*halev*" (the heart), which contains the same letters.
Our translation reflects this assumption, based upon a similar concept in *Likkutim
Yekarim* 118, citing *Chagigah* 20b.

10. *Devarim* 11:16.

11. *Makkos* 23b.

12. See *Likkutei Moharan* II:62.

an unholy form of love, such as a sexual fantasy, he should elevate it to its source, which is the love of God.

There are seven types of thoughts and no more. [These correspond to the seven *sefiros*,] which correspond to the seven days of creation. Thus, each [thought] has an aspect of evening and morning. Evening (*erev*) is related to confusion (*ta'aroves*), which produces alien thoughts. Morning (*boker*) is related to investigation (*bikkur*), for one investigates and searches for God.

These [seven categories comprise] love of God and its opposite, love of transgression (*ahavah*); fear of God and evil fears, such as hatred (*gevurah*); glorification of God and its opposite, such as self-glorification (*tiferes*). Similarly, conquest (*netzach*), thanksgiving (*hod*), and foundation (*yesod*)—which means making connections between things—[all possess holy and unholy aspects. The seventh quality, not mentioned here, is sovereignty (*malchus*)]. Moreover, each quality is a compound of ten facets, [corresponding to the seven lower *sefiros* mentioned above and the three higher *sefiros* of *kesser*, *chochmah*, and *binah*, which express the Divine will and wisdom]. And every unholy thought gives life to ten of the seventy idolatrous nations.

The *Midrash Ne'elam* states: "When the Holy One, blessed be He, first created the world, the world trembled, for it had nothing with which to justify its existence. The Holy One, blessed be He, created Avraham, but the world still trembled—for Yishmael would come from him. Avraham gave birth to Yitzchak, but the world still trembled—for Esav would come from him. But afterward, when Yaakov was born, the world was established, for 'his bed was perfect,' [i.e., his children were all *tzaddikim*]."[13]

Avraham embodied the trait of love, [which is an expression of *chesed* (kindness)].[14] But Yishmael, who came from him, represents love on the side of unholiness.[15] As soon as one experiences an evil love, he enlivens [the aspect of] Yishmael. Yitzchak represents the trait of fear, [which is rooted in the *sefirah* of *gevurah* (severity)]; whereas Esav represents fear in its evil manifestation, such as [the desire to commit] murder, God forbid.[16] Thus, when one succumbs to an evil fear, he

---

13. *Zohar* I, 86b.

14. See *Yeshayahu* 41:8; also *Pardes Rimonim, Sha'ar* 23, *Ahavah*; *Sefer HaBahir*, 49; *Zohar Chadash, Toldos*; and elsewhere.

15. See *Zohar* III, 124a and 246b.

16. See *Sefer HaBahir*, 49; *Zohar Chadash, Toldos*; *Zohar* III, 124a and 246b.

enlivens [the aspect of] Esav and the [other] nine [idolatrous nations] related to him.

However, if one thinks of an evil love, he should say to himself, "What have I done? I have taken something from the World of Thought and brought it to a place of filth." In this way, one may subdue [the Evil Inclination] and cast it down to the earth, while returning the thought itself to the aspect of Nothingness. Then he should reflect, "If I could desire something physical and transitory, such as a beautiful woman, how much more should I love God?" Then he will enter the World of Love.

Similarly, if one hears a humorous remark which makes him happy, he should contemplate that this, too, is a portion of the World of Love. Or if he sees or hears something that gives him pleasure, he should realize that this is a portion of the World of Pleasure. Therefore, he should be extremely careful not to corporealize it. Instead, he should vividly experience [the inner essence of] this pleasure, since it is a portion of the World of Pleasure and can bring him into the World of Pleasure, as well. Thus, he will fulfill the verse, "Then you shall delight in God."[17] The verse actually states *al Hashem*—"above God." [One's actions will also give pleasure to God, so to speak.[18]] For when a *tzaddik* experiences pleasure, he brings Divine pleasure to all the worlds.

If one sees something frightening, he should say, "What is there to be afraid of? Is this not merely another human being like myself [or an animal or another living creature]? It is only frightening because the Creator has clothed Himself in this form. How much more should I fear God Himself!"

Likewise, concerning the trait of glorification (*tiferes*), if one is praised and then, in the midst of prayer, one thinks, "People admire me because I pray with *kavanah*," he should [use this feeling] to apprehend the World of Glorification.

If one experiences a desire for conquest, he should conquer the desire itself by using it to apprehend the Divine trait of conquest (*netzach*). The same applies to [the traits of] thanksgiving (*hod*) and attachment (*yesod*). One should not bind himself [to the outer manifestation of the alien thought] but only to God, may He be blessed (*Likkutim Yekarim* 194).

---

17. *Yeshayahu* 58:14.
18. See *Zohar* II, 83a.

"When you go out to battle against your enemies . . . and you see among the captives a woman (*eishes*) of beautiful (*yifas*) appearance. . . ." (*Devarim* 21:10–11). The word *eishes* (woman) contains the initials of the verse, "*Hashem s'fasai tiftach*"—"O God, open my lips . . ." (*Tehillim* 51:17). The next word, *yifas* (beautiful), contains the initials of [the verse's conclusion,] "And my mouth will utter Your praise"[19] (*Otzar HaChaim, Ki Seitzei*; cited in *Sefer Baal Shem Tov, Ki Seitzei* 3).

In the days of the holy Baal Shem Tov there was a certain spiritual teacher whom some of the disciples wished to visit, just to see what he had to offer. Before leaving, they asked their master how they could tell if this teacher was a true *tzaddik*. The Baal Shem Tov replied that they should ask his advice about the problem of alien thoughts. If he claimed to know a solution, they could be certain that he was a charlatan (*Divrei Yechezkel*).

---

19. Also note *Likkutei Moharan* II:82 on the same verse.

Tikkun Chatzos

"May your fear of Heaven be as great as your fear of flesh and blood" (*Berachos* 28b). If one's teacher were to come and find him asleep, upon awakening, he would recoil and begin to tremble in his master's presence. How much more [should one rise with alacrity] when the Creator awakens him from sleep at midnight [to lament the destruction of the Holy Temple and the exile of the Jewish people] (*Kesser Shem Tov* 205).

One should always be sure to arise at midnight [to mourn the destruction of the Holy Temple and the exile of the Jewish people], as well as to connect the night to the new day [through one's Divine service][1] (*Tzava'as HaRivash* 83).

The importance of arising at midnight on a regular basis should be known [to all]. At the very least, one must be sure to recite the morning prayers—both summer and winter—before sunrise. That is, the greater portion of the prayers preceding the declaration of *Shema* ("Hear, O Israel . . .") should be concluded before dawn. For the difference between praying before sunrise and after sunrise is as great as the difference between east and west. Before dawn one is still capable of nullifying all harsh judgments. When the sun emerges, all of Heaven's decrees are proclaimed, whether for harm or benefit. However, before Heaven's will has been proclaimed, one can still nullify harsh judgments.

Let this [teaching] be your reminder: "And he is like a bridegroom emerging from under the wedding canopy; he will rejoice like a mighty warrior . . . and nothing is hidden from his wrath."[2] Do not read *m'chamaso* ("from his wrath") but *m'chomaso* ("from its heat"). That is, once the sun has shone upon the earth, nothing is hidden from the wrathful angels who execute all severe judgments. Therefore, let this not be a matter of little consequence in your eyes, for it is great.

---

1. See *Likkutei Moharan* I:54, I:149; ibid., II:67; *Sichos HaRan* 301.
2. *Tehillim* 19:6–7.

The Baal Shem Tov, of blessed memory, was very particular about this. At times, when he did not have a *minyan* with which to pray [before dawn], he would pray alone (*Tzava'as HaRivash* 16).

When one arises at midnight and sleep begins to overtake him, he should walk about in his house and sing songs of praise to God—even audibly—in order to drive sleep away from himself.

It is also good to study many different Torah subjects and not to dwell upon only one thing, which would be burdensome. Rather, a person should study many subjects [and this will help him to stay awake] (*Tzava'as HaRivash* 28).

One should turn the nights into days and sleep a few hours [during the afternoon] in order to forego sleep at [the latter part of the] night (*Tzava'as HaRivash* 27).

Torah

The Baal Shem Tov strongly advocated the study of *Shulchan Aruch* without any of its commentaries, both with children and adults. Due to neglect of this area of study, [the prediction of our Sages might be fulfilled, God forbid, that] the Torah will be forgotten among the Jewish people.[1] (However, it is self-understood that an advanced Torah scholar or one who must render legal decisions must thoroughly explore the commentaries)[2] (*Kesser Shem Tov* II:423).

The Baal Shem Tov taught: The letters of the Torah are the chambers of the Divine [Palace] and His vessels. By fixing his awareness [on these letters], one can draw an emanation of the Supernal Light into them; as the *Zohar* states, "The Holy One, blessed be He, and the Torah are one."[3] A person must put all his attention into [the letters of Torah], for [the mind] is the soul itself. And this is the *deveykus* [to which the *Zohar* alludes when it states that] "the Holy One, blessed be He, the Torah and the Jewish People are one"[4] (*Ohr HaGanuz L'Tzaddikim, Miketz*).

"God's Torah is perfect (*temimah*); it renews the soul" (*Tehillim* 19:8). The Baal Shem Tov taught: God's Torah is always perfect and complete, for no one in the world has touched it yet. This is because "it renews the soul" of the person who continually approaches it with fresh enthusiasm. When one studies God's Torah with simplicity (*temimus*), as if he had never done so before, then it renews the soul (*Vay'chal Moshe, Tehillim* 19).

---

1. *Shabbos* 138b.
2. Also see *Sichos HaRan* 29 and 185; *Likkutei Moharan* I, 8:6–7; I:62.
3. *Zohar* I, 24a; also see *Likkutei Moharan* I:281.
4. *Zohar* III, 73a.

"He who studies a subject one hundred times cannot be compared to he who does so a hundred and one" (*Chagiga* 9b). ["A hundred and one"] means that a person's studies must be imbued with the One—the Master of the Universe (*Degel Machaneh Ephraim, Tzav*).

The *Gemara* states: "There are great matters and small matters. A great matter is the *Ma'aseh Merkavah* (the mystical experience). A small matter is the scholarly dialogue between Abaye and Rava" (*Succah* 28a).

It is difficult to understand how the dialogue between Abaye and Rava could be called "a small matter." [These discussions deal with] the fundamentals of our Torah which God gave us at Mount Sinai. However, the explanation is as follows:

In truth, the revealed and the hidden dimensions of Torah are one. Everything depends upon the intent of the individual. If one only wants to acquire knowledge, he will not merit to perceive anything. Regarding him it is written, "All flesh is like grass, and all of its kindness is like the flower of the field."[5]

However, if one longs to cleave to God and to become a vehicle (*merkavah*) for Him, the only way to do so is through the Torah and *mitzvos*. Then, whether one engages in the revealed teachings or the hidden teachings, he will be a *merkavah* for God.

Therefore, the *Gemara* says, "A small matter is the scholarly dialogue between Abaye and Rava." This alludes to one who studies for intellectual pleasure or to fulfill his own needs. Such study is a small thing. He is serving God with something small and insignificant, for to him the Torah is like any other intellectual pursuit.

But when one wishes to become a *merkavah* for God, then it is a great thing. Thus, the *Gemara* says, "A great matter is the *Ma'aseh Merkavah*." This alludes to one who wishes to make himself into a vehicle for Godliness by means of the Torah[6] (*Kesser Shem Tov* 174).

---

5. *Yeshayahu* 40:6.
6. Rabbi Moshe Chaim Luzzatto's views on Torah study are kindred to those of the Baal Shem Tov. See *Rechev Yisrael* by R. Mordechai Sariki citing Ramchal's *Adir Ba Marom*, p. 219.

To study Torah *lishmah* (for its own sake) means with love [of God]. One should attach himself to the letters of Torah in order to become a *merkavah* (vehicle) for the Holy One, blessed be He, who is the source of all life and sublime pleasure. The Infinite Light shines within the letters, and "in the light of the King's countenance is life."[7] This is what I heard from my master, the Baal Shem Tov: [The *mitzvah* of studying Torah] *lishmah* means for the sake of the letter itself; that is, for the Infinite Light and life force hidden within it (*Kesser Shem Tov* 426).

The proper intention (*kavanah*) for Torah study is to attach oneself in holiness and purity to the letters of thought and speech. That is, one should bind his *nefesh, ruach, neshamah, chayah* and *yechidah* (the five levels of the soul) with the holiness of "the candle of *mitzvos* and the light of Torah,"[8] the letters that enlighten and shine and impart true Godly life. When one finally merits to understand and attaches himself to the holy letters, he will be able to perceive through the medium of the letters themselves—even to know future events. Thus it is written that [the words of Torah] "enlighten the eyes."[9] For they enlighten the eyes of those who cleave to them in holiness and purity like the lights of the *Urim* and *Tumim* [on the breastplate of the *Kohen Gadol*][10] (*Sod Yachin U'Boaz, Chapter 2*).

Whenever the Baal Shem Tov was asked a question, he would open a volume of the *Zohar* or *Gemara* and study for a short while. Then he would answer the question. He once said, "The light with which the Holy One, blessed be He, created the world enabled man to gaze from one end of the world to the other. [Subsequently,] He hid it for the *tzaddikim* in the Torah. Thus, when a *tzaddik* studies Torah *lishmah*, he can gaze from one end of the world to the other" (*Notzer Chesed* 5:25).

---

7. *Mishlei* 16:15.
8. Ibid. 6:23.
9. *Tehillim* 19:8–9
10. See *Likkutei Moharan* I:281; II:35.

"If one reads the *Megilla* backwards (*l'mafreia*), he has not fulfilled his obligation" (*Megilla* 17a). The Baal Shem Tov's explanation of this [Mishnah] is well-known: If one studies the *Megilla* and thinks that the tale it tells only happened long ago (*l'mafreia*), and that the miracle is not taking place right now—"he has not fulfilled his obligation." The purpose of reading the *Megilla* is for a Jew to learn from it how to conduct himself today (*Likkutei Sichos, Purim* 5731; based on *Divrei Shalom, Bo*).

[The Midrash states] that the entire Torah was included in the inscription of the Ten Commandments (*Bamidbar Rabba* 13:15). The Baal Shem Tov added that just as the entire Torah is contained in the Ten Commandments, the entire Torah is included in every single word. This is [possible to grasp] if the soul of one's teacher is rooted in the World of Oneness. However, if his soul is rooted in the World of Separateness, the student will only receive isolated pieces of information (*Ben Poras Yosef* 23b).

"And, behold, God stood beside Yaakov and said: 'I am the Lord, the God of Avraham, your father, and the God of Yitzchak. The land upon which you are lying I shall give to you and to your seed'" (*Bereishis* 28:13). On this verse, Rashi comments: "The Holy One, blessed be He, folded up the entire land of Israel beneath him . . ."

My master (the Baal Shem Tov) taught that a person must travel from place to place in order to earn a living, etc., because holy sparks [related to the root of his soul] have fallen there, which he must extract and redeem [from their exile]. Thus, the Holy One, blessed be He, folded up the entire land of Israel beneath Yaakov, so that he would not have to travel from place to place in order to extract his lost sparks. The entire land of Israel was gathered together beneath him, and he was able to extract these holy sparks while remaining in his own place.

One might ask why this was done for Yaakov and not for the other Patriarchs or for anyone else. However, just as ordinary men accomplish

various *tikkunim* (spiritual rectifications) with their deeds, so do scholars through their Torah study. The Torah is the medium through which
everything comes into existence; it is the handiwork of the Holy One,
blessed be He, through which the world was created. Yaakov personified the Torah, as it is written, "The voice is the voice of Yaakov . . ."[11]
[It is also written,] "You grant truth to Yaakov . . ."[12] Likewise, [the
Gemara states that] the Torah is called "truth."[13] Therefore, without
leaving his place, Yaakov was able to accomplish what would have entailed travel and physical effort on the part of others. When the entire
land of Israel folded itself up beneath Yaakov, he was able to extract [all
of his holy sparks] in that very place by means of his Torah study[14]
(*K'tones Pasim, B'ha'aloscha,* 35b; *Tzafnas Pane'ach* 114a).

From the power of the Torah one has studied on a given day, he
can subsequently know what to do when there are difficult decisions to
be made. As long as one cleaves to God, he will always know [what to
do] from the power of the Torah [he has studied].[15]

However, if a person relates to his circumstances as if they did not
reflect the Divine will, God relates to him accordingly. He will not prepare food and clothing that contain holy sparks related to the root of
that person's soul in order for him to [elevate and] perfect them (*Tzava'as
HaRivash* 31).

When one studies Torah, he should rest a bit every so often in order
to cleave to God, may He be blessed. It is impossible for most people to
experience *deveykus* while engaged in Torah study, for not every mind
is capable of continually studying in a state of love and fear of God. Only
exceptional individuals such as Rabbi Shimon bar Yochai and his disciples [can do so], as the *Zohar* states. Nevertheless, one must always

---

11. *Bereishis* 27:22.
12. *Michah* 7:20.
13. *Berachos* 5b.
14. Note *Sichos HaRan* 28.
15. See *Likkutei Moharan* I:1.

study, for Torah causes the soul to shine, and it is "a Tree of Life to all who grasp it."[16] If one did not study, he would not have the intelligence to cleave to Him; as the Mishnah states, "An empty-headed man has no fear of sin, and an ignoramus cannot be pious . . ."[17] Also, if a person sits idle, the Evil Inclination and its cohorts may bring him to improper thoughts, evil passions, and worthless discussion, since the faculty of thought is always active and never rests.

If, with the wonder of the Torah's wisdom, a person could contemplate the power of the Creator within all things, he could certainly discern that the kindness of the Creator and His beneficence is unceasing. [Such contemplation] would cause him to cleave to God with a complete love, and he would long to perform God's will, to serve Him and to give up his very soul[18] for the holiness of His Name. [He would strive] to attain oneness with God through all his deeds, without any compromise, like the Early Chasidim, whose thoughts were always attached only to God, may He be blessed; and this was considered to be as meritorious as Torah study or perhaps more so.[19] Thus, the saintly [Rabbeinu Bachya ibn Pakuda], author of *Chovos HaLevavos* (Duties of the Heart), and the eminent [Rabbi Yeshaya Horowitz], author of *Sh'nei Luchos HaBris* (Two Tablets of the Covenant), state that *deveykus* is sometimes a greater occupation than Torah study.[20]

However, in these times, it is difficult enough for us to attempt to cleave to the Creator during the three daily prayer services and while reciting the blessings over food. If we were to neglect Torah study, we would remain empty of both. [Therefore], at least one should not study constantly, without interruption. [This practice] befit earlier generations, who were much stronger and whose spiritual refinement and fear of Heaven were constant and did not require great effort. Reverence was always upon their faces, and they studied Torah in a lofty state of holiness, with love and fear of God. They were involved in [mystical knowledge of God] even while studying the revealed dimensions of the Torah—for "the Torah and the Holy One, blessed be He, are one"[21]—and they made themselves a vehicle for the *Shechinah*. Thus,

---

16. *Mishlei* 3:18.
17. *Avos* 2:5.
18. Lit., *nefesh*, *ruach*, and *neshamah*.
19. *Berachos* 32b.
20. *Chovos HaLevavos, Sha'ar Ahavah*, 5; *Sh'nei Luchos HaBris, Masechtas Shavuos*.
21. *Zohar* II, 60a.

they were able to accomplish a great deal in Torah study. But if people such as ourselves, whose minds are weak and whose abilities are inferior, were to study Torah constantly, without interruption, we would forget all about fear of Heaven or improving ourselves or unifying our actions with God. And this is the main thing, as it states, "The beginning of wisdom is fear of God."[22] Thus, the saintly author of *Chovos HaLevavos* (Duties of the Heart) chastised a certain individual who asked a strange [theoretical] question concerning the Laws of Divorce [when he lacked the Torah knowledge necessary for everyday life].[23] And the Ari *z"l* also stated that [even] an astute and knowledgeable scholar should only study the *Gemara* in depth (*b'iyun*) for an hour or two every day.[24]

Therefore, one should pause occasionally during one's studies and contemplate the greatness of the Creator, in order to love and fear Him, to be diffident before Him, to long to perform His *mitzvos*—and not to be busy with many thoughts, but to think one thought, as stated above, (*Likkutei Amarim* of Rabbi Menachem Mendel of Vitebsk, 14b; also see *Tzava'as HaRivash* 29).

"And the sound of a rustling leaf shall pursue them . . ." (*Vayikra* 26:36). The holy Rabbi Uri of Strelisk said in the name of the Baal Shem Tov that this verse alludes to those who do not study Torah *lishmah* (for its own sake)—particularly those who do for intellectual sport. As Tosefos states, it would have been better for such people never to have been born.[25] "The sound of a rustling (*nidaf*) leaf shall pursue them . . ." The *daf* (page) of the *Gemara*, the leaf [of the holy text], shall pursue them [in vengeance] (*Ohr Tzaddikim, Likkutim,* cited in *Sefer Baal Shem Tov, Bechukosai*).

One may experience a greater degree of *deveykus* while speaking [with others] than while engaged in Torah study. While speaking one

---

22. *Tehillim* 111:10.

23. *Chovos HaLevavos, Hakdamah.*

24. *Sha'ar HaMitzvos, Va'eschanan,* 33a; *Sha'ar Ruach HaKodesh* 11b; *Pri Eitz Chaim, Hanhagas HaLimud,* 83b.

25. *Tosefos on Pesachim* 50b.

must concentrate on cleaving to God, may He be blessed. [However], while studying, one must think about the subject before him, and through this he will be enabled to cleave to God, as is proper.

It is necessary to engage in Torah study assiduously, for it is "a Tree of Life to all who grasp it."[26] But when one speaks only of mundane matters and relies upon his *deveykus*, he must be careful not to [let himself] occasionally fall from his state of cleaving to God. In speech, too, there are aspects of greatness and smallness. At times one may be attached to the Creator in a state of smallness, and, at other times, in a state of greatness. [On the other hand, when one studies Torah in an uninspired state, he is still attached to God] (*Likkutim Yekarim* 51; *Tzava'as HaRivash* 30).

When one studies Torah, he must bear in mind before Whom he studies. Sometimes one can actually distance himself from the Creator through [improper] Torah study. Therefore, one must be aware of this at all times (*Tzava'as HaRivash* 54).

When one studies Torah, he should recall the words of the Talmud, "Since the destruction of the Holy Temple, no place remains for the Holy One, blessed be He, in His world but the four *amos* (cubits) of *halachah* (Torah law)."[27] And he should reflect, "Does not [the Creator] constrict Himself and dwell right here?" Then he will study with joy, reverence and love of God (*Tzava'as HaRivash* 119).

"The words of his mouth are iniquity and deceit; he has ceased using his intellect to do good" (*Tehillim* 36:4). That is, the words of the Evil Inclination's mouth are iniquity and deceit. However, the Evil Inclination certainly does not try to entice a person to stop studying Torah entirely, for it knows he would not listen to its advice. After all, if one

---

26. *Mishlei* 3:18.
27. *Berachos* 8a.

did not study Torah, he would no longer have any social status; no one would call him a *lamdan* (an expert scholar). Instead, the Evil Inclination tells him not to study anything that might instill fear of Heaven in his heart, such as *mussar* (ethical works) or the *Shulchan Aruch*, in order to gain a practical knowledge of Torah law. Rather, he should spend all his time studying the *Gemara* with all its commentaries in order to flaunt his mental prowess.

Thus, the verse concludes, "He has ceased," i.e., the Evil Inclination has caused him to cease, "using his intellect to do good." That is, it deters him from also engaging in the kind of study which brings a person to improve himself [by instilling within him] the fear of Heaven[28] (*Tzava'as HaRivash* 117).

"For I have given you a good teaching; do not forsake My Torah" (*Mishlei* 4:2). The "good teaching" refers to the revealed aspect of the Torah. Concerning this, it is possible to think that it has been given "to you" and thus forget about the One who gave the Torah. One looks for legal loopholes, one asks questions. But when it is "My Torah,"—when one [also] studies the inner dimension of Torah and believes in Divine Providence—then he will surely fulfill [the latter half of the verse], "do not forsake it"[29] (*Sefer HaSichos* 5702, p. 128).

Rabbi Nosson of Nemirov once told his disciple, Rabbi Nachman of Tulchin, "The Baal Shem Tov said that he came to the world just to do away with the ill-tempered Torah scholar" (*Avanehah Barzel* 41).

---

28. See *Zohar* III, 253a; *Likkutei Moharan* 28:1.
29. See *Likkutei Moharan* I:31.

Trust in God

Once [Rabbi Nachman of Breslev] was discussing the subject of trust in God and remarked: There are some *tzaddikim* who do not let any money remain in their possession from one day to the next. This was true of many of our predecessors, such as the Baal Shem Tov and the *tzaddik*, our holy master, Rabbi Elimelech [of Lizhensk], and others like them. Each day they would distribute all of their money, not leaving any of it for the following day (*Chayei Moharan* 499).

[The Baal Shem Tov taught]: A person's thoughts should be in the Supernal World, engaged in Divine service [and not sunken in mundane matters]. One should attach himself to God and trust that he will obtain whatever he needs (*Tzava'as HaRivash* 24).

One should contemplate that "the whole world is full of His glory,"[1] and that the *Shechinah* is always with him. [God] is the Subtlest of the subtle, the Master of all that transpires in the world, and He can accomplish whatever one desires. Therefore, one should not trust in anything but God, may He be blessed[2] (*Tzava'as HaRivash* 137).

"Rabbi Shimon bar Yochai and his son, Rabbi Elazar, were forced to go into hiding for teaching Torah during the Roman occupation of the land of Israel. After sitting in a cave for twelve years . . . they went out and saw a man tilling the earth. Rabbi Shimon exclaimed, "These people have put aside eternal life in favor of the transitory!" Wherever he gazed, a fire came forth and destroyed it . . ." (*Shabbos* 32b).

The Baal Shem Tov explained: Rabbi Shimon knew that even when he had been confined to a cave, God provided him with sustenance. Thus,

---

1. *Yeshayahu* 6:3.
2. R. Avraham ben HaRambam devotes an entire chapter to this subject in his *Sefer HaMaspik L'Ovdei HaShem*. Also note *Sichos HaRan* 2.

he looked [in disfavor] upon people who did not involve themselves in Torah study [and instead pursued physical livelihood].

"A Heavenly voice ordered Rabbi Shimon and his son to return to the cave for another twelve months. When they emerged a second time, they saw an old man hurrying along, holding two sprigs of myrtle in honor of Shabbos . . ." (ibid.)

[Honoring the Shabbos showed that the mundane acts of ordinary people need not entail putting aside eternal life.] Thereupon, Rabbi Shimon ceased to be distressed (*Ohr Yitzchak, Vayeitzei*).

Truth

"Truth will sprout from the earth" (*Tehillim* 85:12). When one is like the earth, which allows everyone to walk upon it, the seed of truth can sprout.

[The Baal Shem Tov] also remarked on this verse, "If someone sees something valuable lying on the ground, he immediately picks it up. Why doesn't anyone pick up [the truth]? Really, everyone wants to—but no one is willing to stoop so low" (*Geulas Yisrael*).

The Baal Shem Tov once told his disciples: "My children, you only need to be very careful not to lie, and you will surely become good people" (*Imrei Pinchos* 878).

Our master, the Baal Shem Tov, pointed out that the eye fools a person. [Regarding a Heavenly vision], the *Gemara* states, "I see an upside-down world: the above is below, and the below is above" (*Pesachim* 50a). The same thing may be seen in this world: the "above" is not truly superior, and the "below" is not truly inferior (*Sefer HaMa'amarim* 5710, cited in *Kesser Shem Tov, Hosafos, Masechtas Pesachim*, 75).

There is a popular saying: "With the truth, a person can go all over the world." The Baal Shem Tov explained, "That's because he will get thrown out of one place after another" (*Toldos Yaakov Yosef*, Bo, 46b, cited in *Sefer Baal Shem Tov*, Vayeira 10).

During the period of opposition to the Baal Shem Tov, a woman once attempted to pick up a rock in order to throw it at him. Due to the stone's heaviness, she was unable to lift it. "Master of the World," she prayed aloud, "May it be accounted before You as if I had thrown it at him." The Baal Shem Tov said, "In Heaven, this woman's sincerity has caused great delight" (*Siach Sarfei Kodesh* III:641).

Tzaddik

"A Heavenly voice came forth and proclaimed: 'The entire world is sustained because of Chanina, My son. And as for Chanina, My son, a *kav* of carobs suffices for him from one *erev* Shabbos to the next'" (*Taanis* 24b).

The Baal Shem Tov explained this passage from the *Gemara* as follows: The *tzaddik* is like a *sh'vil* (conduit) and a channel which draws forth various effluences. By means of his holy actions, [the *tzaddik*] draws forth blessings to the world. And just as a channel does not benefit from that which passes through it, so does the *tzaddik* only wish to give to others. Thus, the Heavenly voice proclaimed: "The entire world is sustained *bish'vil* (because of) Chanina, My son . . ." That is, the world is sustained by the *sh'vil* (conduit) made by Chanina. And like a conduit and a channel which does not seek its own benefit, he was content with the barest minimum. "A *kav* of carobs suffices for him . . ."[1] (*Avodas Yisrael, Likkutim, Taanis*).

"Righteous (*tzaddik*) is God in all His ways . . ." (*Tehillim* 145:17). If one is a *tzaddik* and binds himself to the Creator, then God will be with him in all his ways (*Ohr HaEmes* 37b; attributed in a manuscript version to the Baal Shem Tov).

"This is the Gate to the Lord; *tzaddikim* . . ." (*Tehillim* 118:20). That is, the *tzaddikim* are the gate to the Lord (*Butzina D'Nehora*).

"Day to day, speech flows . . ." (*Tehillim* 19:3). The Baal Shem Tov rendered this interpretively: Each day boasts to the next about a good deed a *tzaddik* performed on it (*Divrei Shalom, Ki Sisa*, cited in *Sefer Baal Shem Tov, Emor* 2).

---

1. See *Likkutei Halachos, Orach Chaim, Hilchos Taanis* 3:2.

All of a person's spiritual attainments—whether in the perfection of his character traits or his speech—are possible only because of the *tzaddikim* and leaders of the generation. The *tzaddik* can elevate everything.[2]

The *tzaddik* can elevate certain individuals through his Torah study and prayer. However, there are others he can elevate only through the informal remarks he makes while traveling . . . Even his ordinary remarks have a purpose, although they may seem to be of no consequence.[3] In truth, the *tzaddik* elevates the person with whom he speaks by his mundane words. This is what I heard from my grandfather (the Baal Shem Tov); but few men are able to do this[4] (*Degel Machaneh Ephraim, Metzora*).

The Baal Shem Tov taught: Why are only Avraham, Yitzchak and Yaakov called the Patriarchs, and why is the merit of our ancestors primarily identified with them? Because throughout their lives, their Divine service and prayers were for the sake of their entire generation and for all generations to come (*Ohr HaGanuz L'Tzaddikim, Ki Setzei*).

The holy *Zohar* mentions several Tannaim, such as Rabbi Hamnuna Saba and his son, whose souls came back [to this world] after death in order to teach the secrets of Torah to Rabbi Shimon bar Yochai and his disciples. Others, however, did not return after death, even as souls.

The Baal Shem Tov explained: If during his lifetime, a *tzaddik* always prayed and served God for the sake of his generation, then even after death, he remains the same, and [his soul] comes back to spiritually perfect the generation by teaching them Torah, etc. The holy *Zohar* states, "Moshe Rabbeinu's influence extends through the generations . . . to every sage and *tzaddik*."[5] This is because he exerted himself selflessly

---

2. See *Likkutei Moharan* I, 2:6; 10:2–4; 13:5–6; 22:4; ibid., II:7; *Sichos HaRan* 111.
3. *Sukkah* 21b.
4. See *Likkutei Moharan* I:81; ibid., II:91.
5. *Tikkunei Zohar, Tikkun* 69.

on behalf of the entire Jewish people. [Moshe prayed,] "If you will forgive their sin—and if not, please blot me out of the book which You have written."[6] Therefore, after his death, he continues to spiritually perfect every sage and *tzaddik*, and through him the entire generation is rectified[7] (*Ohr HaGanuz L'Tzaddikim, Ki Seitzei*).

"The *tzaddik* knows the nature of his beast, but the mercy of the wicked is cruel" (*Mishlei* 12:10). The word *yodei'a* (knows) implies attachment [as in the verse, "Adam knew Chava, his wife"[8]]. Thus, [the proverb] means that the *tzaddik* can bind even his own animal nature to the service of the Creator (*Tzava'as HaRivash* 99).

"The *tzaddik* will blossom like a date palm; like a cedar of Lebanon he will grow tall" (*Tehillim* 72:13). There are two types of *tzaddikim*—they are both perfect *tzaddikim*, yet there is a difference between them. The first *tzaddik* is continually in a state of *deveykus* and serves the Creator as he should. But he is only a *tzaddik* unto himself, not for others. He does not impart his spirituality to anyone else. Thus, he is like the cedar, of which our Sages state that it does not bear fruit.[9] He is a *tzaddik* by himself and does not "bear fruit" by influencing others for the good and by increasing the number of *tzaddikim* in the world. He only works on himself; nevertheless, "he will grow tall" and receive a great reward.

However, the second *tzaddik* is compared to the date palm, which does produce fruit. He will blossom; he will extract "the precious from the vile"[10] and cause virtue to blossom and increase in the world. Thus, our Sages taught, "In the place where *baalei teshuvah* (penitents) stand, even perfect *tzaddikim* cannot stand."[11] The second type of *tzaddik* is called a *baal teshuvah*—literally, "a master of penitence"—because he

---

6. *Ki Sissa* 32:32.

7. See *Likkutei Halachos, Choshen Mishpat, Sh'luchin* 5:13–18; ibid., *Orach Chaim, B'tzias HaPas* 5:30; ibid., *Yoreh De'ah, Basar V'Chalav* 5:1; *Korcha U'Kisivas Ka'akah* 3:3.

8. *Bereishis* 4:1.

9. *Taanis* 25b; *Bamidbar Rabba* 3:1.

10. *Yirmiyahu* 15:19.

11. *Berachos* 34b.

returns others to the good. He brings many other people to renounce transgression and effects an awakening of *teshuvah* in the world. His reward is far greater than that of the first type, even though he, too, is a perfect *tzaddik* (*Tzava'as HaRivash* 125).

"And he brought back all the wealth and also Lot . . ." (*Bereishis* 14:16). The *Ohr HaChaim* (Rabbi Chaim ibn Attar) asks why this verse does not first mention Lot and then his wealth. According to my humble understanding, this difficulty may be resolved by examining a previous verse.

"And they took Lot and his wealth, the son of the brother of Avram, and they departed . . ."[12] One might also ask why the Torah does not state that Lot was Avram's brother's son before it mentions his wealth. [This would be more correct grammatically.] I saw in a Kabbalistic text that the initial letters of the three words *R'chusho Ben Achi* ("his wealth, the son of the brother") spell the name "Rava" [one of the Talmudic sages].[13] This alludes to the fact that Lot possessed a holy spark of the soul of Rava, and this was his true wealth.[14]

"And he brought back all the wealth . . ."[15] In other words, [Avram brought back] the precious and holy spark of Rava's soul, which had been captive among the forces of impurity, and returned it to its source in the realm of holiness.

"And also Lot . . ." For [Lot] was subordinate to the soul of the *tzaddik* (Rava) . . .[16]

My grandfather (the Baal Shem Tov) taught that every *tzaddik* has holy sparks that are related to the root of his soul, and it is his task to rectify and elevate them. Even his servants, livestock, and possessions contain holy sparks, which he must rectify and elevate to their source.

---

12. *Bereishis* 14:12.

13. *Likkutei Torah of the Ari z"l, Lech Lecha.*

14. Wealth, as understood in the present context, is an intrinsic part of Lot. Thus, the verse actually puts the phrase, "the son of the brother of Avram," in its proper place. The question was only valid if "wealth" meant material possessions. (Also, the acronym R-B-A must emerge from this particular juxtaposition of words.)

15. *Bereishis* 14:16.

16. This explains why "all the wealth" is mentioned before "Lot." According to this Kabbalistic interpretation, Lot's wealth was the precious spark of Rava's soul.

[He also taught that] a person's source is his soul; and one's soul is identical with his name.

Rabbi Nachman Horodenker [a close disciple of the Baal Shem Tov] related this concept to the verse, "And whatever the man would call every living creature (*nefesh chayah*), that was its name."[17] This verse could also be read to mean that the *nefesh chayah*, the inner vitality and soul of a person, is identical with his name.

If you will carefully examine the verse, "And they took Lot and his wealth, the son of the brother of Avram . . ." you will find a basis for our words. For [Lot and his possessions] were sparks of the *tzaddik's* soul; and [Avram] was required to rectify and elevate them to their source. [Therefore, the Torah places the words, "and they took Lot and his wealth, the son of his brother . . ." before "Avram," because they all were spiritually related to the root of the latter's soul[18]] (*Degel Machaneh Ephraim, Lech Lecha*).

At times a person is inspired in Torah study and prayer; he feels like singing praises to the Creator, may He be blessed, and does not know what has come over him. However, he has experienced this arousal because of the *tzaddikim*, who, in their great holiness, light up the hearts of the people of their generation. The illumination of their holiness is what causes him to experience a spiritual awakening. (*Maharid, Chukas*, cited in *Meir Einei Yisrael* p. 178).

"[Rabbi Chanina ben Dosa] used to say: 'If the spirit of one's fellow-man is pleased with him, the spirit of the Omnipresent One is pleased

---

17. *Bereishis* 2:19.

18. According to *gematria*, the name "Avraham" (248) is equivalent to "Rava" (203) plus "Lot" (45). This alludes to the fact that Rava and Lot were both parts of him. Similarly, all other subordinate souls and possessions would be related to his name by other Kabbalistic letter-permutations, etc. However, the author indicates that the simple meaning of "his possessions" still stands firm: for these "holy sparks" are nevertheless bound up with the *tzaddik's* actual physical belongings until they have received their *tikkun* (spiritual rectification) (R. Shmuel Teich).

with him. But if the spirit of one's fellow-man is not pleased with him, the spirit of the Omnipresent One is not pleased with him'" (*Avos* 3:13).

Man is called a "small world." [This applies not only to man as an individual but to the collective body of mankind.] One person is [comparable to] a head and another to a foot; and some are called the heads of the generation and the "eyes of the congregation." When the heads of the generation make themselves a vehicle for the indwelling of the *Shechinah*, this [revelation] extends to the rest of the generation. Thus the Mishnah uses the term *nochah heymenu*—literally, "rests because of him"—to indicate that the spirit of one's fellow-man is pleased with him. The spirit of the Omnipresent One rests upon the entire world because of him. Therefore, the spirit of his fellow-man is pleased with him.

The converse is also true. If there is no indwelling of the *Shechinah*, one should not attribute this lack to the generation, but only to oneself. Thus, the latter part of the Mishnah states that [when the spirit of one's fellow-man is not pleased with him,] the spirit of the Omnipresent One *einah nochah heymenu*—literally, "does not rest because of him." In other words, he himself has brought about this state of affairs (*Toldos Yaakov Yosef, Acharei*).

The Baal Shem Tov taught: How is it possible for the *tzaddik* to arouse the hearts of the Jewish people to *teshuvah* and to benefit them in every way? How can a perfect *tzaddik* have any connection or relationship with such [ordinary] people? The answer is related to the teaching of our Sages that "all Israel are guarantors for one another."[19] This applies particularly to those who are close to [the *tzaddik*], who are like branches attached to their source. [However,] since all the Jewish people are mutual guarantors, they each share a portion of the *tzaddik's* purity. Thus, [the *tzaddik*] has the power to arouse them to *teshuvah*, to awaken Divine mercy on behalf of the Jewish people, and to sweeten all severe judgments against them[20] (*Nahar Shalom,* cited in *Meir Einei Yisrael,* p. 184).

---

19. *Rosh Hashanah* 29a.
20. See *Likkutei Moharan* I:13 ("*hiskabtzus hanefashos*"); 34:4; ibid., II:42 ("*chirik*").

"These are the accounts of the Tabernacle of the Testimony, as they were accounted according to the commandment of Moshe . . ." (*Shemos* 38:21). Throughout this section of the Torah, after describing each particular task related to the Tabernacle and its vessels, it states, "As God commanded Moshe." Why did this need to be repeated after every task? Could it not have summarily stated at the end, "And it was done as God commanded Moshe"?

However, [in this way] the Torah alludes to an important principle in Divine service and the performance of *mitzvos* in general. Whether it be [the *mitzvah* of] *shofar* or Pesach or *tefillin*, etc., everything possesses three aspects: action, word, and desire (which is the aspect of thought). The *kavanah* (mystical intention) within each *mitzvah* or prayer is great and awesome, and few, even among the loftiest individuals, possess the least insight into the *kavanos* of the Men of the Great Assembly when they composed the prayer service. This also applies to the *kavanos* of the *mitzvos*.

In truth, every member of the Jewish people must participate in all three aspects. From the action of each *mitzvah* a garment is made for the soul in the lower Garden of Eden. From the *kavanah* within each *mitzvah* a garment is made for the soul in the upper Garden of Eden. In order to accomplish this, one must bind his *kavanah* together with those other Jews, whose faith is complete and who know the mysteries of the *kavanos* appropriate to each act of Divine service as established by the Men of the Great Assembly. [This applies to both] prayer and the performance of *mitzvos*, to one's *kavanah* while eating during the week and all the more so during the three meals of Shabbos.

Thus, the Ari taught that before one prays it is necessary to mention the positive *mitzvah* to love one's fellow as oneself.[21] In this way, one can bind his *kavanah* and prayer together with those who know how to unify the supernal Divine attributes.

The *kavanah* of constructing the Tabernacle entailed binding one's thoughts to the construction of the Supernal Tabernacle. On the phrase, "The Tabernacle was erected . . ."[22] our Sages taught, "When the Tabernacle was erected below, it was erected Above."[23] This was accomplished by the thoughts and *kavanos* corresponding to the physical components

---

21. *Sha'ar HaKavanos, Birchos HaShachar.*
22. *Shemos* 40:17.
23. *Tanchuma, Naso* 18; *Zohar* II, *Pekudei*, 240a.

of the Tabernacle below. Spiritually, the intention was to build a Supernal Tabernacle. [This touches upon the deepest] mysteries of the
creation of heaven and earth and all the worlds. However, not every
mind can grasp this. Therefore, with each act of constructing the Tabernacle, [the Torah] clearly states that we acted according to the
kavanah that God commanded Moshe. [Only he was capable of these
lofty intentions.]

This is also why before performing any *mitzvah* [it is customary to
recite the prayer of Moshe], "May the pleasantness of my Master, our
God, be upon us, and the work of our hands established for us—and
the work of our hands, establish it."[24] [In this way, we bind our thoughts
and actions to Moshe, whose prayer, in turn, supplicates the Creator on
behalf of the Jewish people] (*Ben Poras Yosef, Hakdamah,* as cited in *Sefer
Baal Shem Tov, Pekudei,* 1).

"Warm yourself by the fire of the Sages, but beware of their glowing embers, lest you be burned . . . for all their words are like coals of
fire" (*Avos* 2:10).

The Baal Shem Tov taught: [The text of this Mishnah seems prob-
lematic.] If embers are by definition glowing, why does [the Mishnah]
subsequently need to employ the phrase "coals of fire"? And if the embers
have burned out, why must one be careful to avoid being hurt by them?
Have they not already become cold?

[However, the matter is as follows.] Sometimes even a perfect
tzaddik falls from his spiritual level and must serve God in a state of
constricted consciousness. That is, he does not pray and study with
intense concentration [but] spends his time involved in ordinary pursuits. Upon seeing that the *tzaddik* cannot pray or study Torah with any
particular inspiration and even seems to waste his time, one might conclude, "If the *tzaddik* can act this way, so can I!"

That is why the Mishnah warned that one should not put himself
on the same plane as the Sages and *tzaddikim.* For when the *tzaddik*
awakens from his spiritual sleep and begins to study and pray as before,

---

24. *Tehillim* 90:17. Concerning the role of the *tzaddik* in elevating the prayers of
the Jewish people, see *Likkutei Moharan* I, 2:6, 9:3. This is also the reason for the custom to declare before praying or performing any *mitzvah,* "I bind myself to the *tzaddikim*
of the generation . . ." as recommended in *Sichos HaRan* 296.

then all the idle words he spoke and all the mundane deeds he performed will ascend Above, as is known [to those familiar with the Kabbalistic doctrine] concerning the ascent of the holy sparks hidden in even the lowest things. But an ordinary person who does not know the first thing about the inner world of Divine service, how could his heart ever persuade him to compare himself to the *tzaddik*?

Thus, the Mishnah states, "Beware of their glowing embers . . ." Even when they have fallen from their spiritual level and are like burned-out embers, i.e., they speak and act in an ordinary manner, be careful not to emulate them. "For all their words are like coals of fire." Even their mundane words will be like coals of fire when they awaken from their spiritual sleep[25] (*Tzava'as HaRivash* 96).

In every generation there must be *tzaddikim*, "foundations of the world," of whom it is written, "Light is sown for the righteous (*tzaddik*) and joy for the pure of heart."[26] [They must exist,] for all beneficial influences come through the *tzaddik*. This was revealed to us by the Baal Shem Tov, whose light fills the world; indeed, without attachment to the Sages of the generation, we would not be able to endure at all[27] (*Tiferes Shlomo, Vayeishev*).

Rabbi Mordechai of Lechovitch once said, "Ever since the Baal Shem Tov came to the world, no one is able to fulfill his potential in Divine service, however great his efforts, without a *rebbe*"[28] (*Toras Avos, Hiskashrus L'Tzaddikim*).

I heard from the Rav of Polonoye and the Rav of our community (Rabbi Gedaliah of Linitz) that the Baal Shem Tov said, "When one recounts the praises of the *tzaddikim*, it is as if he engages in the mysteries

---

25. See *Likkutei Moharan* II:116.
26. *Tehillim* 97:11.
27. See *Likkutei Moharan* I:8; ibid., 240.
28. See ibid. I:17, I:30, II:39.

of the *Ma'aseh Merkavah* (the mystical experience)"[29] (*Shiv'chei Baal Shem Tov* 158).

Rabbi Nachman [of Breslev] said: Many mysteries and lofty matters are contained in the stories that the world tells. These stories, however, are deficient, for they leave out many things. They are also confused, and people don't tell them in the right order. [Sometimes,] what begins a story should be told at the end, and so forth. Nevertheless, the folk tales that the world tells contain extremely lofty sublime mysteries.

The Baal Shem Tov, of blessed memory, was able to bring about a mystical unification (*yichud*) through telling a story. When he perceived that the supernal channels were defective, and it was not possible to rectify them through prayer, he would rectify and unify them by telling a story (*Sippurei Ma'asios, Hakdama*).

The Baal Shem Tov taught that every day one should tell a friend a story about the deeds of a *tzaddik* (*Divrei Shalom*).

---

29. Rabbi Menachem Mendel of Rimanov explained that a story ("*ma'aseh*") about a *tzaddik* is comparable to the *Ma'aseh Merkavah*, because, as the Kabbalists state, "the *tzaddikim* are the *Merkavah* (Divine Chariot)" (*Gan Hadasim* 2b).

II

Customs of the Baal Shem Tov

Although the following collection is by no means complete, it represents those customs and specific practices of the Baal Shem Tov for which we were able to find reliable sources. Virtually all Chasidic traditions agree that the Baal Shem Tov generally followed the viewpoint of the *Zohar* and the Ari *z"l*. However, many of his customs were simply those of the communities in which he lived. Almost as soon as he passed away, a host of diverse customs and approaches to Divine service developed within the Chasidic movement, reflecting the views of subsequent leaders who lived in various parts of Eastern Europe. Inevitably, many traditions were lost or became subject to dispute. Thus, although every contemporary Chasidic group follows some of the Baal Shem Tov's customs, no one knows or observes them all.

All Jewish customs rooted in *halachah* are meaningful and holy. In this sense, preoccupation with such matters would seem to be unwarranted. On the other hand, by preserving and emulating customs of the *tzaddikim* with whom we feel an affinity, we reinforce our bond of attachment to them. As such, our customs reflect the beauty of the Jewish way of life and the way it is transmitted from one generation to the next. It is in this spirit that these customs of the Baal Shem Tov are presented.

Arising From Sleep

One should cultivate the trait of alacrity (*z'rizus*) and wake up from sleep with enthusiasm, for he has been created anew and has become a different person, fit to engender, like the Holy One, blessed be He, who engenders worlds. Whatever a person does should be with alacrity, for one may serve God with everything that exists[1] (*Tzava'as HaRivash* 20).

This is a basic principle: According to the first thought one conceives upon arising from bed, so goes the rest of the day—and with no other thought (*Tzava'as HaRivash* 25).

---

1. Also see *Shnei Luchos HaBris* II, *Acharei; Kuntres Poke'ach Ivrim* III:1.

Tikkun Chatzos

The Baal Shem Tov strongly urged his followers to awaken at midnight in order to mourn the destruction of the Holy Temple and the exile of the Jewish people, as is stressed in the *Zohar* and the works of the Ari z"l[1] (*Tzava'as HaRivash* 16; *Kesser Shem Tov* 205).

---

1. See *Shulchan Aruch, Orach Chaim,* 1:3; *Zohar* III, *Acharei,* 68a; ibid., *Balak,* 46a; *Zohar Chadash, Balak,* 23b; *Sha'ar HaKavanos, D'rushei HaLayla* 6, 54b; ibid., *D'rush Tikkun Chatzos,* 58b. Also see *Likkutei Moharan* I:149; ibid. II:67; *Avodas Yisrael, Haftoras Vayeira; Siddur Shel HaBaal HaTanya, Seder Hashkamas HaBoker; R. Yeshaya Asher Zelig Margolius, Sefer Kumi Roni* (printed together with *Sefer Shimush Chachamim*).

Mikveh

The Baal Shem Tov said that every spiritual level he had reached was due to his diligence in purifying himself by immersing in a *mikveh*. The regular use of a *mikveh* is more efficacious than fasting, which weakens the body and [adversely effects one's] Divine service. It is better to use the strength one would have lost by fasting by studying Torah or praying with enthusiasm and *kavanah*. In this way, one can attain a high spiritual level[1] (*Likkutim Yekarim* 178).

In the winter, at times he would even break the ice in order to immerse in a nearby stream (*Sippurei Baal Shem Tov*).

The Baal Shem Tov stressed the importance of observing the decree of Ezra HaSofer [to don *tefillin* and pray in a state of ritual purity]. He once remarked that if one needs to immerse in a *mikveh*, and it is difficult to do so because of the cold, etc., he should immerse one time, and no harm will befall him (*Mishmeres Shalom* 2; *Shulchan HaTahor, Hilchos Krias Shema* 88:2).

He also cautioned that, in any event, one should never let three days pass without immersing in a *mikveh* (*Even HaShoham* 7).

The Baal Shem Tov once said: A *shochet* (ritual slaughterer) who needs to immerse in a *mikveh* [to fulfill the decree of Ezra HaSofer] and

---

1. The Baal Shem Tov's *kavanos* for immersing in the *mikveh* may be found in *Sefer Baal Shem Tov, Yisro; Kesser Shem Tov* 2; *Siddur Shel HaBaal HaTanya, He'aros U'Maftechos*, 5a. His *kavanos* for washing one's hands when one cannot immerse in a *mikveh* are given in *Tzava'as HaRivash*, 28b. However, it should be stressed that such practices are not meant for the ordinary person.

does not do so will fail to notice if his knife becomes defective (*Ner Yisrael* III, *Tzaddik*, p. 173).

He once said, "When a person immerses in a *mikveh* in the morning, the Holy One, blessed be He, accounts it to him as if he had fasted one day" (*Sippurei Tzaddikim HeChadash* 16).

He also said that immersing in a cold *mikveh* can nullify a Heavenly decree of death [may the Merciful One spare us] (*Sur Mei'ra* 7).

I heard [from Rabbi Yaakov Yosef of Polonoye] that the Baal Shem Tov once asked him, "Why do you remain in the *mikveh* for so long? When I go to the *mikveh*, I just close my eyes once and behold all the worlds" (*Shiv'chei Baal Shem Tov* 170).

The Baal Shem Tov taught: Prophecy cannot exist outside of the Land of Israel—except in a place of water. Thus, Yechezkel HaNavi spoke words of prophecy while standing in the River Khebar, even though he was not in the Land of Israel (*Degel Machaneh Ephraim, Bo*).

Mezuzah

I heard in the name of the Baal Shem Tov that one should not place a *mezuzah* in an iron case. [Concerning the prohibition to touch the altar-stone in the Holy Temple with an iron implement], our Sages taught, "It is not fitting to associate that which shortens [life] with that which lengthens [life]."[1] Similarly, concerning the *mitzvah* of *mezuzah*, it is written, "In order that you should increase your days . . ."[2] Moreover, one should not use any sort of metal [case for the *mitzvah* of *mezuzah*][3] (*Da'as Kedoshim, Hilchos Mezuzah* 287:1, cited in *Sefer Baal Shem Tov, Va'eschanan,* 85).

---

1. *Middos* 3:4.

2. *Devarim* 11:21.

3. It is unclear whether the Baal Shem Tov or the anonymous disciple who preserved this custom extended it to include all metal coverings.

Tzitzis

The Baal Shem Tov taught that one should make knots at the ends of the strings of one's *tzitzis*. Not only does this prevent them from unraveling, but it bears Kabbalistic significance. The sum of these knots (32) plus the five doubled knots on each of the four *tzitzis* (40) equals seventy-two. This is the *gematria* (numerical value) of the word *chesed* (kindness). However, one should not tie them on the same day as the *tzitzis* themselves, in keeping with the ruling of the Magen Avraham[1] (*Midrash Pinchos* 13, cited in *Sefer Baal Shem Tov, Shelach*, 4).

---

1. *Shulchan Aruch, Orach Chaim* 11:23, ad loc.

Tefillin

The Baal Shem Tov was particular to put on his *tefillin* at the beginning of the prayer service, prior to reciting the first paragraph of *Shema* and *Korbanos* (sacrificial offerings) (*Pe'er L'Yesharim* 78; *Ta'amei HaMinhagim, Birchos HaShachar*).

He was accustomed to tie the strap of the *tefillah shel yad* on his upper arm in the form of the Hebrew letter *shin*, winding the strap away from himself in the manner of the Sephardim[1] (*Trisker Maggid*, as cited in *Sefer Baal Shem Tov, Va'eschanan*, 84).

He recited a separate blessing on each *tefillah*, following the view of the Ashkenazim.[2] Since he felt that there was no question about this, he did not recite the words, *Baruch shem k'vod malchuso l'olam va'ed.* (However, the Maggid of Mezeritch recited only one blessing, following the view of the Ari z"l)[3] (*Shulchan HaTahor, Hilchos Tefillin* 25:4, *Ze'er Zahav* 3; *Beis Rizhin*).

---

1. This custom or variations of it are also mentioned in *Likkutei Maharich, Tefillin; Siddur HaAri of Rabbi Shabbsai of Rashkov*, based on *Pri Eitz Chaim, Sha'ar HaTefillin* 10, 24a; *Siddur Tefillah Yesharah of Rabbi Aharon of Zelichov, Seder Hanachas Tefillin; Sefer HaMinhagim Chabad*. However, see *Shulchan HaTahor* 27:2, which contends that this only applies to one who puts on the *tefillin* of Rashi and Rabbeinu Tam simultaneously.

2. See the Rama on *Shulchan Aruch* 25:5; also *Zohar Chadash, Tikkunim*, 119b; *Midrash Tanchuma, Bo; Tosefos on Menachos* 36a.

3. *Sha'ar HaKavanos, D'rushei Tefillas HaShachar* 3, 12b. Also, see Rashi on *Menachos* 36a; *Berachos* 60b; *Mishneh Torah, Hilchos Tefillin* 5; *Shulchan Aruch, Hilchos Tefillin* 25:5.

Prayer

The Baal Shem Tov instructed his disciples to study a section of the holy *Zohar* every morning before praying[1] (Rabbi Mordechai of Tchernoble, *Likkutei Torah, Hadrachah* 7).

Some individuals are accustomed to drink tea before the morning prayer service in order to concentrate better. Concerning this practice the Baal Shem Tov once remarked, "It would be better for them to stir up their prayers than to stir up their tea beforehand"[2] (R. Levi Yitzchak Bender, *Siach Sarfei Kodesh* II, 1–57).

He prayed at the earliest time possible, reciting the *Shemoneh Esrei* prayer with the first light of dawn (*k'vasikin*)[3] (*Tzava'as HaRivash* 16; *Imrei Pinchas* 389).

There is a tradition among Breslever Chasidim that the Baal Shem Tov told his followers to pray together at dawn (*k'vasikin*) on five occasions in particular: Hoshana Rabbah, Purim, the seventh day of Pesach, the first day of Shavuos and Tisha B'Av[4] (*Chasidei Breslev*).

---

1. See *Imrei Pinchos, Inyanei Limud HaTorah,* 47–65; *Sichos HaRan* 108.
2. See *Shulchan Aruch, Orach Chaim* 89:3; *Be'er Heiteiv,* ad loc., 89:11; *Zohar* II, 215b; *Tzetel Katan* 11; *Sichos HaRan* 277.
3. *Shulchan Aruch, Orach Chaim* 89:1. Also see *Eishel Avraham,* ad loc., where it seems that the Baal Shem Tov prayed before HaNeitz HaChamah.
4. For a possible variant of this tradition, see *Likkutei Maharich, Shacharis Shel Rosh Hashanah.*

The Baal Shem Tov once saw one of his disciples kiss his little son. He remarked, "I love the lowest and worst Jew in the world even more than you love your only son . . ." In this spirit, the Baal Shem Tov always prayed with a *minyan* except during the period of secluded meditation (*hisbodedus*) and intensive self-purification of his youth (*Shulchan HaTahor, Hilchos Tefillah* 109:1, *Ze'er Zahav* 12).

He prayed according to the Ashkenazic prayer ritual as modified by the Kabbalistic customs of the Ari z"l.[5] The various *siddurim* which reflect these and other Chasidic modifications are today called *Nusach Sephard* or *Nusach Ari*. (These basically Ashkenazic prayer books are not to be confused with those of the Sephardic communities) (*Shulchan HaTahor, Birchos HaShachar* 46:2, *Ze'er Zahav* 5; ibid., *Hilchos Tefillah* 112:1, *Ze'er Zahav* 1; *Shiv'chei Baal Shem Tov* 211).

He also instructed his disciples to follow the Sephardic custom of adding the words, *V'yatzmach purkanei vi'karev Meshichei . . .* ("He brings forth His redemption and brings nigh his Anointed One") to the Kaddish prayer (*Shulchan HaTahor, Birchos HaShachar* 56:1, *Ze'er Zahav* 4).

Upon arriving in the synagogue in the morning, he would recite the order of blessings (*Birchos HaShachar*) according to the Ashkenazic rite. (However, the Maggid of Mezeritch recited them at home prior to *Tikkun Chatzos*, according to the Sephardic rite, following the view of the Ari z"l)[6] (*Shulchan HaTahor, Birchos HaShachar* 46:2, *Ze'er Zahav* 5; *Beis Rizhin*).

He used to begin the order of blessings with the prayer *Adon Olam* (*Shulchan HaTahor, Birchos HaShachar* 46:3, *Ze'er Zahav* 2).

---

5. *Pri Eitz Chaim, Sha'ar HaAmidah,* Chapter 20; *Sha'ar HaKavanos, Aleinu,* 50b.
6. *Sha'ar HaKavanos* 3.

The Baal Shem Tov and his disciples would only perform *nefilas apayim* (covering one's face during the *Tachanun* prayer) in the synagogue after having completed the *Shemoneh Esrei*, together with a *minyan*.[7] He also would not perform *nefilas apayim* during the *Selichos* prayers, even after sunrise. According to the Ari *z"l*, this practice is dangerous[8] (*Shulchan HaTahor, Hilchos Nefilas Apayim* 131:9).

------

7. The custom cited by the Rama on *Shulchan Aruch* 131:2 is to do so in the presence of a Sefer Torah.

8. *Siddur HaAri of R. Shabbsai of Rashkov, Nefilas Apayim.*

Studying Torah After Prayer

The Baal Shem Tov stressed the importance of studying Torah, however much or little, after praying in a state of *deveykus*. One must guard against the Forces of Unholiness, which will attempt to bring him down from his spiritual level through anger or another evil trait. But when one studies Torah after prayer, the power of the holy letters prevents these forces from having any grasp (*Kesem Ofir, Esther* 1:8; *Heichal HaB'racha, Devarim* 11a; *Degel Machaneh Ephraim, Tzav; Shulchan HaTahor* 155:1).

Tehillim

The Chabad *Rebbeim* have preserved a tradition from the Baal Shem Tov to recite the chapter of *Tehillim* (Psalms) appropriate to the number of one's years (including the present year) after concluding the *Shir Shel Yom* in the morning prayer service[1] (Letter of R. Yosef Yitzchak of Lubavitch, 9 Teves 5709, cited in *Sefer HaMinhagim Chabad*).

---

1. A similar custom existed among Breslever Chasidim in Uman, the center of this community before the Holocaust, according to Rabbi Levi Yitzchak Bender *z"l*.

Birkas HaMazon

The Baal Shem Tov was careful to pour the water used to wash his hands at the end of a meal (*mayim acharonim*) into a vessel and not under the table or onto the ground, in keeping with the ruling of Rambam[1] (*Shulchan HaTahor, Hilchos B'tzias HaPas* 181:2, *Zer Zahav* 1).

It was the custom of the Baal Shem Tov and his family to conclude the first blessing of *Birkas HaMazon* with the words, *hazan b'rachamav es hakol* ("Who sustains everyone with mercy")[2] (*Chasidei Breslev; Chasidei Skolye*).

---

1. *Mishneh Torah, Hilchos Berachos* 6:16; also *Zohar* II, *Vayakhel*, 203b.
2. See *Likkutei Maharich, Seder Birkas HaMazon*, citing Rabbi Meir ibn Gabbai's commentary on the *siddur, Tola'as Yaacov*.

Ma'ariv

He was particular to recite the verses beginning *Baruch Hashem l'olam amen v'amen* prior to the *Shemoneh Esrei* prayer during the weekday evening service, in keeping with the Ashkenazic custom (*Mishmeres Shalom* 23:2; *Imrei Pinchos* 432; *Shulchan HaTahor, Tefillas Arvis* 236:1).

Before Going to Sleep

The Baal Shem Tov taught that before sleep one should recite the words, *Havadai sh'mo, kein tehilaso*—"His name is Certainty; such is His praise," from the *Mussaf* prayer service of Rosh Hashanah. This will destroy all forces of unholiness that might seek to harm one during sleep (*Sippurei Tzaddikim* 11, cited in *Sefer Baal Shem Tov, Noach*, note 165).

Before going to sleep, one should contemplate that his consciousness is returning to the Holy One, blessed be He, in order to be strengthened anew in Divine service (*Tzava'as HaRivash* 22).

Parshas Hashavua

Before a child is born, he is taught the entire Torah.[1] I heard from my master, the Baal Shem Tov, that on Thursday nights they teach the [unborn] child the weekly Torah portion with the commentary of Rashi. Indeed, when one grows up and studies the Torah portion with the commentary of Rashi on Thursday nights, if God graces him with a good memory, he will recall the feeling he had as an infant when they taught it to him for the first time[2] (*HaTamim*, cited in *Kesser Shem Tov*, *Hosafos*, 95).

---

1. *Niddah* 30b.
2. See *Sichos HaRan* 223.

Erev Shabbos

The Baal Shem Tov instructed his followers to immerse in the mikveh every erev Shabbos [and erev Yom Tov], as well as before praying on Shabbos morning (*Sefer HaSichos* 5702, cited in *Sefer HaMinhagim Chabad*; *Siddur HaAri of Rabbi Shabbsai of Rashkov*).

The Baal Shem Tov did not use costly silver candlesticks or vessels for Shabbos or Yom Tov (*Shiv'chei Baal Shem Tov* 122).

He instituted the practice of reciting Chapter 107 of *Tehillim* ("*Hodu*") and the hymn *Yedid Nefesh* composed by Rabbi Eliezer Azkari before the erev Shabbos afternoon prayer service (*Me'or Einayim, Beshalach*; *Ateres Tzvi, Terumah*; *Siddur HaAri of Rabbi Shabbsai of Rashkov*; *Sefer HaMinhagim Chabad*; *Darkei Chaim V'Shalom* 369).

He was accustomed to begin the prayers of *Kabbalas Shabbos* in the early afternoon (*Mishmeres Shalom* 26; *Shiv'chei Baal Shem Tov* 212; *Adas Tzaddikim*).

Shabbos Kodesh

The Baal Shem Tov and his disciples dressed in white garments on Shabbos and Yom Tov in keeping with the view of the Ari z"l[1] (*Shiv'chei Baal Shem Tov* 6; *Siddur HaAri of Rabbi Shabbsai of Rashkov*; this is also one of the points of objection stated in the anti-Chasidic tract, *Zemir Aritzim*).

After filling the cup for *Kiddush*, many Chasidim are careful not to leave the wine bottle open. Some say that this alludes to the "wine" (i.e., secrets of Torah) which is put away for the *tzaddikim* in the Garden of Eden. It is said that the Baal Shem Tov revealed a Kabbalistic reason for this custom to his disciple, Rabbi Pinchos of Koretz (*Yalkut Mahariya D'Ziditchov, Hanhagos*, 52; *Tiferes Avos* 329).

He would recite the entire evening *Kiddush* for Shabbos (and Yom Tov) while standing. Also, he recited the version of the Ari z"l, which contains seventy words[2] (various Chasidic traditions).

---

1. On the subject of white garments, see *Shabbos* 25b; ibid., 114a; ibid., 119a (with Rashi, ad loc.); *Bava Kama* 59b (with *Tosephos*, ad loc.); *Kiddushin* 73a (with Rashi, ad loc.); *Sha'ar HaKavanos, Inyan Rechitza*, 63a-b; *Pri Eitz Chaim, Sha'ar HaShabbos, Perek* 4; *Ben Ish Chai, Halachos* II, *Lech Lecha*, 18; *Shulchan HaTahor, Hilchos Shabbos* 262:8; *Zohar Chai, Vayeishev* 182b; *Darchei Chaim V'Shalom, Seder Erev Shabbos*, 365; *Divrei Torah* 141:79; *Zichru Toras Moshe*, cited in *Likkutei Maharich, Hanhagos Erev Shabbos*; white garments are also discussed in *Likkutei Moharan* I, 29:3.

2. See *Zohar* I, *Hakdamah*, 5b; *Sha'ar HaKavannos, Kiddush*, 71a; *Mishnas Chasidim, Leil Shabbos* 3:7.

Following the custom of the Ari z"l, he used twelve *challos* at the Shabbos table, corresponding to the twelve loaves (*Lechem HaPanim*) used in the Holy Temple[3] (*Shiv'chei Baal Shem Tov* 6).

He greatly praised the singing of *zemiros* (religious songs) at the Shabbos table and told his followers to ignore those who disparage this custom[4] (*Mishmeres Shalom* 27, in the commentary *Hadras Shalom*).

The Baal Shem Tov loved all Jews—especially the simple Jewish masses, whose humble faith in God he often praised. He invited them to his Shabbos and Yom Tov table, and together they would sing the Shabbos *zemiros* with great joy (Rabbi Yosef Yitzchak of Lubavitch, *Igros Kodesh*).

He would dance with his followers on Shabbos nights, for this nullifies harsh Heavenly decrees. Once he remarked, "Dancing brings joy to the Supernal Family [i.e., the Creator and the Ministering Angels] and blessings to the Jewish people, along with happiness, mercy, and great kindness" (*Zera Baruch, Hosafos*).

Although he usually served fish at each Shabbos meal, in keeping with the custom of the Ari z"l, the Baal Shem Tov was particular to do so at *shalosh se'udos* (the third meal eaten at the conclusion of the holy day) (*Yishrei Lev* 4:1).

---

3. *Sha'ar HaKavannos, Inyan HaShulchan*; also see *Tikkunei Zohar, Tikkun* 47. According to *Raya Mehemna, Pinchos*, 245a, one may use four *challos* at each of the three Shabbos meals for the same purpose. This is discussed by Rabbi Yosef Chaim of Baghdad in *Halachos* II, *Vayeira* 15.

4. This custom is also mentioned by the anti-Chasidic polemicist Rabbi David Makover, cited in Rabbi Mordechai Vilnik's *Chasidim and Misnagdim*.

He and his disciples were accustomed to extend the third Shabbos meal well into the night (*Zohar Chai*, *Hakdamah*).

Melave Malka

After the *havdalah* ceremony, the Baal Shem Tov used to sit quietly, smoking his pipe, and recount what had been revealed to him on Shabbos (*Shiv'chei Baal Shem Tov* 98).

The Baal Shem Tov taught that if one lights four candles and prepares a meal in honor of *Melave Malkah*, he can rest assured that David HaMelech, peace be upon him, will be present [in spirit] at his feast. Also, he will merit to actually see David HaMelech during his lifetime. If he or a member of his family is sick or in distress, he should pray, "Master of the Universe! In the merit of David HaMelech, please answer my prayer (and then specify his request)," and surely God will help him. However, one must try to the best of his ability to prepare a meal for *Melave Malkah* every week (*Imrei Aish*).

A *segulah* attributed to the Baal Shem Tov is to eat something prepared with garlic during the *Melave Malkah* feast (*Sefer Ma'aseh Yechiel*, 16b, cited in *Sefer Baal Shem Tov*, *Yisro*, 51).

Rosh Chodesh

The Baal Shem Tov would fast on every *erev* Rosh Chodesh (*Yom Kippur Katan*) until the "birth" of the new moon (*molad*) (*Tz'ror HaChaim*).

He would recite the entire book of *Tehillim* without interruption every Rosh Chodesh (*Imrei Pinchas* 435).

It is a tradition passed down by the Maggid of Mezeritch and his disciple, Rabbi Levi Yitzchak of Berditchev, that when the Baal Shem Tov would partake of the Rosh Chodesh feast, the Seven Shepherds would join him (attributed to Rabbi Yisrael Shosek; see *Siddur Tz'losa D'Yisrael*, p. 533).

Elul

Beginning with the second day of Rosh Chodesh Elul, the Baal Shem Tov would recite three chapters of *Tehillim* every day and conclude the remaining chapters after the final prayers of Yom Kippur[1] (*Sefer HaMinhagim Chabad*).

---

1. The particular chapters corresponding to each day and to the prayer services of Yom Kippur are listed in the back of the Kehot edition of *Sefer Tehillim*.

Yomim Noraim

The Ari z"l recited the additional *piyutim* (hymns) included in the blessings before *Krias Shema* during the morning prayer service of Rosh Hashanah and Yom Kippur, as well as on other holidays. However, the Baal Shem Tov did not say them, and this has remained the common Chasidic custom (*Shulchan HaTahor, Hilchos Krias Shema* 68:2; ibid., *Hilchos Tefillah* 112:1, *Ze'er Zahav* 1).

The Baal Shem Tov personally sounded the *shofar* on Rosh HaShanah, utilizing his own Kabbalistic *kavanos*[1] (various Chasidic traditions).

---

1. These *kavanos* were preserved by his disciples and may be found in the *Siddur Shel HaBaal HaTanya, He'aros U'mafteichos,* 6a-7b; *Kiddushas Levi, Likkutim L'Rosh Hashanah,* pp. 495–497.

Rosh Hashanah

It has already become the established custom of all who follow the path of the Baal Shem Tov to sound thirty *shofar* blasts after the Torah reading, thirty blasts during the silent *Shemoneh Esrei* of *Mussaf*, thirty blasts during the Reader's Repetition of the *Mussaf Shemoneh Esrei*, and ten blasts during *Kaddish* prior to the phrase, "*Tiskabel* . . ." (*Mishmeres Shalom* 41:7, cited in *Sefer Baal Shem Tov, Rosh Hashanah V'Yom Kippur*, 44).

Yom Kippur

The Baal Shem Tov taught: Prior to the *Ne'ilah* service on Yom Kippur, one should pray from the *machzor* (holiday prayer book) in a state of constricted consciousness in order to pray the *Ne'ilah* service in a state of *deveykus* (*Tzava'as HaRivash* 39).

I heard from the sons of our saintly master, Rabbi Yaakov, may his light shine, who heard from our master, Rabbi Nachman, head of the rabbinical court of the holy community of Kolomaye, in the name of our master, the Baal Shem Tov, of blessed memory: The day after Yom Kippur is customarily called *Gott's Nomen* (God's Name) because we cease to refer to God [in the *Shemoneh Esrei* prayer] as *HaMelech HaKadosh* (the Holy King) but thenceforth call Him *HaE-l HaKadosh* (the Holy Lord)[1] (*Eishel Avraham*, Section II, *Orach Chaim* 624, cited in *Sefer Baal Shem Tov, Yom Kippur*, 51).

---

1. See *Likkutei Moharan* II:66.

Succos

Our master, the Baal Shem Tov, had a well-built, warm *succah* (*Kovetz Lubavitch 5, Sichas Chol HaMoed Succos* 5706).

The Baal Shem Tov once remarked that the beauty of his *succah* was [his guests]: the simple *kabbalas ol* ("Bearers of the Yoke of Heaven") Jews, who cause delight Above by rejoicing in the performance of *mitzvos*, due to their simple faith in God (*Sichas L'eil Succos* 5706, cited in *Kesser Shem Tov, Hosafos*, 112).

"In *succos* you shall dwell, seven days . . ." (*Vayikra* 23:22). In other words, you shall cause the Supernal Seven Days to dwell in your *succos*. These are the seven Supernal Guests (*Ushpizin*) [through whom the lights of the seven lower *sefiros* are revealed to the world] (*Likkutim Yekarim* 31b, cited in *Sefer Baal Shem Tov, Emor* 8).

Hoshanah Rabbah

It was the custom of the Baal Shem Tov to recite the *Hoshanah* supplications immediately after *Hallel* (*Rabbanei Medzhibuzh*).

Rabbi Yaacov Yitzchak, the Chozeh of Lublin, said that Eliyahu HaNavi taught our master, the Baal Shem Tov, that whoever prays with *kavanah* on the three days of Hoshanah Rabbah, Shemini Atzeres and Simchas Torah will be able to pray with *kavanah* for the entire year (*Sha'ar Yissaschar, Z'man Simchaseinu*, 32).

On Hoshanah Rabbah, the disciples of the Baal Shem Tov would come to him to discuss any questions of unusual difficulty, for at that time his mind was exceptionally lucid, and he could see "from one end of the earth to the other" (*Notzer Chesed*).

Shemini Atzeres

The Baal Shem Tov sanctified himself to such an extent that on Shemini Atzeres he did not dwell in the *succah*, like those who live in the Land of Israel. (However, the Maggid of Mezeritch did so the entire day, as stated in *Shulchan Aruch*)[1] (*Esser Oros* 70b; *Beis Rizhin*).

---

1. See *Shulchan Aruch, Orach Chaim* 668:1; *Minchas Elazar* IV, 31, *Otzar HaChaim, VaYikra* 244, *Devarim* 85, citing *Korban Nesanel* on the *Rosh, Perek Lulav V'Aravah*, 7.

Chanukah

The Baal Shem Tov used to recite the last verse of Chapter 90 of *Tehillim* (*V'hi noam . . .*) followed by Chapter 91 (*Yosheiv b'seiser . . .*) seven times while seated near the Chanukah candles. The Ramban stated that this is a *segulah* for Divine protection. According to the Tashbatz, the Chashmonaim used to recite this seven times before going into battle (*Siddur HaAri of Rabbi Shabbsai of Rashkov; Likkutei Maharich, Dinei U'Minhagei Chanukah*).

He also would recite each word of the prayer of Rabbi Nechunya ben HaKana (*Ana b'koach. . .*) seven times with a certain beautiful melody (*Zera Boruch*).

The holy Baal Shem Tov used to celebrate the eighth night of Chanukah together with his disciples. After lighting the candles, they would sing and dance and then share a festive meal (*Sippurei Baal Shem Tov*).

Shabbos Chazon

Shabbos Chazon should be observed [with joy] like every other Shabbos. This applies even when Tisha B'Av falls on Shabbos. One may eat the *shalosh seudos* meal together with one's household [or comrades] and partake of fish and meat [until shortly before sundown]. This was the practice of the Baal Shem Tov and his disciples (*Mishmeres Shalom* 40:1, based on *Shulchan Aruch* 552:10).

Pesach

On *erev* Pesach, the Baal Shem Tov and his disciples would bake *matzos mitzvah* [*matzos* to be used at the *seder* meals] while singing the words of Hallel[1] (*Shiv'chei Baal Shem Tov* 199; also see *Siddur HaAri of Rabbi Shabbsai of Rashkov, Seder Erev Pesach*).

The Baal Shem Tov and his disciples recited the full *Hallel* on the first two nights of Pesach in the synagogue after the *Ma'ariv* prayers, following the view of the Ari *z"l* and the Talmud Yerushalmi[2] (*Rabbanei Medzhibuzh*).

The Baal Shem Tov used only *shmurah matzos* throughout the Pesach holiday and was careful not to cook *matzos* with liquid or to eat those that had become wet (*gebrochts*) (various Chasidic traditions).

He would prepare a special meal, which he ate together with his disciples at the end of the last day of Pesach. Today, the Chasidim of Skolye and Breslev call this "the Baal Shem Tov's *Seudah*" and, during the meal, tell the story of the Baal Shem Tov's attempted journey to the Land of Israel and his miraculous rescue at sea. This custom was once widespread among Chasidim. According to a tradition of the Chabad Chasidim, the Baal Shem Tov called this meal "*Moshiach's Seudah*" (*Chasidei Skolye and Breslev; Sefer HaSichos* 5702, cited in *Sefer HaMinhagim Chabad*).

---

1. *Shulchan Aruch, Orach Chaim,* 458:1.
2. *Sha'ar HaKavanos, D'rushei Pesach* 3, 81b; *Yerushalmi, Arvei Pesachim, Halachah* 1; ibid., *Sofrim, Halachah* 2:9; *Shulchan Aruch, Orach Chaim* 487:4 with the gloss of R. Moshe Isserles, ad loc.

Chol Hamoed

He and his followers did not wear *tefillin* during the intermediate days of Pesach (*Chol HaMoed*), in conformity with the view of the *Zohar*[1] and many Rishonim[2] (*Imrei Pinchas* 751; *Shiv'chei Baal Shem Tov* 6; *Shulchan HaTahor, Hilchos Tefillin* 31:1, *Ze'er Zahav* 1).

---

1. *Zohar Chadash, Shir HaShirim*, 64b; also note *Sha'ar HaKavanos, Drushei Chazoras HaAmida, Drush* 2, 38b.

2. *Tosefos on Menachos* 36b; *T'shuvos HaRashba* and *Ra'avad*, as cited in *Beis Yosef, Hilchos Tefillin*, 31:2; *Shulchan Aruch*, op. cit.

Chadash (New Wheat)

The Baal Shem Tov once made a *she'eilas chalom* (dream-request) concerning the prohibition of eating from the new crop of wheat (*chadash*) at the present time. [In the days of the Holy Temple, it was Scripturally forbidden to do so until the *omer* offering had been brought on the second day of Pesach]. He was told that when the Bach (Rabbi Yoel Sirkis) passed away, the fires of *Gehenna* were cooled off in his honor for forty days. Upon awakening, the Baal Shem Tov sent for a bottle of liquor made from *chadash* and drank from it. He explained, "It is sufficient for us to rely upon the Bach, who permitted this"[1] (*Zichron Tov* 12b, cited in *Sefer Baal Shem Tov, Emor* 6).

At first the Baal Shem Tov was lenient about *chadash*. But once he was traveling with Rabbi Yechiel, after he had been appointed rabbi of Horodno, and saw that the latter was stringent about *chadash*. Then the Baal Shem Tov became stringent, too (*Imrei Pinchos* III:201, cited in *Sefer Baal Shem Tov, Emor* 7).

---

1. Note the commentary of the Bach on *Shulchan Aruch, Yoreh Deah* 293, which states: "No authority in matters of Torah law should contradict the prevailing custom, which follows those authorities who permit [the consumption of *chadash* in these times]. Whoever wishes to be strict with himself may do so as a matter of personal piety, but he should not tell others to follow his example . . ."

Sefiras Ha'Omer

The Baal Shem Tov counted the first night of the *omer* in the synagogue after the evening prayer service, not after the second *seder* meal. (However, the Maggid of Mezeritch did so after the *seder*)[1] (*Kedushas Aharon—Komarna; Beis Rizhin*).

The Baal Shem Tov and the Maggid of Mezeritch were both accustomed to lead the *minyan* in reciting the blessing and counting the *sefiras ha'omer* in the synagogue (*Kovetz Lubavitch* 11, *Sichas* 20, *Kislev* 5706).

The Baal Shem Tov did not cut his hair for the entire period of *sefiras ha'omer* until *erev* Shavuos, following the view of the Ari *z"l*.[2] (various Chasidic traditions).

---

1. In keeping with the Baal Shem Tov's view, see *Siddur Nahar Shalom* of Rabbi Shalom Sharabi and the *Siddur Shel HaBaal HaTanya, Seder Sefiras HaOmer*. However, in support of the custom to count after the second seder meal, see *Mishnas Chasidim, Masechtas HaOmer* 1:1, and Rabbi Menachem Azariah of Fano, *Mayan Ganim, Seder Shel Pesach*, 35b.
2. *Pri Eitz Chaim, Sha'ar Sefiras HaOmer* 7, 124b.

Pesach Sheini

It was the custom of all the Baal Shem Tov's disciples to celebrate Pesach Sheini by making a festive meal on the fourteenth day of Iyar. This commemorates the offering of the *Korban Pesach* (Passover sacrifice)—although it was actually eaten in the evening, on the fifteenth day of the month (*Darchei Chaim V'Shalom, Y'mei Sefiras Ha'Omer* 631).

Shavuos

The Baal Shem Tov would stay awake throughout the first night of Shavuos reciting the *Tikkun* (selections from Tanach, etc.,) following the custom of the Ari *z"l*. He would not engage in mundane speech until after the repetition of the *Mussaf Shemoneh Esrei*, for this is when all the efforts of the previous night ascend Above. Therefore, it is necessary to guard one's thoughts exceedingly (*Shiv'chei Baal Shem Tov* 211; *Siddur HaAri of R. Shabbsai of Rashkov, Seder Chag HaShavuos*).

It was his custom to pour a small glass of liquor for each of his disciples after the morning prayers on the first day of Shavuos. On one such occasion, he remarked, "I am giving *maharitch* (liquor given as a reward) for the receiving of the Torah" (*Sefer Baal Shem Tov, Ki Savo*, 12, in the footnote, citing a letter of the Maggid of Mezeritch).

Our master, the Baal Shem Tov, had great affection for the second day of Shavuos. Immediately after the Baal Shem Tov revealed [his teachings to the world] . . . he instituted the practice of praying with the first light of dawn on the second day of Shavuos. Afterward, he would share a small repast with those present in order to recite the *Birkas HaMazon* (Grace After Meals) over a cup of wine. Later in the afternoon, there would be a large festive meal, during which the Baal Shem Tov would sit and speak with his disciples at length. Thus did the Baal Shem Tov conduct himself until the day he passed away[1] (*Sefer HaSichos* 5704, p. 135.)

He once said, "If the Jewish people would sanctify themselves with Torah and *mitzvos*, they would continually hear the voice of God speaking as from Mount Sinai" (*Kesser Torah*).

---

1. However, according to a tradition of the Breslever Chasidim, the Baal Shem Tov was particular that his disciples pray together *k'vasikin* on the first day of Shavuos.

Stories of Tzaddikim

The Baal Shem Tov taught: "When one recounts the praises of the *tzaddikim*, it is as if he engages in the mysteries of the *Ma'aseh Merkavah*" (*Shiv'chei Baal Shem Tov* 158).

He said that every day a person should tell one of his friends a story about the deeds of a *tzaddik*[1] (*Divrei Shalom*).

---

1. On the virtues of recounting the deeds of *tzaddikim*, see Rambam, *Pirush al HaMishnayos*, *Avos* I:17; Rabbeinu Bachya, *Pirush al HaTorah*, *Vayishlach*; also note *Likkutei Moharan* I:234; *Sichos HaRan* 138.

Segulos

I heard the following *segulah* in the name of the Baal Shem Tov: One who needs to be healed from a sickness should resolve to make a festive meal in honor of B'eiri HaNavi and recite the following two verses (which are attributed to him).

"And when they shall say to you, 'Consult the necromancers and the sorcerers who chirp and mutter,' shall not this people inquire of its God? For the sake of the living shall we inquire of the dead, for Torah and for testimony? [Even righteous non-Jews] would not agree to such [counsel], which has no light."[1]

Then, on the third day (Tuesday) of the first week after God brings about his recovery, one should actually fulfill his pledge[2] (*R. Yitzchak Isaac of Ziditchov, Likkutei Torah V'Shas, Emor, 107b*).

Following the meal in honor of a *bris milah*, one should fill the cup over which the blessings will be recited with honey wine (*mead*). If *mead* is not available, one may mix honey and water instead. This is a *segulah* for the child to become a Torah scholar (*Chok Olam*, included in *Sefer Bris Olam*, 23b, cited in *Sefer Baal Shem Tov, Segulos* 1).

[Rabbi Shneur Zalman of Liadi] once remarked: "While I was in Mezeritch I heard from the *Rebbe* (Rabbi Dov Ber) in the name of the *Zeide* (the Baal Shem Tov) that honey cakes made from grain cause one's heart to be drawn to the Torah—because grain and honey in their spiritual source are vessels for the Torah" (*Likkutei Dibburim* II, p. 265).

If a woman experiences difficulties during childbirth, God forbid, her husband should immerse in a *mikveh* (*Sifran Shel Tzaddikim*, cited in *Sefer Baal Shem Tov, Yisro*, 14, note 25).

---

1. *Yeshayahu* 8:19–20, according to *Targum Yonasan*; also see *Vayikra Rabba* 6:6.
2. It is assumed that this pledge should be made without an actual vow.

To eliminate the evil trait of anger, it is a *segulah* to recite the verse, "How can a young man keep his way pure? By guarding Your word" (*Tehillim* 119:9) (*Yismach Moshe, Vayigash*, cited in *Sefer Baal Shem Tov, Vayigash*, 2; ibid., *Segulos* 7).

The Baal Shem Tov said that one should not give a knife as a present (*Sichos HaRan* 9).

The holy Rabbi Yisrael, the Maggid of Kozhnitz, said in the name of the Baal Shem Tov that one should not wish another person *l'chayim* over beer (*Sifran Shel Tzaddikim* 1:8, cited in *Sefer Baal Shem Tov, Pekudei*, 3).

Health

When the Baal Shem Tov visited the city of Uman, he instituted a number of practices. One of them was that when a person recovers from a serious illness, he should make a thanksgiving feast for at least ten poor people and give them charity as well (R. Levi Yitzchak Bender, *Siach Sarfei Kodesh*, vol. II, 1–329).

He cautioned against eating raw onions, even when mixed with oil and eggs, etc., whether on weekdays or the holy Shabbos. Onions should only be eaten when cooked [or, according to a reliable tradition, when prepared in a pungent brine] (*Sichos HaRan* 265).

III

Letters of the Baal Shem Tov

The following letters may be found in *Sefer Baal Shem Tov*, the classic anthology of the Baal Shem Tov's teachings edited and annotated by Rabbi Shimon Mendel of Givartshov, first published in Lodz, Poland (1938) and more recently reprinted by Machon Daas Yosef in Jerusalem, Israel (1991). The letter to Rabbi Yaacov Yosef HaKohen of Polonoye was originally included in *Shiv'chei Baal Shem Tov*, compiled by Rabbi Dov Ber of Linitz, published in Kopust (1815). The letter to Rabbi Avraham Gershon Kitover was first printed in *Ben Poras Yosef* by Rabbi Yaacov Yosef HaKohen of Polonoye (1780), an early Chasidic text which recently has been republished with annotations and appendices by Rabbi Avraham Laufer. The latter document also appears as the first entry in Rabbi Aharon HaKohen of Zelichov's collection of the Baal Shem Tov's teachings, *Kesser Shem Tov* (1794), reprinted with critical notes, indexes and supplementary material by Kehot, New York (1973).

Both letters bespeak the lofty spiritual realms to which their author was privy, as well as the intimacy and directness with which he related to his disciples. We are particularly fortunate to have the letter to Rabbi Gershon Kitover. This extraordinary testimony was apparently never sent to its intended receiver, who had emigrated to the Holy Land. Thus, the letter remained within the Baal Shem Tov's immediate circle until its eventual publication almost thirty years later.

Letter to Rabbi Yaacov Yosef of Polonoye
(author of *Toldos Yaacov Yosef,*
Tsafnas Pane'ach, Ben Poras Yosef)

To my beloved friend, the great light of the Diaspora, the mighty hammer, famed for piety, the perfect and lofty sage who performs wonders, cherished of my heart, who is closer to me than a brother, our esteemed master, Rabbi Yosef HaKohen, may his light shine:

I received the letter written by your holy hand and read in the first two lines[1] your declaration that you feel compelled to fast. This news greatly disturbs me, and I adjure you by the angels and by the name of the Holy One, blessed be He, and His *Shechinah* not to enter into this dangerous practice. For [fasting] is an act of melancholy and gloom, and the *Shechinah* does not rest upon sadness but only upon the joy of a *mitzvah*[2] as you well know and as I have often taught you. May these words be upon your heart.

As for the conflicting thoughts that have prompted you to consider this, I will advise you. "The Lord is with you, O mighty warrior."[3] Every morning, when you study Torah, attach yourself to the letters with complete *deveykus* in the service of the Creator, may His Name be blessed. Then all the forces of strict judgment will be sweetened in their Source, and you will be relieved from them. "Do not hide yourself from your own flesh,"[4] God forbid, by fasting more than is necessary and obligatory. And if you will surely hearken unto my voice, God will be with you.

With this, I shall be brief and wish you peace from one who ever desires your well-being,

Yisrael Baal Shem Tov

P.S. Greetings to your only son, the great rabbi, my friend, the esteemed and pious Rabbi Shimshon, may his light shine. Also, greetings to my only son, the distinguished Rabbi Tzvi, may his light shine, and his wife and children, together and individually.

---

1. *Pesachim* 2a.
2. *Shabbos* 30:2.
3. *Shoftim* 6:12.
4. *Yeshayahu* 58:7.

Letter to Rabbi Avraham Gershon Kitover

To my beloved brother-in-law, my friend who is dear to me as my own heart and soul, the exalted rabbi and *chasid*, renowned for his Torah scholarship and fear of Heaven, our master, Rabbi Avraham Gershon, may his light shine. Peace unto him and his family, his modest wife, Bluma, together with all their children; may they be blessed with life, *amen, sela*.

I received the letter written by your holy hand, which you sent by means of the emissary from Jerusalem, at the fair of Luka in the year 5510 (1750 C.E.). It was written with extreme brevity, explaining that you had already written at length to each of us individually and had sent those letters by means of a certain man en route to Egypt. However, the letters never arrived, and I was sorely grieved that I never saw the work of your holy hand which was written in greater detail. Assuredly this is due to the calamitous state of the many lands in which the plague has spread because of our many transgressions. Not far from our region the pestilence has reached the holy community of Mohilev, as well as Wallachia and Turkey.

[Your letter] also states that the Torah teachings and mystical revelations which I sent you through the rabbi and preacher of the holy community of Polonoye did not reach you; this, too, caused me great distress. It certainly would have given you great joy if they had reached you. I have since forgotten many [of those teachings]. However, the few details I still remember I will write to you in brief.

On Rosh Hashanah of the year 5507 (1746 C.E.), I made a [Kabbalistic] oath and elevated my soul in the manner known to you. I saw wondrous things in a vision, the like of which I had never witnessed since the day my mind first began to awaken. The things which I saw and learned when I ascended there would be impossible to communicate, even if I could speak to you in person. When I returned to the lower Garden of Eden, I saw many souls, both living and dead, some known to me and others unknown—their number was beyond reckoning. They were hastening to and fro in order to ascend from one world to another through the Column known to those initiated into the Mysteries. Their joy was too great for the mouth to express or the physical ear to hear. Also, many evil-doers were repenting, and their sins were being forgiven, since it was a special time of Divine favor. Even to me, it was amazing

212

how many of them were accepted as penitents, a number of whom you also know. There was great joy among them, too, and they ascended in the same manner.

Together they begged and implored me unceasingly, "Because of the glory of your Torah, God has granted you an additional measure of understanding to grasp and to know these matters. Ascend with us so that you can be our help and support."

Because of the great joy that I beheld among them, I agreed to go up with them. I besought my master (Achiyah HaShiloni) to accompany me, for the ascent to the Supernal Worlds is fraught with danger. From the day of my birth until now, I never experienced such an ascent as this.

I went up from level to level until I entered the Palace of Moshiach, where Moshiach studies with the Tannaim and *tzaddikim*, as well as the Seven Shepherds.[1] There I found extremely great rejoicing, but I did not know the cause of this delight. At first I thought that it might be due to my having passed away from the physical world, God forbid. Later they told me that I had not yet died, for they have great pleasure on high when I effect mystical unifications in the world below through their holy Torah. However, to this very day, the nature of their joy remains unknown to me.

I asked Moshiach, "When will you come, master?"[2]

And he replied, "By this you shall know: it will be a time when your teachings become publicized and revealed to the world, and your well-springs have overflown to the outside.[3] [It will be when] that which I have taught you—and that which you have perceived of your own efforts—become known, so that others, too, will be able to perform mystical unifications and ascents of the soul like you. Then all the evil *klippos* will be destroyed, and it will be a time of grace and salvation."

I was amazed at this and greatly troubled, since a long time must pass for this to be possible. But while I was there I learned three *segulos* and three Holy Names which are easy to learn and explain. My mind was then set at ease, and I thought that with these teachings the people of my own generation might attain the same spiritual level and state as myself. They would be able to elevate their souls and to learn and per-

---

1. Adam, Sheis, Mesushelach, Avraham, Yaacov, Moshe and David, as stated in *Succah* 52b. However, in common usage the Seven Shepherds are the Holy Guests (*Ushpizin*) associated with the festival of Succos: Avraham, Yitzchak, Yaakov, Moshe, Aharon, Yosef, and David.

2. See *Sanhedrin* 98a.

3. *Mishlei* 5:16.

ceive just as I do. However, I was not granted permission to reveal this
during my lifetime. I pleaded for your sake to be allowed to teach you;
but I was denied permission altogether and took an oath to that effect.

Yet this I can tell you, and may God assist you, that your way may
be pleasant to the Lord,[4] and that you do not go astray (particularly in
the Holy Land). Whenever you pray or study—and with every utterance
of your lips—intend to bring about the unification of a Divine Name.
For every letter contains worlds and souls and Godliness, and they ascend
and combine and unite with one another. Then the letters combine and
unite to form a word, and they are actually unified with the Divine
Essence—and in all these aspects, your soul is bound up with them. All
of the worlds become unified as one, and they ascend and bring about
great joy and delight without measure. Consider the joy of a bridegroom
and bride in this lowly physical world, and you will realize how much
greater is the joy on such a lofty spiritual level.

God will surely help you. Wherever you turn, you will succeed and
become enlightened. "Give wisdom to the wise, and he will become wise
all the more."[5] Please pray for my sake, that I might be privileged to dwell
in God's land during my lifetime; and pray for the remnant of our people
who still remain in the Diaspora . . .

These are the words of your brother-in-law who longs to see you
face-to-face, who prays that length of days be granted to you and your
wife and children, and who wishes you peace "all your days—including
the nights,"[6] for many good years, *amen, sela.*

Yisrael Baal Shem Tov
of the Holy Community of Medzhibuzh

---

4. *Shoftim* 8:6.
5. *Mishlei* 9:9.
6. *Berachos, Mishnah* 1:5.

APPENDIX I: *"Everything Is Godliness"*

One of the controversial issues which led to the persecution of the Baal Shem Tov and his disciples was his assertion that "everything is Godliness, and Godliness is everything." Mystics have their own way of speaking—sometimes to the chagrin of rationalists, who, after all, account for the greater part of the population. To some of his rabbinic contemporaries, the Baal Shem Tov's statements sounded dangerously like pantheism.

Of course, the Baal Shem Tov never identified God with nature—it is a fundamental belief of Judaism that, before or after creation, God is immutable, infinite and transcendent.[1] What the Baal Shem Tov wished to communicate was the oneness of all things within God and the presence of God's Oneness within all things. (In the language of the Kabbalah, these two perceptions are called *yichuda ila'ah* and *yichuda tata'ah*—the Higher Unification and the Lower Unification.[2]) This experience of Divine Oneness gave rise to the surpassing love—for God, for the Jewish people, for all creatures great and small—which the Baal Shem Tov uniquely expressed.

So the question immediately arises: How can this love be applied to evil? And if everything is Godliness, how can it not? In fact how can evil exist at all?

The manifestation of all phenomenal reality is a consequence of what the Kabbalah calls *tzimtzum* (constriction). This term refers to the withdrawal of God's Infinite Light when it arose within the Divine will to create the universe. As a result of the *tzimtzum*, an "empty space" was formed.[3] This empty space is the precondition for creation to possess an appearance of independent existence; and, since it is the antithesis of revelation, the empty space is the source of the potential for "evil,"

---

1. *Mishneh Torah, Yesodei HaTorah*, Chapters 1 and 2; *Derech HaShem*, Section I, Chapter 1.

2. See *Zohar* I, 18a; *Sefer HaTanya, Sha'ar HaYichud V'haEmunah*; *Likkutei Moharan* I:11; *Likkutei Halachos, Orach Chaim, Birchos HaShachar*, 5; ibid., *Yoreh De'ah, Simonei Ohf Tahor*, 3; ibid., *Yoreh De'ah, Kalei Ilán*, 1; ibid., *Choshen Mishpat, Eidus*, 4.

3. Terms such as *tzimtzum* and *empty space*—indeed the entire Kabbalistic description of creation—must not be taken literally. No spatial or temporal concept can be applied to God, nor can transcendental realities be understood in physical terms. Rather, such Kabbalistic descriptions should be understood in a metaphorical sense.

i.e., an act which could appear to contradict the Divine will. Basing himself on the teachings of both the Ari z"l and the Baal Shem Tov, the Chasidic master Rabbi Nachman of Breslev defines the issues in the following way:

> When God wanted to create the world, there was no place to do so, since everything was infinite. Therefore, He withdrew the [Infinite] Light to the sides, and by means of this act of withdrawal (tzimtzum), an empty space was formed. Within this empty space were brought into being all the various finite entities (midos) which comprise the creation of the universe. This empty space was necessary, for without it, there would have been nowhere for creation to take place. [However,] the tzimtzum which produced the empty space is impossible to understand or grasp. [Its essence will become known] only in the Ultimate Future. For [concerning the empty space] one must say two opposite things: it is both something and nothing. The empty space came about through the tzimtzum: [the Creator] withdrew His Godliness from there (so to speak), and no Godliness remained (so to speak). Otherwise, the space would not have been empty. Everything would have remained infinite, and there would have been no room at all for creation. But the real truth is that Godliness surely exists there too, for nothing can exist without His life force. Therefore, it is absolutely impossible to grasp the aspect of the empty space until the Ultimate Future.[4]

Chasidic doctrine fully agrees that from the standpoint of creation, evil exists and must be repudiated, according to the Torah's dictates. Man possesses free will and is, accordingly, subject to reward and punishment. At the same time, from God's perspective (so to speak), evil has no *essential* existence—everything is perfect, subsumed within His absolute Oneness. And, according to the degree to which a person can

---

4. *Likkutei Moharan* I, 64:1. The primary discussion of *tzimtzum* in the works of the Ari z"l may be found at the beginning of *Eitz Chaim, Drush Igulim V'Yosher, Anaf* 2; *Sha'ar HaHakdamos, Hakdamah* 4, p.14; *Mevo Shearim* I, 1:1. Statements of *Chazal* germane to the subject may be found in *Berachos* 10a, *Bereishis Rabba* 12:4; *Shemos Rabba* 2:9; *Shir HaShirim Rabba* 3:15; *Sefer HaBahir* 1:1, *Zohar* I:15a, III:225a and 227b; *Zohar Chadash* 35c; *Tikkunei Zohar* 5 (19a), 57 (91b), and 70 (122b). The writings of Rabbi Moshe Cordovero are often cited in favor of the Baal Shem Tov's view, especially *Shiur Komah, Machshava* 40; ibid., *Torah* 13:22; *Pardes Rimonim* IV:10; ibid., VI:8; *Elima Rabasi, Mayan* I: *Tamar* 1, 4–22; ibid., *Tamar* IV:1. For an overview of this key issue, see R. Shmuel Teich's *Lahavas Aish*, a survey of Kabbalistic concepts as seen in the light of Chasidic thought.

sanctify himself, he can receive a glimmer of this higher reality. The position taken on this issue by Rabbi Chaim of Volozhin, one of the most prominent leaders of the Misnagdim, is essentially the same.[5]

So, if the ultimate truth is that "everything is Godliness," what is the substance of creation? What is the nature of the empty space which is the precondition of all phenomenal reality?

As Rabbi Nachman states, there is no answer to this paradox—not one that the rational mind can grasp. When man is finally granted this perception, he will transcend his status as a mortal who must chose between good and evil and attain the level of the angels.[6]

---

5. See *Nefesh HaChaim, Sha'ar* III.
6. *Likkutei Moharan* I, 21:4.

APPENDIX II: *Chasidic Mysticism Today*

The teachings of Chasidism have both strengthened and transformed Jewish spirituality. Perhaps the Baal Shem Tov's greatest success was in promoting his values—joy in the performance of *mitzvos*, love of God as the greatest incentive for ethical behavior, an appreciation of the inestimable worth of the simplest Jew and the smallest good deed, and attachment to *tzaddikim* as the key to spiritual survival and growth. Not only is the master's influence still felt in the Chasidic world, but, in one way or another, there is almost no sector of *K'lal Yisrael* it has not affected.

But as for the quest for *deveykus*, there is hardly a *yeshiva*, even among the Chasidim, where the subject is so much as mentioned. Yet this was probably the Baal Shem Tov's central concern. What happened?

To give this question the attention it deserves, one would have to explore the entire history of the Chasidic movement, its ongoing ideological diversities, and the various currents in Jewish life to which Chasidism has responded. Such a study could easily fill another book. But, without having done my homework, I would still venture an unscholarly guess: it is impossible to "mass produce" something as subtle and personal as the experience of *deveykus*. Indeed, such experiences are inherently elusive. Rabbi Nachman of Breslev taught:

> "For I know that God is great; our God above all others" (*Tehillim* 135:5). You may have a vision, but you cannot even share it with yourself. Today you may be inspired and see a new light. But tomorrow you will not be able to communicate it, even to yourself. "I know." I—as I am now. For the vision cannot be brought back . . .[1]

The dangers of charlatanism on the one hand and self-delusion on the other often seemed to vindicate the opponents of the movement. Thus, the communal aspects of Chasidic life have fared better over the years than its mysticism. When on a long Shabbos afternoon a Chasid in Borough Park or Williamsburg looks into his *Kedushas Levi* or *Ma'or VaShemesh*, he is usually content to savor a *Chasidishe vort*—a sagacious insight. But, in the practical sense, he is not much more of a mystic than his non-Chasidic counterpart.

---

1. *Sichos HaRan* 1.

Despite all this, searching individuals may be found in almost every group who still pursue the Baal Shem Tov's inner path. Certainly, among the leaders of the various communities there have always been accomplished Kabbalists. Some even persisted in the attempt to include the common folk in the mystical quest.

After the original fervor of the Baal Shem Tov's movement began to fade, a number of Chasidic masters developed innovative schools of their own. It is beyond the scope of this work to discuss them all; however, I would like to mention several that incorporate not only mystical concepts, but mystical practices. My purpose in doing so is not to reduce any school to the dimensions of a thumbnail sketch, but merely to highlight this latter point. Thus, the interested reader may conclude this book with at least a sense of where to inquire further.

Perhaps the first attempt to create a technique not reserved for a spiritual elite was the approach to the daily prayer service conceived by Rabbi Aharon HaKohen of Zelichov. His commentary, *Kesser Nehora*, attempts to summarize the *kavanos* of the Ari *z"l* in a way that addresses both the mind and heart. He defines the parameters of "the service of the heart" according to four basic themes: awe of God, love of God, praise of God, and the acceptance of God's Kingship. These four categories correspond to the four letters of the essential Divine Name, YHVH. Thus, by praying in the manner he describes, one fulfills the Psalmist's words, "I have placed God (YHVH) before me always." First published in 1794 together with the *Siddur Tefillah Yesharah* (his own redaction of the formal prayers according to the Chasidic custom), R. Aharon's system of *kavanos* is still used by many Chasidim today.

One of the most profound thinkers to develop the Baal Shem Tov's teachings was Rabbi Shneur Zalman of Liadi (1745–1812). His highly intellectual approach came to be known as Chabad Chasidism, borrowing the Kabbalistic acronym for the three *sefiros* of *chochmah* (wisdom), *binah* (understanding) and *daas* (knowledge). Born of the dispassionate Lithuanian temperament, Chabad distrusted the fervor of many Chasidim as a "delusion of the blood," the self-serving pursuit of an emotional high. Alternately it developed a philosophical-contemplative method by which the seeker might spontaneously experience an intuitive sense of his own nothingness (*bittul ha-yesh*) and the omnipresence of the Divine. The emotional consequences of such contemplation would be a natural by-product of the search for unity. In this way, Chabad sought to kindle a steady inner flame in the heart rather than fan the fires of sporadic— and possibly false—ecstasy. The basic practice, still employed by contemporary devotees of Chabad, entails intensely and systematically contemplating the metaphysical order of the universe. In Kabbalistic terms, this is known as the *Seder HaHishtalshelus*, and the exploration of its intricacies produced a profound literature and a unique spiritual path. The core of these teachings may be found in R. Shneur Zalman's famous *Sefer HaTanya*, especially in the second section, *Sha'ar HaYichud V'Ha-Emunah* (translated into English as "The Gate of Unity and Faith"). Other key works are *Ner Mitzvah V'Torah Ohr* and *Kuntres HaHispa'alus* by Rabbi Dov Ber of Lubavitch. However, virtually all Chabad texts work out the implications of R. Shneur Zalman's ideas in various contexts.

More distrustful of rational intellect than the founder of Chabad, Rabbi Nachman of Breslev (1772–1810) wanted the individual to attain a realization of Godliness through the fabric of life itself. He stressed the path of *hisbodedus*—secluded self-examination and spontaneous personal prayer. One sets aside one hour every day to pour out his heart to God, preferably in a secluded place in the middle of the night. R. Nachman encouraged the seeker to overcome his worldly attachments by stripping away one level after another of the "false self" until all that remains is the subtlest trace of ego—and then one may let go of this, too, permitting the Infinite Light to shine through at last. This process necessitates reflecting upon one's life circumstances and experiences, especially by using the Torah one has studied (and R. Nachman's discourses in particular) as a springboard for meditation and prayer. A general description of *hisbodedus* is given in *Likkutei Moharan* I:52, as well as in the anthology *Hishtapchus HaNefesh* (translated into English as "Outpouring of the Soul" by Rabbi Aryeh Kaplan). But, actually, the possibilities of *hisbodedus* are unlimited— for according to R. Nachman, every aspect of the human condition can be a starting point in one's search for God.

Rabbi Zvi Hirsch (Eichenstein) of Ziditchov (1765–1831) and his nephew and disciple, Rabbi Yitzchak Isaac Yechiel (Safrin) of Komarna (1806–1874), saw the teachings of the Ari *z"l* and those of the Baal Shem Tov as part of both an essential and historical continuity, an ongoing revelation of the deepest levels of Torah. Therefore, they discussed the mysteries of Lurianic Kabbalah more openly than any other Chasidic leaders, even delving into the use of *kavanos* and *yichudim*—meditations upon various Divine names and combinations of holy letters. When performed by a worthy individual in a state of purity and with holy intent, these meditations can restore spiritual harmony to the universe and elicit Divine mercy and favor. (However, as the Rebbes of Ziditchov and Komarna also warned, when *kavanos* and *yichudim* are employed indiscriminately, the results may be catastrophic.) Perhaps the best introduction to this path is R. Yitzchak Isaac Yechiel's *Netziv Mitzvosecha*. His diary of dreams and visions, *Megillas Sesarim*, is one of the most revealing personal testimonies written by a Chasidic master. (In a similar vein, some of R. Nachman of Breslev's dreams and visions may be found in *Chayei Moharan*, translated by Avraham Greenbaum and published in English as "*Tzaddik*." The dream-journal of another major Chasidic thinker, Rabbi Tzadok HaKohen of Lublin, was published as *Kuntres Divrei Chalomos*.)

Rabbi Kalonymus Kalman (Shapira) of Piaseczno (1889–1943), a more recent Chasidic leader who perished in the Warsaw Ghetto, brought an illumination of mysticism to the masses through his innovative educational methods. By imbuing the student (or disciple) with a deep sense of his own essential spiritual nature, the Piaseczno Rebbe initiates him into Torah study, prayer, and the performance of *mitzvos* by using visualization techniques. These improvisational *kavanos* are sometimes derived from the Kabbalah but avoid its more esoteric aspects. The Piaseczno Rebbe's ultimate goal is not only to bring the everyday practices of Judaism to life but to initiate his disciples into the ethereal realms of the spirit. His best-known works are *Chovos HaTalmidim* (translated into English as "A Student's Obligation" by Micha Odenheimer, Aronson 1991) and *Hachsharas Avreichim*. But perhaps the clearest exposition of his approach may be found in a small booklet entitled *Bnei Machshavah Tovah*. These works began attaining popularity during their author's lifetime and have more recently inspired a growing number of devotees in many Chasidic *yeshivos*, especially in Israel.

However, like everything else in Torah, one can learn only so much from texts. Ever since Sinai, the Jewish tradition has been passed down from master to disciple, and especially in this area of Torah, one must find a teacher. Some Chasidim would argue that this master-disciple relationship is even more important than the particular school to which one belongs.

The *Gemara* tells us to search for a teacher who is comparable to a *malach Hashem Tz'vaos*—"an angel of the Lord of Hosts."[2] But the question is: Where can one find such a teacher? And how can one know if he is making the right choice? The answer I received from my teachers is that you have to be willing to search as long as it takes—and, like everything else (and maybe more than everything else), you have to pray for Divine assistance.

---

2. *Moed Katan* 17a.

Glossary

Ad Bias Goel Tzedek—"until the coming of the Righteous Redeemer."

Adon Olam—"Master of the Universe;" a liturgical poem attributed to Rabbi Shlomo ibn Gabirol (11th century), usually recited at the beginning of the morning prayer service.

Ahavah Rabbah—the prayer immediately preceding the *Shema* in the morning service.

Ahavas Yisrael—love of the Jewish people.

Alef-Beis—the Hebrew alphabet.

Aleinu—"It is incumbent upon us . . ." the prayer with which each of the three daily services concludes.

Am Ha'aretz—"people of the land"; a peasant or ignoramus.

Amora/Amoraim—Talmudic teachers in the period after the redaction of the Mishnah (approx. 200–500 C.E.).

Amud—prayer stand (lit. "pillar").

Ari z"l—acronym for *Eloki Rabbi Yitzchak*—the Divinely inspired Rabbi Yitzchak Luria (1534–1572)—whose teachings became central for virtually all Kabbalists thereafter, Ashkenazim and Sephardim alike.

Ashkenazim—originally referring to the Jewish community of medieval Germany, the term has come to be used for Jews of European descent.

Ashur—Assyria.

Asiyah—World of Action, lowest of the four worlds discussed in the Kabbalah, characterized by the greatest sense of separateness and alienation from God.

Atzilus—World of Emanation, the highest of the four worlds discussed in the Kabbalah, in which "lights and vessels are one." In terms of Divine service, this corresponds to a level of *deveykus* in which one does not experience himself as an autonomous entity.

Avraham/Avraham Avinu—The Patriarch Abraham.

Baal Teshuvah/Baalei Teshuvah—a penitent; especially one who returns to belief in God and the observance of *mitzvos* after having been estranged from Judaism.

Bar Mitzvah—a boy over the age of thirteen, who is then responsible for his own conduct by Torah law and may be counted in a *minyan*.

Beiri HaNavi—Beiri the Prophet.

Binah—"understanding"; the ability to infer one thing from another; the eighth *sefirah* in ascending order, characterized by suprarational perception; the apprehension of Godliness granted to souls in the Garden of Eden.

Birkas HaMazon—Grace After Meals.

B'riah—World of Creation, characterized by the Divine Throne and the loftiest angels; second in descending order of the Four Worlds described by the Kabbalah.

Bris Milah—the covenant of circumcision as prescribed by the Torah.

Chadash—the new crop of wheat, barley, spelt, rye and oats, as yet unredeemed by the *omer* offering; see R. Shlomo Ganzfried's *Concise Code of Jewish Law*, Chapter 172.

Chai—"living"; in the four categories of existence, this refers to animals, fish, and birds, all of which possess a *nefesh* (living soul).

Challah/Challos—actually the portion of dough tithed for the Kohen (Priest) in the Holy Temple; more commonly, the loaves served at the Shabbos meals.

Chasid/Chasidim—a pious individual; often refers to a member of the Chasidic movement founded by the Baal Shem Tov in the 18th century.

Chayah—the fourth level of the soul in ascending order, corresponding to the *sefirah* of *chochmah*.

Cheder (Yid.)—school for small children.

Chesed—kindness; first of the seven lower *sefiros*; personified by Avraham Avinu.

Chiddush/Chiddushim—an original idea or interpretation.

Chochmah—wisdom; the ninth *sefirah* in ascending order; the seminal spark or flash of insight that implicitly contains all possible ramifications thereof, down to the most intricate physical details; the root of intellect.

Chomer—physicality; outer form.

Da'as—knowledge, especially knowledge of God; sometimes counted as a *sefirah* in its own right, *da'as* is actually the conclusion of the interaction of *chochmah* and *binah* and provides the common root of the seven lower *sefiros* (*chesed* through *malchus*).

David HaMelech—King David.

Derech—path or way.

Deveykus—cleaving or attachment; mystical communion with God.

Domem—the inanimate realm; lowest of the four levels of existence described by the Kabbalah.

D'rush—homiletical meaning; the third level of Torah interpretation as classified by the Talmudic rabbis (*peshat-remez-d'rush-sod*).

D'varim K'gachalei Eish—"words like coals of fire" (paraphrase of *Avos* 2:10).

Elisha HaNavi—Elisha the Prophet.

Eliyahu HaNavi—Elijah the Prophet.

Emunah—faith or belief.

Erev Shabbos (or Yom Tov)—the day prior to Shabbos or Yom Tov.

Gehenna—"Valley of Hinnom"; Purgatory.

Gemara—the Talmudic arguments, discussions, laws and sermons based upon the Mishnah. Compiled in its present form by Ravina and Rav Ashi in approximately 500 c.e.

Gematria—the science of numerology in rabbinic thought; since each Hebrew letter possesses a numerical value, words can be rendered as numbers and interrelated symbolically according to certain principles.

Ge'ulah—redemption (esp. Messianic Redemption).

Gevurah—power or might; the second of the seven lower *sefiros*, characterized by restraint, severity, and fortitude; personified by Yitzchak Avinu.

Hakafos—circuits; esp. the rings of dancers formed during Simchas Torah celebrations.

Halachah—Torah law.

Havdalah—the rite by which Shabbos or Yom Tov is terminated and mundane work may be resumed.

Hisbodedus—seclusion; any of several forms of meditation or personal prayer.

Hod—splendor; the fifth of the seven lower *sefiros*; together with *netzach*, *hod* is the source of prophecy; personified by Aharon HaKohen.

Hoshana Rabbah—last of the intermediate days of the Succos festival, Hoshana Rabbah is thus called after the ritual of circling the table on which the Torah is read seven times while reciting prayers of supplication both for rain and Divine mercy.

Kabbalah—"that which has been received"; the Jewish mystical tradition. Some divide the Kabbalah into three distinct but interrelated areas: *Kabbalah Iyunis*—metaphysical and theological teachings, as well as esoteric readings of Torah; *Kabbalah Ma'asis*—mystical practices (forbidden by most later authorities) which can affect the world in supernatural ways; and the meditative Kabbalah.

Kabbalas Ol—acceptance of the yoke of the Kingdom of Heaven.

Kameyah/Kameyos—a Kabbalistic amulet usually containing Divine names.

Kavanah/Kavanos—intention, focus, or concentration; sometimes refers to specific Kabbalistic concepts or Divine Names to be borne in mind during prayer, ritual acts, or other spiritual practices.

Keruvim—the angelic forms over the Ark in the Holy Temple that served as the channel for prophecy and Divine inspiration.

Kesser—"crown"; the highest of the *sefiros*, tenth in ascending order; considered removed from the rest of the sefirotic structure, *kesser* is characterized by the mystery of the Divine will (*ratzon*) and sublime unity and delight (*oneg*); it is also the source of the Thirteen Attributes of Divine mercy (*rachamim*).

K'fitzas HaDerech—a miraculous contraction of distance, often mentioned in tales of the Baal Shem Tov.

Kiddush—the rite of sanctification of Shabbos or Yom Tov, usually recited over a cup of wine.

Kiddush HaLevanah—prayer service in commemoration of the new moon which alludes to the renewal of the Jewish people, who are likened to the moon.

Klippah/Klippos—"husk"; in Kabbalistic thought, the aspect of evil or impurity that obscures the holy and the good.

Kohen Gadol—the High Priest in the Holy Temple.

Korban—sacrifice.

Korban Pesach—the Passover lamb.

K'rias Shema—the recitation of the *Shema* prayer ("Hear O Israel, the Lord, our God, the Lord is one") during the morning and evening prayer services, as well as upon retiring before sleep.

K'vasikin—"like the Vasikin," i.e., a Jewish pietist sect that flourished before the Mishnah was redacted, whose members prayed with the first light of dawn.

Lashon HaRa—harmful speech or gossip.

Lechem HaPanim—"showbread"; the twelve loaves offered in the Holy Temple.

Limud—lesson; instructive concept.

Lishmah—"for its own sake."

Ma'ariv—"west"; often refers to the evening prayer service (*arvis*).

Machzor—the holiday prayer book.

Maggid—lecturer; often refers to an itinerant preacher or a rabbi known for his speaking abilities.

Malchus—kingship, sovereignty; in Kabbalah, the seventh and last of the lower *sefiros*, *malchus* expresses the feminine principle of receptivity and peace; symbolically associated with prayer, the wife, Shabbos, and the Jewish people; personified by David HaMelech.

Mashgiach Ruchani—the rabbi entrusted with the spiritual welfare of the students in a *yeshiva*.

Matzah/Matzos—unleavened bread, especially that eaten during Passover.

Mayim Acharonim—water used to cleanse the fingers at the conclusion of a meal.

Medaber—"speaker"; mankind, the highest of the four categories of existence.

Megilla—a scroll, usually that of Esther, read on the holiday of Purim.

Melave Malkah—"escorting the Queen"; the meal eaten on Saturday night when the Shabbos has already departed but its spirit of sanctity still lingers on.

Memalei Kol Almin—the aspect of Godliness that permeates all the worlds; Divine immanence.

Merkavah—the Divine Chariot in Ezekiel's prophetic vision; sometimes refers to ancient Jewish mystical practices by which one could attain a vision of God.

Mesiras Nefesh—self-sacrifice.

Mezuzah/Mezuzos—holy scroll containing portion of the *Shema* affixed to the doorpost of a Jewish home.

Mikveh—pool for ritual immersion.

Minchah—"offering"; the afternoon prayer service.

Minyan—a prayer quorum of ten Jewish males above the age of thirteen.

Mishnah—the fundamental body of rabbinic law which the *Gemara* elucidates and develops; or a subsection of this body of teachings. The Mishnah was compiled in its present form by Rabbi Yehudah HaNassi in approx. 200 C.E.

Misnaged/Misnagdim—an opponent of the Chasidic movement and its teachings.

Mitzrayim—Egypt.

Mitzvah/Mitzvos—Divine commandment (whether Scriptural or of rabbinic origin).

Mochin—"brains," which, according to the Kabbalah, are threefold, corresponding to the *sephiros* of *chochmah*, *binah*, and *da'as*; consciousness or intellect in general.

Moshe Rabbeinu—Moses, our teacher.

Moshiach—the Messiah.

Motza'ei Shabbos (or Yom Tov)—the evening after Shabbos or Yom Tov.

Mussaf—prayer service commemorating the additional sacrifice offered in the Holy Temple on Shabbos or Yom Tov.

Mussar—reproof; especially teachings that guide one to improve himself morally and spiritually; an introspective, pietistic movement initiated by Rabbi Yisrael Salanter in the late 19th century that greatly influenced the Lithuanian *yeshiva* system down to the present day.

Nefesh—soul; in Kabbalistic doctrine, lowest level of the soul that vitalizes the body.

Nefilas Apayim—"falling upon the face"; part of the *Tachanun* prayer.

Neila—last section of the Yom Kippur prayers.

Neshamah—soul; in Kabbalistic doctrine, the Divine soul possessed only by humans; or the third level of the soul, which is the seat of intellect.

Netzach—victory or eternity; fourth of the lower seven *sefiros*, *netzach* breaks through obstacles by drawing upon the transcendent Divine will (*kesser*). In conjunction with *hod*, it is the source of prophecy and Divine inspiration; personified by Moshe Rabbeinu.

Nigleh—revealed Torah teachings.

Nistar—esoteric or mystical Torah teachings.

Nitzachon—the determination to achieve victory at all costs.

Nosson HaNavi—Nathan the Prophet.

Nusach Ari—the prayer rite according to the customs of 16th-century Kabbalist Rabbi Yitzchak Luria (known as the Ari z"l).

Nusach Ashkenaz—the prayer rite according to the customs of European Jewry.

Nusach Sephard—the Ashkenazic prayer rite as modified by various Kabbalistic and Chasidic customs; so named because of certain similarities to the true Sephardic (Mediterranean and Middle Eastern) prayer book.

Pasul—ritually invalid.

Pesach—Passover.

Pesukei D'Zimrah—psalms recited during the morning prayer service.

Peyos—the locks of hair in front of the ears that the Torah forbids Jewish men to remove; many Jews, especially Chasidim, customarily let them grow long.

P'nimius HaTorah—the inner aspect of Torah; Jewish mystical teachings.

P'shat—the plain meaning of Scripture; first of the four levels of interpretation according to rabbinic tradition (*p'shat-remez-d'rush-sod*).

Rabbi—title of Talmudic teachers in the Land of Israel; in contemporary usage, a Jewish religious leader.

Rav—title of Talmudic teachers in Babylonia.

Rebbe (Yid.)—rabbi or teacher; especially a Chasidic master.

Rosh Chodesh—first day of the Jewish month.

Rosh Hashanah—Jewish New Year (which is actually two days considered as one).

Ruach—spirit; second of the five levels of the soul and seat of the emotions.

Ruach HaKodesh—Divine inspiration.

Seder—"order"; usually, the elaborate ritual meal of Passover eve commemorating the exodus from Egypt in Biblical times.

Sefer Torah/Sifrei Torah—Torah scroll.

Sefirah/Sefiros—Divine emanations or attributes that manifest themselves in each of the Four Worlds and are the source of the ten faculties of the soul.

Sefiras HaOmer—the counting of the Omer, a measure of barley offered in the Holy Temple beginning on the second day of Passover and ending the day before Shavuos. It is still customary to recite a blessing and count each of these days in commemoration of the Omer offering.

Segulah/Segulos—treasure or prized possession; sometimes refers to a charm or remedy.

Selichos—penitential prayers recited before Rosh Hashanah and Yom Kippur.

Sephardim—Originally referring to the Jewish community of medieval Spain, the term has come to be used for Mediterranean and Middle Eastern Jews in general.

Seraphim—fiery angels.

Seudah—meal or feast.

Shabbos—the Jewish Sabbath.

Shalosh Seudos—the third Shabbos meal, which the Kabbalists describe as *Ra'ava d'Ra'avin*, the spiritual peak of the holy day.

Shechinah—the Divine Presence; sometimes identified as the *sefirah* of *malchus* or *Knesses Yisrael*, the collectivity of Jewish souls.

She'eilas Chalom—a Kabbalistic practice by which a request, usually for spiritual guidance, may be answered in one's dreams.

Shefa—the flow of Divine life force into creation.

Shemoneh Esrei—the silent prayer of eighteen benedictions (nowadays, nineteen) which is the core of the morning, afternoon and evening prayer services.

Shemurah Matzah—Passover *matzos* made from wheat that has been guarded with utmost stringency against contact with water or leaven (*chametz*).

Sh'lita—acronym for "may his days be long and good, amen."

Sh'tetl (Yid.)—a small Jewish village in Eastern Europe.

Shul (Yid.)—synagogue.

Shulchan Aruch—Rabbi Yosef Karo's classic code of Jewish law.

Siddur—the formal prayer book.

Sovev Kol Almin—the aspect of Godliness that transcends creation.

Succah—a booth in which one eats and dwells during the autumn holiday of Succos.

Succos—the Festival of Booths, which commemorates God's care for the Jewish people during their journey through the wilderness in Biblical times. Succos is also a harvest festival.

Tachanun—supplications; especially after the morning or afternoon *Shemoneh Esrei* prayer.

Tallis—prayer shawl.

Talmud—the combined teachings of the Mishnah and *Gemara*, which is the basis of rabbinic Judaism.

Tanna/Tannaim—a rabbinic authority during the period of the Mishnah.

Techeiles—the thread of blue that the Torah mandates be tied in ritual fringes (*tzitzis*) at the corners of a Jewish man's *tallis* or other four-cornered garment.

Tefillin—two leather cases containing Scriptural passages which Jewish men strap to their arm and head during the weekday morning prayer service.

Teshuvah—return to God, repentance.

Tiferes—the third of the seven lower *sefiros* that represents harmony and beauty; the synthesis of *chesed* and *gevurah*.

Tikkun—rectification, repair, perfection.

Tikkun Chatzos—the midnight prayer service mourning the destruction of the Holy Temple and the exile of the *Shechinah* and the Jewish people.

Tisch (Yid.)—table.

Tzaddik/Tzaddikim—a righteous or holy man; in Kabbalistic and Chasidic thought, one who has completely overcome his physical passions and ego.

Tzedakah—charity.

Tzitzis—ritual fringes that a Jewish male must tie at the corners of his *tallis* or four-cornered garment.

Tzome'ach—vegetative or plant life.

Tzurah—form or design; the inner spiritual aspect of a physical entity.

Urim V'Tumim—the breastplate worn by the Kohen Gadol in the Holy Temple, composed of twelve precious stones which served as a Divine oracle to be used in times of national crisis, etc.

Yaakov/Yaakov Avinu—the Patriarch Jacob.

Yechezkel HaNavi—Ezekiel the Prophet.

Yechidah—the highest level of the soul, in which it is utterly one with God.

Yesh M'Ayin—"something from nothing"; the unique characteristic of the Divine act of creation.

Yeshiva/Yeshivos—"sitting"; a school dedicated to Torah study.

Yesod—"foundation"; the sixth *sefirah* of the lower seven (in descending order), which establishes connections, especially with the *sefirah* of *malchus*; personified by Yosef HaTzaddik.

Yetzirah—"formation"; the World of Formation, which is the abode of the angels.

Yichuda Ila'ah—Higher Unification.

Yichuda Tata'ah—Lower Unification.

Yitzchak/Yitzchak Avinu—the Patriarch Isaac.

Yom Kippur—the Day of Atonement.

Yom Tov—a Jewish holiday.

Yosef HaTzaddik—Joseph, the Biblical figure who especially personified the ideal of the *tzaddik*.

Zeide (Yid.)—grandfather.

Zemer/Zemiros—religious song.

Z'rizus—alacrity.

Bibliography

PRIMARY SOURCES

Kahan, R. Avraham Yitzchak, ed. *Likkutim Yekarim*. Jerusalem: Yeshivas Toldos Aharon, 1974.

R. Moshe Chaim Ephraim of Sudylkov. *Degel Machaneh Ephraim*. Jerusalem, 1986.

Rubenstein, Avraham, ed. *Shiv'chei Baal Shem Tov*. Jerusalem: Reuven Mass., Ltd., 1991.

Schochet, R. Immanuel, ed. *Tzava'as HaRivash*. Brooklyn, NY: Kehot, 1975.

Tzeinvirt, R. Avraham Abbish, ed. *Tzava'as HaRivash*. Jerusalem: Machon Daas Yosef, 1991.

R. Yaakov Yosef of Polonoye. *Ben Poras Yosef*, ed. R. Avraham Laufer. Brooklyn, NY, 1995.

———— *K'tones Pasim*. New York, 1940.

———— *Toldos Yaakov Yosef*. Jerusalem, 1973.

———— *Tsafnas Panc'ach*. Brooklyn, NY, 1991.

ANTHOLOGIES

R. Aharon HaKohen of Zelichov. *Kesser Shem Tov*. Kfar Chabad: Kehot, 1981.

Goldstein, R. Nachman. *Leshon Chasidim*. Jerusalem: Chasidei Breslev, 1978.

Kornblit, R. Yehoshua Yosef. *Meir Einei Yisrael*. Jerusalem: Machon Daas Yosef, 1991.

R. Shimshon Menachem Mendel of Gevartchov. *Sefer Baal Shem Tov*. Jerusalem: Machon Daas Yosef, 1993.

Index

235

ABOUT THE AUTHOR

David Sears is best known for the many Jewish children's books he has illustrated and written, the most recent of which is *The Lost Princess* (1996), one of Rabbi Nachman's famous mystical tales. An alumnus of Brooklyn's Darchei Noam Yeshiva (founded by the previous Bostoner Rebbe, *zt"l*), he received his grounding in Chasidic literature through the Breslev Kollel and from teachers in Israel and the United States. Among his other fields of interest is traditional Jewish music. In 1991, he and Klezmer clarinetist/mandolinist Andy Statman founded Shoresh, an archive of Jewish folk music. They have also coproduced two commercial recordings (*Songs of the Breslever Chasidim: Today* and *Between Heaven and Earth*). David and his wife, Shira, live in the Borough Park section of Brooklyn.